Reading Raps

Reading Raps

A Book Club Guide for Librarians, Kids, and Families

Rita Soltan

A Member of the Greenwood Publishing Group

Westport, Connecticut • London

Library of Congress Cataloging-in-Publication Data

Soltan, Rita.
    Reading raps : a book club guide for librarians, kids, and families / by Rita Soltan.
      p. cm.
    Includes bibliographical references and indexes.
    ISBN 1-59158-234-2 (pbk. : alk. paper)
  1. Children's libraries—Activity programs. 2. Book clubs (Discussion groups) 3. Children's literature—Stories, plots, etc. 4. Children's literature—Bibliography. 5. Reading promotion. 6. Children—Books and reading—United States. I. Title.
  Z718.1.S63 2006
  027.62'5—dc22   2005030842

British Library Cataloguing in Publication Data is available.

Library of Congress Catalog Number: 2005030842
ISBN: 1-59158-234-2

First published in 2006

Libraries Unlimited, 88 Post Road West, Westport, CT 06881
A Member of the Greenwood Publishing Group, Inc.
www.lu.com

Printed in the United States of America

♾™

The paper used in this book complies with the Permanent Paper Standard issued by the National Information Standards Organization (Z39.48-1984).

10 9 8 7 6 5 4 3 2 1

To Eva and Robert
—your teaching and creative writing are my inspiration.

Contents

Chapter 4: Father-Son Book Club 169

Chapter 5: Readers' Rap 249

Acknowledgments

This effort is a culmination of numerous book discussion programs I have planned, led, and supervised over many years as a public children's librarian. I am indebted to the families—children, parents, guardians, and mentors—with whom I have worked over the years who helped me understand the importance of good children's literature, its vibrancy, strength, and beauty. I also wish to thank all my colleagues and friends at the Bloomfield Township Public Library in Bloomfield Hills, Michigan, specifically Marian Rafal and her staff, whose constant support and combined knowledge and experience guided me through hours of research and reading. In addition, I am grateful for Bloomfield Township's wonderfully comprehensive children's and young adult collection of which there is no equal in Michigan.

I would also like to thank my acquisitions editor, Barbara Ittner, for her smooth direction and advice throughout my writing and to my production editor, Elizabeth Budd, for her capable guidance in making my thoughts on paper cohesive and clear.

Finally, thank you to Sam for loving me, always, and to Robert, Eva, and Ari who told me to keep going. You are all the source of my happiness and love.

Introduction

The concept of reading to discuss books is now quite the rage. It is advocated in the media on television talk shows such as *Good Morning America* and by parents in organized clubs such as the Mother-Daughter Book Club (notably highlighted by Shireen Dodson in her 1997 book of the same name). Politicians, too, have highlighted the value of book clubs; for example, Chicago's Mayor Richard Daley actively supported the city's "One Book, One Chicago" program, modeled after "If All of Seattle Read the Same Book."

Of course, libraries serving children and youth have offered and conducted book discussion programs for years, but the promotion (or visibility) and expansion of groups throughout the community have become a popular and alternative venue for parents and children to share noncompetitive, structured time in a nonmedia, nonsport setting.

A primary goal of a book club is to encourage both parents and kids to think creatively, to express ideas, and to socialize in a relaxed and comfortable milieu. A second goal is to develop an appreciation for reading and a general sense that good literature can be enjoyable and recreational.

Teachers also use children's literature regularly as part of the literacy curriculum by incorporating literature circles and book discussion groups into classroom activities. Research on classroom discussion sessions shows a variety of positive outcomes for children's intellectual development and reading proficiency. As Linda B. Gambrell and Janice F. Almasi (1996, p. xi), coeditors of *Lively Discussions! Fostering Engaged Reading,* note, "it is through the personal interpretation of both narrative and informational text that learners come to better understand themselves, others, and the world in which we live."

The public library, viewed as an extension and supplement to formal academic education, serves as a logical locale to implement and conduct discussion groups for both children and families. In contrast to the school setting, where a discussion program has a literacy curriculum focus, the public library can offer a more light-hearted, social exchange that provides encouragement in a comfortable, welcoming environment to

- read voluntarily,

- widen participants' experience and knowledge of children's literature,

- promote library services in general, and

- develop social and public-speaking skills.

Gambrell (1996, p. 26) believes that "discussion brings together listening, speaking, and thinking skills as participants engage in exchanging ideas, responding and reacting to text as well as to the ideas of others." Encouraging free thought and expression helps children feel confident and valued, that their voiced opinions count.

Adults can benefit and bond in two ways when participating in family or parent-child discussion programs: by sharing a unique experience with their child and by coming together with peers to appreciate literature to which they may not have been exposed. After one of my first Father-Son programs, one dad remarked to me that he never knew a "kid's" book could present so much substance for discussion. Discussion groups allow the librarian or group leader to promote some of the best literature, and they allow kids to read without the requirement of reporting back in a prestructured, instructional environment. Just as traditional story times generate an early appreciation of art, poetry, music, and literature, exposure to different genres, writing styles, and formats through discussion will further children's understanding of the world around them and foster a fondness for reading pleasure and fun.

It is hoped that this guide with ready-made discussion plans for one hundred books will facilitate the youth librarian, teacher, parent, or even scout leader and camp counselor in designing, implementing, and conducting discussion groups for children and parents. With some encouragement, settings beyond the library can be employed, including scout troops, after-school care programs, summer-camp sessions, and in-school lunchtime groups. A chapter is included with specifics for starting and running a group, helpful hints on how to develop questions, tips on icebreakers, and the basic brief rule of thumb for leading a discussion.

The book is then divided into four chapters, each representing a particular type of discussion group and providing nuts-and-bolts information on using the book for discussion—titles with plot summaries, character sketches, themes, suggested questions, and ideas for similar readings. In addition to the now popular Mother-Daughter series, a Father-Son Book Club and Family Book Group are included as alternative parent—child programs. Finally, a traditional child-only program, Readers' Rap, rounds out the assortment. Besides gender-specific communities, keep in mind that groups may be formed around a multitude of themes or genres. Science fiction buffs can meet regularly to discuss both classic and new titles; fantasy aficionados, mystery fans, and so on can create their own networks. In addition, the numerous titles featuring children in foreign settings provide opportunities to form a group with an "around the world literature" theme.

Easy accessibility of discussion guides and titles is given with appended indices by title, author, theme, subject, and grade level. A bibliography for further professional reading is also included. The titles reflect a broad range of themes, interests, and genres, taking into account a multicultural approach and highlighting timeless classics from Roald Dahl's *James and the Giant Peach* (1961) and Oliver Butterworth's *The Enormous Egg* (1956) to new and imminent titles such as Sharon Creech's *Granny Torelli Makes Soup* (2003) and Blue Balliett's *Chasing Vermeer* (2004). At the same time, very popular books such as the Harry Potter or Lemony Snicket series or even Louis Sachar's *Holes* have be consciously eliminated because they have been in the mainstream through mass-marketing and feature films. Although these are wonderful books for discussion, my intention was to offer a more versatile and perhaps unique variety of lesser known but equally worthwhile books. Rationale for selections for each group is stated in the chapters' opening statements. All of the books suggested are just that—suggestions; they may be interchanged, when appropriate, between groups. Finally, although most books are intended for readers between Grades 3 and 8, it should be noted that certain picture books, and in particular the Caldecott Medal and Honor Books, have been included and should be incorporated for their unique art and literary value. Read, discuss, appreciate, and enjoy!

References

Dodson, Shireen, and Teresa Baker. *The Mother-Daughter Book Club.* New York: HarperCollins, 1997.

Gambrell, Linda B., and Janice F. Almasi, eds. *Lively Discussions! Fostering Engaged Reading.* Newark, NJ: International Reading Association, 1996.

Goldstein, Bill. "TV Book Clubs Try to Fill Oprah's Shoes." *New York Times* 16 December 2002, p. C17.

Ramirez, Marc. "On the Same Page? The Plot's Thickened as Other Cities Copy Seattle's Novel Reading Idea." *The Seattle Times* 24 March 2002, p. B1.

Chapter 1

Book Discussion Basics

Getting Started

The basic requirements for starting a book discussion group include four ingredients— kids, parents, books, and a plan. Your library has three of the four (parents, kids, and books), and creating the fourth is feasible with a little foresight and organization. Knowing your community is critical to determining which kind of group you should offer initially. A simple place to start is with your summer reading program participants. Registration information such as grade levels and ages can be useful in creating an initial list of possible discussion group members. These children and parents, already coming to the library, are a built-in target audience. Summer brings the added advantage of a relaxed, out-of-school period, when kids may be less pressured with extracurricular activities and homework. From this initial list of possible participants, you can host one or two summer sessions as part of the overall summer reading program.

Your first sessions can be children-only meetings, which I call Readers' Rap; parent-child meetings, which I call Family Book Group; or a combination of both. There are many other possibilities, including gender-oriented parent-child groups such as Mother-Daughter and Father-Son groups, which are explored in this guide.

After determining your format, evaluate your summer reading community's needs and decide whether daytime or evening programs work best. For parent-inclusive groups, the early evening is usually a safe bet. Meetings for kids only may be scheduled during the day.

Invitation is the key to creating a strong following. Introductory flyers, library and school newsletter announcements, Parent-Teacher Organization (PTO) bulletins, and last-minute reminder calls to attend ensure steady participation. As with any other library program, a following can develop in which participation is invited on a monthly or six-week basis. Building a dedicated group can also extend beyond your specific library by partnering with a neighboring community institution that also provides group programming for children. Introduce the idea of bringing the book discussion session to their site and taking turns co-leading with staff at the local after-school day-care center, a neighboring public library or branch serving both communities, or the local community center.

1

Choosing Titles

The realm of children's literature is widespread across genres, time periods, and levels of difficulty and substance. What makes a book discussable and what engages both kids and parents in conversation that brings together ideas from both an adult and child's perspective? Good novels have four components:

1. characterization

2. plot

3. conflict and resolution

4. theme

Individually and combined, these components produce situations and issues for a book's characters that are provocative, providing further opportunities for thinking and perhaps analysis. Engaging, well-developed characters with unique personalities or distinct and compelling issues or needs can encourage exploration or inquiry into what that character does or how and why that character behaves, acts, or thinks. For example, in William Steig's classic, *The Real Thief,* Derek's behavior as a thief and his refusal to come forward create circumstances that only he can correct, yet he continues to makes choices that implicate and harm his falsely accused friend, Gawain. Conflict within Derek's own feelings of guilt and greed are clearly portrayed in this moralistic tale.

Controversial themes set within a historical time period, for example, or in modern or fantasy settings make for critical, meaty subjects. Jerry Spinelli uses themes of trust, peer acceptance, fear, and courage in his novel *Wringer,* all easily understood by today's youth. Palmer's upcoming tenth birthday with the promised ritual of performing as a wringer on Pigeon Day challenges his beliefs and physical aptness, placing his position within his circle of friends in jeopardy.

An author's writing style and how points are carried through symbolism, imagery, and other literary devices is another criteria to use when selecting. In *Protecting Marie,* Kevin Henkes employs the use of a paper doll, Marie, as a symbol of Fanny's feelings of security, privacy, control over herself, and trust. Henkes also uses a literary descriptive technique to emphasize through metaphor the emotions of Fanny and her father, Henry. In a kitchen scene when Henry's anger and frustration over his struggling art career is a strong issue, the accidental turnover of the dog's food bowl filled with kibbles is a wonderfully descriptive passage to explore.

> On her knees, Fanny cleaned up the kibbles, some had ended up in Dinner's water dish. Already they were saturated, breaking apart—miniature fireworks exploding in a dish on the kitchen floor in a warm old house on a cold first day of the year.

The image of the kibbles "breaking apart" represents Fanny's confidence and even her heartbreak as she fears Dinner (her dog) will be taken away from her. Henry's anger is paralleled through the visually descriptive "fireworks exploding in a dish." Fanny's mother and the comfort she provides is represented through the detailing of the "warm old house" as it contrasts with her father's selfish concerns and impatience of "a cold first day of the year." The use of language and imagery should not, however, turn the discussion into a literary lesson, but an introduction to some examples, if available, can launch some meaningful exchanges between participants and especially between adults and children.

Finally, books that have solutions to conflict or situations that seem debatable, controversial, or even unresolved create a basis for discussion. Again, in the book *Wringer,* Spinelli leaves us wondering on the last two pages if the yearly pigeon shoot will continue to take place after Palmer bravely rescues Nipper from the fallen pigeons, and a child asks if she might not have a pigeon for a pet. Will

Palmer start a campaign to end it? How will his response to the shooting be received by his peers and at school?

Controversial themes and conflicts may spark concern among parents and participating adults if not chosen or handled correctly. Often, reading level does not parallel a child's emotional or maturity level. However, if chosen correctly, many of these highly discussable topics can kindle positive conversation in the group. Look for issues that relate to behavior and moral dilemmas based on your group's age and experience rather than on its cognitive reading ability. Survey reviews in both professional journals and mainstream media venues. Track award winners, talk to your potential group members about their interests, scout out books that similar groups have selected for discussion, and perhaps provide a forum for group selection by either voting or creating a list of suggested titles. Most importantly, you should read the books ahead of time to preview your possible choices before making decisions; this will allow you to judge whether a book is appropriate for the group's age, gender, and so forth and also to ascertain the book's potential for discussion.

Providing Books

Once you have chosen a selection of titles that will work for your target group, making them available in multiple copies at the time of registration is another key to running a successful discussion club. Large library systems have the advantage of interlibrary loaning between branches or of actually keeping a core collection of book discussion paperbacks available in a central location for distribution when needed. A smaller library may take advantage of an active Friends group and have it sponsor the program by providing the funds for paperback purchasing. Some libraries make these purchases part of a core collection, labeled as such, and others even provide the new paperbacks to participants as gifts from their Friends organization. Developing a core collection of multiple copies can also allow a small library to interchange books with other neighboring libraries on a special loan policy. In addition, cooperating with a local bookstore, where participants can receive a discount if they purchase their own copies, may be another solution. The point here is to make it easy for your participants to find copies and to have them available as soon as registration begins. This will encourage reading ahead of planned session dates so that meaningful time can be spent at the meetings. It will also allow your participants to watch for segments or questionable morsels that might pique their attention or curiosity as they continue to read.

Questions That Inspire and Promote Great Discussion

Carefully thinking about and creating questions that lend themselves to interpretation rather than evaluation or factual content is the critical link to get your participants—young and old—to think about and express their views. As you read and prepare for the session you will lead, begin to think about and write down what the prevalent question, issue, or concept is in the story and then develop and cluster several related questions to that main one. Keep in mind that answers can be varied, displaying an assortment of opinions that are neither right nor wrong. Answers should also be interpreted from sample passages in the text you might use to question why, what if, or how characters act and situations develop. For example in the book *Wringer,* teasing and mental torture is a running theme that is clearly displayed in the scene where Dorothy, Palmer's friend, is "treestumped" by Beans, the boys' ringleader, everyday after school. An interpretive question can be asked after reading the following passage from the book.

> For a while it had been enough just to bother Dorothy Gruzik, enough to hear the laughter of himself and his pals. Now he wanted more. He wanted something from Dorothy. He wanted her to scream or laugh or cry or kick or sling a book bag. Or even scowl. A good scowl, that would do for starters. Anything but ignore them.

This question can then elicit discussion on the behavior and rationale of both Beans and Dorothy: "Why did Beans insist on a stronger reaction from Dorothy, and how did Dorothy deal with the constant torment?" Interject a factual question whenever you want to remind participants of specific plot advancements or character motivation. In the same scene, Dorothy finally reacts. "What does Dorothy do specifically to make the boys stop?" Clarify the answer by reading from the text. Use evaluative questions to initiate some criticism of an author's strategy or perspective, such as asking, "Why did the author write the ending as he did? Did you feel another ending was more realistic, better, etc.?"

In addition, consider the book's overall appeal to brainstorm and develop questions. Does the book have a character with an engaging personality, a particular writing style that the author has employed, a setting in a specific time period in history, or simply an intriguing plot line?

Leading the Discussion

The first session of any new book group is the one that brings new participants together and can hopefully encourage continued gatherings as you, the leader, make everyone feel welcome. Food is an excellent way to entice a relaxed comfort level, whether it is pizza or cupcakes or a treat related to the book being discussed. I led a discussion on the offbeat mystery by Kate Klise, *Regarding the Fountain,* and served pumpkin muffins with honey, an added feature in the story's school cafeteria menu. Serving food at the beginning stimulates some mingling at the treats table, and as everyone is filling out a nametag and settling in around a circle of chairs, you can then begin with an easy icebreaker activity or introduction.

Icebreakers

This can be as simple as asking everyone to introduce themselves. However, an approach that is less intimidating and more fun might be to use a riddle game in which everyone picks a riddle from a basket, takes turns reading it out loud, and waits for the group to call out an answer. The purpose here is to get everyone to talk and connect a bit before the real discussion begins. Using an icebreaker that is related to the book is always a good idea. Again, with the book *Regarding the Fountain,* Klise employs the use of puns throughout the story. I created a series of puns on separate small papers held in a basket and had the kids and adults take turns reading and figuring them out. We then began to talk about the puns in the story. An easy segue into the discussion becomes natural this way. If the book you are discussing has a setting in another culture or historical time period, finding a simple game to play from that country or era might be a creative beginning to your session.

Icebreakers also help both children and adults become familiar with each other more quickly so that equal participation is promoted and the feeling of "adult superiority" is removed. In joint adult-children programs, all members should be treated as co-participants; regardless of age, participants respect and listen to each other and acknowledge each other's views, feelings, and ideas. Also, icebreakers help in a group that has fluctuating attendance by making newcomers and children, who do not come on a regular basis, feel welcome.

Once everyone is comfortable both physically and verbally, you can begin to explain and get members to buy into the brief ground rules to the program.

- Respect everyone.

- All answers are correct.

- Find your time to speak.

- Respond to others.

- State your opinion.

Respect for everyone's opinions and thoughts is first and foremost. There are no right or wrong answers. Although no one needs to wait to be called on, waiting for an appropriate time to speak is expected. Responding to fellow members' ideas as well as stating one's own opinions is the way to converse with each other.

Managing Challenges

As leader, you will have to step back and facilitate, rather than participate. This might include subtly and tactfully managing certain behaviors in the group to encourage equal participation and move the discussion forward. Behavior that might hamper good discussion could be present in someone who dominates the conversation without giving someone else a chance to speak. Interject politely by verifying this person's comments and asking the group whether anyone agrees or disagrees and why. There might also be someone who leads the group astray on an unrelated tangent. Refocus the discussion by discreetly mentioning the point being discussed and asking if anyone else has an idea. In addition, there will inevitably be children or even parents who feel more at ease listening than talking. The challenge is to gently include them once or twice in the conversation to keep the balance. In this case, use a round-robin approach for one or two questions, asking for a one-line answer from everyone as you go around the circle. Use answers that participants provide as launch pads for follow-up questions and refrain from providing your own answers. The rule of thumb for a good discussion leader is to listen as much as possible.

When the discussion has fully developed and is complete, you can offer a routine closing activity that will allow everyone to give his or her final thoughts on the session by using one simple question for everyone to answer. Final questions might be as follows:

- Who was your favorite character and why?
- What was your favorite part of the book?
- Why did you like or not like the book?

You may then offer some extra information about the author, background material on any historical era or setting used in the story, provide a suggested follow-up list of books and perhaps booktalk one or two of them as a conclusion to the program. In addition, you can introduce the next book for the following meeting.

With these basics in tow, you can now begin to select, read, and plan for your book discussion program.

Books Cited

Henkes, Kevin. *Protecting Marie*. New York: Greenwillow Books, 1995.

Klise, Kate. *Regarding the Fountain: A Tale in Letters of Liars and Leaks*. New York: Avon Books, 1998.

Spinelli, Jerry. *Wringer*. New York: HarperCollins, 1997.

Steig, William. *The Real Thief*. New York: Farrar, Straus & Giroux, 1973.

Resources

Fineman, Maria. *Talking about Books: A Step-by-Step Guide for Participating in Book Discussion Groups*. Rockville, MD: Talking about Books, 1997.

Jacobsohn, Rachel W. *The Reading Group Handbook: Everything You Need to Know, from Choosing Members to Leading Discussions*. New York: Hyperion, 1998.

Moore, Ellen, and Kira Stevens. *Good Books Lately: The One-Stop Resource for Book Groups and Other Greedy Readers*. New York: St. Martin's Press, 2004.

Slezak, Ellen, ed. *The Book Group Book*. 3rd edition. Chicago: Chicago Review Press, 2000.

Web Sites

Book Spot Book Discussion Center: http://www.bookspot.com/discussion/ (accessed 1 November 2004).

Reading Group Choices: http://www.readinggroupchoices.com/ (accessed 1 November 2004).

Book Muse: http://www.bookmuse.com/pages/notes/kidscategory.asp?group=none (Accessed 1 November 2004).

Chapter 2

Family Book Group

Today's families reside in many different types of households. Children are raised in numerous situations beyond the traditional nuclear setting. A family book group offers the child between the ages of nine and fourteen the opportunity to come to the program with a special adult, be it a parent, grandparent, aunt, uncle, college-age sibling, favorite caregiver, or other person in his or her life. Groups can also be divided by age: nine to eleven year olds and twelve to fourteen year olds, for example.

Planning for and leading a multigenerational coed group is not without its challenges. Wide and varied interests and opinions may exist when adult role models range in ages from young adult or college-age individuals to the elder grandparents. Such a group may also present a multitude of reading levels and perhaps adult limitations in our ever-growing multicultural school and community settings. However, these challenges can also produce benefits as an eclectic intergenerational group when various opinions and views may spark greater discussion and offer opportunity to develop a healthy respect for diverse ages and cultures of both genders. Encouraging your families to read together and to read aloud as a regular routine in preparation for the program will not only provide a more focused and readied group for discussion, it will also allow for the slower, less interested reader to participate more wholly by coming to the group with a positive involved feeling.

Titles in this chapter reflect an array of genres of fiction as well as some picture books with issues and themes that lend themselves to varied interpretation and thought. Picture books can be a good opener to the series of sessions offering an illustrated story as a read aloud with provocative questions to encourage discussion at the end of the reading. This defines the concept and structure of your discussion group, especially for adults who need a clearer understanding on why they must read together with their child, as well as for adults whose first language is not English and are concerned about participating in a literature program with their English-dominant child for the first time. A wordless picture book, such as David Wiesner's *Sector 7,* can cultivate imaginative thought expressed more simply. In addition, gender is not a focus of any of the main protagonists in the selections for this chapter; rather, both male and female characters are represented, expressing universal conflicts, qualities, and concepts. Books with animal protagonists such as Dick King-Smith's *Martin's Mice* or William Steig's *The Real Thief* with such powerful themes of right and wrong are non-gender-based and can be appreciated by all readers. Fantasy-based stories such as Bill Brittain's *The Wish Giver* posing dilemmas, outcomes, and solutions will also work well. Keeping with universal themes such as the concept of war in Mem Fox's *Feathers and Fools* in addition to choosing more family-oriented issues such as those in Namioka's *Yang the Youngest and His Terrible Ear* is the basic key to successfully choosing books for this group.

Baseball in April and Other Stories

Gary Soto

San Diego: Harcourt, Brace, Jovanovich, 1990

Reading Level: . . . . Grades 5–7
Genre: . . . . Realistic fiction/short stories
Themes: . . . . Hope, dreams/aspirations, success versus failure
Awards: . . . . Pura Belpre Honor Book

Plot Summary

These eleven short stories center around a community of Hispanic school kids growing up in a working-class area of Fresno, California. Each story reflects a particular issue that its main character deals with as he or she lives a daily routine; in essence, all the characters are trying to do and be their best. These are all good kids living within the limitations of their circumstances, hoping to break away from constraints that hold them back and attain an unexpected goal, no matter how small or insignificant it might appear to others.

Main Characterization

Alfonso in "Broken Chain" would like to begin a new relationship with a girl he has met and has the typical early-adolescent concerns about his appearance and acceptance of his peers.

Jesse in "Baseball in April" aspires to join the little league team, practices, and tries out, but he is rejected because of his poor batting skills. He joins an unofficial team that forms in the park, where he scores a hit during the season and makes it to third base.

Hector in "Two Dreamers" has difficulty coping with his grandfather's dream of buying a better house to show off to his Mexican family and is uncomfortable about having to make the phone calls to the real estate office for his non-English-speaking *abuelo*.

Veronica in "Barbie" would love to own and play with a real Barbie doll and is terribly disappointed when her well-meaning uncle gives her a cheaper copy of the prestigious doll.

Fausto and his mother find a way to acquire a guitar without the usual expense involved in "The No-Guitar Blues."

Victor in "Seventh Grade" decides to take French instead of his first language, Spanish, and gets into amusing trouble when he attempts to answer his teacher.

Yollie in "Mother and Daughter" suffers the embarrassment of her dyed, old dress washing out in a rainstorm the night of the school dance.

Gilbert is convinced that he can be "The Karate Kid" he's seen in the movies and convinces his mother to spend hard-earned money on lessons, only to later find he is bored and unhappy with the sport and doesn't have the heart to admit it to his parents.

Manuel bravely enters the talent show where he will lip-sync to "La Bamba" with unexpected, humorously different results.

Lupe strives at succeeding in a sport, even though she has always been awkward and clumsy. She ultimately becomes "The Marble Champ."

Maria in "Growing Up" learns a lesson in life when she convinces her parents she is too old to go on vacation with them and stays behind.

Themes

Each of these stories represents the ordinary person's dreams and aspirations for either a better life or a desired accomplishment. Hope and uncertainty, success and failure, play opposite each other as the characters enter and exit a moment in life that will have a certain impact on their awareness and development.

Books with Similar Issues or Themes

Short story collections centering around young people's lives.

American Eyes: New Asian-American Short Stories for Young Adults. Edited by Lori M. Carlson. New York: Henry Holt, 1994.

America Street: A Multicultural Anthology of Stories. Edited by Anne Mazer. New York: Persea Books, 1993.

Avi. *What Do Fish Have to Do with Anything? And Other Stories.* Cambridge, MA: Candlewick Press, 1997.

Join In: Multiethnic Short Stories. Edited by Donald R. Gallo. New York: Delacorte Press, 1993.

13: Thirteen Stories That Capture the Agony and the Ecstasy of Being Thirteen. Edited by James Howe. New York: Atheneum, 2003.

Author-Related Sources

Berger, Laura Standley, ed. *Twentieth-Century Young Adult Writers.* Detroit: St. James Press: 1994, 600–2.

Gary Soto official Web site: http://www.garysoto.com/ (accessed 12 February 2005).

Hipple, Ted, ed. Vol. 3 of *Writers for Young Adults.* New York: Charles S. Scribner's Sons, 1997, 183–92.

Holtze, Sally Holmes, ed. *Seventh Book of Junior Authors and Illustrators.* New York: H. W. Wilson, 1996, 303–4.

Silvey, Anita, ed. *Children's Books and Their Creators.* Boston: Houghton Mifflin, 1995, 613–15.

Discussion Questions

For *Baseball in April and Other Stories*

1. What do these stories say about the lives of all these characters?

2. What do all of the characters in these stories have in common besides their Hispanic heritage?

3. Why are the problems and issues these characters bring up in each story really about all kids?

4. Why is hope an important theme throughout all these stories?

5. How does each of these characters succeed in their goals?

6. Which story could you identify with most? Why?

7. Which story did you like the most or least? Why?

Beast

by Donna Jo Napoli

New York: Atheneum, 2000

Reading Level: . . . . Grades 6–8
Genre: . . . . Fantasy
Themes: . . . . Survival, faith, forgiveness
Awards: . . . . School Library Journal Best Books

Plot Summary

Orasmyn, Prince of Persia, makes the difficult choice to use a camel with a scar on its neck as the sacrificial animal for the holy Feast of Sacrifices day. The teachings of Muhammad clearly state that an animal that has suffered or been defiled cannot be used for religious sacrifice. Reasoning that all animals have some imperfections, Orasmyn wrestles with the dilemma and concludes that this particular camel is the best choice available. On the holy day, Orasmyn has an encounter with a *pari,* or fairy, who is displeased with his decision, telling him that he has failed a "royal test" and would now have to suffer the curse of being killed by the hand of his own father, the shah of Persia, before midnight of the next day. Vowing to elude the curse, Orasmyn and his father devise a plan to avoid each other all day as Orasmyn plans to spend the time in prayer locked in his room. On his way back to his quarters, a woman—the *pari,* once again—lures Orasmyn from his room and transforms him into a lion. Living in the body of a beast with the mind of a man, Orasmyn becomes acutely aware of how the curse will be fulfilled, for he cannot go to his room now and will become the object of a hunt led by his father. The story quickly evolves into one of survival for the prince who journeys to India, where he thinks he might live out his life within a pride of lions learning their behavior and habits, and then to France, a place for love, hoping that if he is able to attract the affection of a woman, the curse, as professed by the *pari,* will be undone. As in the traditional "Beauty and the Beast" fairy tale, Orasmyn lives the life of the beast taking advantage of a serendipitous visit by a father to lure and attract a daughter to his world and thus reverse the curse.

Main Characterization

This is clearly Orasmyn's story, describing the blending of his life in the dual animal and human worlds. As a lion, he is not accepted in the home of his birth, where he is feared and misunderstood, but he is equally unwelcome within the habitat of lions and struggles with the animalistic ways of killing, feeding on raw flesh and blood, and mating. Ostracized, the curse lives on beyond the first day, dooming him to perpetual loneliness. Always thinking as a man, survival becomes his utmost motivation; a secondary focus is to change his fate through calculated planning and forethought. His daily life in the abandoned castle in France underscores the human need to create a homelike atmosphere complete with a garden while meeting his beastly needs of sustenance through his foraging, ransacking, and hunting small prey. Belle is the young woman who will relieve Orasmyn of his malediction. She is brave, persistent, patient, loyal, and kind hearted. As in the fairytale, she is able to see within the beast's soul to understand his needs.

Themes

Survival becomes the main theme of the story from the moment that Orasmyn has his encounter with the *pari*. He is immediately faced with the challenge of outwitting the *pari*'s fatal plan, eventually coming to terms with the devious strategy the fairy has chosen. His human–animal existence affords him the intellectual ability to pursue his survival with foresight, expressing faith in the future. His religious beliefs give him the courage to feel remorse and hope for forgiveness. Belle's love for her father and family provides the strength she needs to come, stay, and return to the castle. Surviving in the home with a carnivorous wild animal, having faith to pursue her promise to her father, and forgiving both father and Orasmyn for her situation are interwoven themes.

Books with Similar Issues or Themes

Brooke, William J. *A Telling of the Tales*. New York: Harper & Row, 1990.

Five original renditions of the classic fairy tales—*Sleeping Beauty, Paul Bunyan, Cinderella, John Henry,* and *Jack and the Beanstalk*—with intriguing new contemporary endings.

Fletcher, Susan. *Shadow Spinner*. New York: Atheneum, 1998.

A fictional telling of how thirteen-year-old Marjan joined the sultan's harem in ancient Persia and gathered enough stories to tell Shahrazad, saving herself and the other young women.

Haddix, Margaret Peterson. *Just Ella*. New York: Simon & Schuster, 1999.

Following her romantic courtship and marriage, Ella must face the reality of a boring life in the castle with a dull, uninteresting husband. She takes steps to escape to a better life. A feminist approach to the traditional Cinderella story.

Levine, Gail Carson. *Ella Enchanted*. New York: HarperCollins, 1997.

The curse of obedience bestowed on her at birth makes Ella's life more difficult as she grows. This fantasy novel is based on the traditional Cinderella tale.

McKinley, Robin. *Beauty: A Retelling of the Story of Beauty & the Beast*. New York: Harper & Row, 1978.

A novel version told from the perspective of the young woman who is forced to leave her home to join the beast in his castle as payment for her father's act of taking a rose.

Napoli, Donna Jo. *Zel*. New York: Dutton Children's Books, 1996.

Based on the Rapunzel character, the lives of Zel, her mother, and suitor Konrad are explored from a psychological perspective in alternating chapters.

Author-Related Sources

"Donna Jo Napoli." In vol. 51 of *Children's Literature Review*. Farmington Hills, MI: Gale Group, 1999, 152–68.

"Donna Jo Napoli." In vol. 137 of *Something about the Author*. Farmington Hills, MI: Gale Group, 2003, 154–60.

Donna Jo Napoli Web site: http://www.donnajonapoli.com/ (accessed 30 May 2004).

Hipple, Ted, ed. *Writers for Young Adults*. New York: Scribner's, 2000, 217–26.

Silvey, Anita, ed. *Essential Guide to Children's Books and Their Creators*. Boston: Houghton Mifflin, 2002, 320.

Discussion Questions

For *Beast*

1. Why did Orasmyn justify the use of a scarred camel for the Feast of Sacrifices?

2. Why did the *pari* or fairy choose to change Orasmyn into a lion rather than into another animal?

3. What makes Orasmyn a creature existing in both the animal and human worlds?

4. How is religion important in Orasmyn's life? How does he try to follow the rules and beliefs of his religion, even as he needs to behave as a lion to survive?

5. Orasmyn is a gardener. Why are roses so important to him?

6. When Belle arrives at the castle, she finds weapons there and has the opportunity to protect herself by killing Orasmyn. Why doesn't she use the weapons?

7. *Mon ami* means "my friend" in French. Why does Belle choose to call Orasmyn *mon ami*?

8. Belle keeps a diary in the margins of a Chinese book. Why does she finally decide to show it to Orasmyn?

9. Why does Orasmyn need Belle?

10. Why does Belle return to the castle after visiting her family?

11. Why does Belle need Orasmyn?

12. Why did the *pari* include a way for Orasmyn to reverse the curse by gaining the love of a woman?

Because of Winn-Dixie

By Kate DiCamillo

Cambridge, MA: Candlewick Press, 2000

Reading Level: . . . . Grades 4–6

Genre: . . . . Realistic fiction

Themes: . . . . Friendship, sadness, loneliness, acceptance

Awards: . . . . Newbery Honor, School Library Journal Best Books, ALA Notable Children's Book, Michigan Mitten Award

Plot Summary

India Opal Buloni is adjusting to her new life in the southern town of Naomi, Florida, where her father is the preacher at the Open Arms Baptist Church. Finding it difficult to make friends her age, she explores her surroundings and recounts her observations from a ten-year-old's perspective. A chance visit to the local supermarket provides the opportunity to make a best friend—a dog she rescues from the angry grocer, promptly naming it after the grocery store chain, Winn-Dixie. Girl and dog quickly become inseparable, as Opal confides her deepest feelings of longing for her mother, who left when she was three. Opal is confident Winn-Dixie is listening and comprehending in his own way. Her newfound relationship forges a connection with other, rather eccentric town residents. These friends include Otis the pet store clerk, who gives her a job sweeping the store, her pay being a new collar and leash for Winn-Dixie; the town librarian, Miss Franny Block, who has old stories to tell; Gloria Dump, who is unjustly labeled "an old witch" and lives out her days alone in her house; and an assortment of children—the Dewberry brothers, Amanda Wilkinson, and five-year-old Sweetie Pie. All the while, Opal yearns to learn everything possible about her mother. She questions her father, asking for ten things related to her mama, one for every year Opal has been alive. As the summer progresses, Opal gains insight into everyone's peculiar behavior and situation as she visits with Miss Block in the library, reads *Gone with the Wind* aloud to Gloria Dump (who cannot see very well), encourages Otis to play his guitar and enjoy his music, and treats Amanda kindly despite her nasty behavior. Opal succeeds in bringing together this unlikely group of characters at a summer barbecue hosted at Gloria's house, where everyone appreciates the friendship and respect they have for each other. Ultimately Opal realizes, after almost losing Winn-Dixie in a thunderstorm, the value of cherishing life and what you make of it.

Main Characterization

India Opal Buloni is a ten-year-old girl struggling to feel whole without a mother. Friendless in a new town, she bonds first with several adults whose lonely existences seem to draw her into their lives. Unable to confide her true thoughts and emotions to her father, a preacher, she talks to her dog and gathers adult wisdom from her newfound friends. Her nonjudgmental personality allows her to accept the eccentricities of these adults, yet she is leery of developing relationships with her peers, Stevie and Dunlap Dewberry and Amanda Wilkinson, whose attitudes and behaviors are initially negative.

The preacher is Opal's father, who appears to be withdrawn, sad, and lonely. He focuses on his work and gives Opal the basic love and parental support of a single, hardworking parent.

Opal's mother is a shadow figure, mostly revealed through Opal's yearning to know more about her. Her alcoholism and abandonment of the family is revealed through Opal's conversations with her father and Gloria Dump.

Winn-Dixie is a charming, loveable, friendly dog that wins the heart of Opal and represents a confidante, best friend, and companion to a girl who is searching for more than childhood camaraderie. His panicky behavior in a thunderstorm indicates that a terrible experience may have left him fearful of rainstorms.

Miss Franny Block is the town librarian, operating out of a library started by her family. Her advanced age does not deter Opal from befriending her, offering an ear for old family stories.

Gloria Dump is the misunderstood resident of the town. Labeled a witch by the Dewberry brothers, her quiet life is enhanced by Winn-Dixie's entrance into her yard and Opal's attempt to retrieve him. A daily relationship grows as Opal learns about Gloria's former alcoholism, paralleling that of Opal's mother, and is guided to understand others, their emotional pain, and the reactive behavior it can cause.

Otis is a clerk in the pet store who has a passion for music and has been jailed for disobeying and hitting a police officer. His shyness and lack of confidence is countered by Opal's assertiveness and resolve.

The Dewberry boys, Stevie and Dunlap, are brothers, aged nine and ten, who continually tease Opal, unable to understand her willingness and need to maintain a relationship with her eccentric adult friends. Dunlap is more willing to accept Opal's friendship and is easier to convince than his brother Stevie.

Amanda Wilkinson is a girl who is reserved and unfriendly, quietly suffering from her own loss, her younger brother's accidental drowning. Her need for peer companionship is not evident at first, until a sympathetic and patient Opal returns her aloofness with kindness.

Sweetie Pie is a five-year-old girl who looks up to Opal as an older friend and whose innocence allows her to accept everyone equally.

Themes

Friendship and the importance of showing understanding for each other's circumstances is a dominant theme of this book. Many of the people whom Opal befriends, as well as Winn-Dixie the dog, are coping with a loss or a bad experience; sadness and loneliness appear in the story as recurring themes. Interaction with both adult and child characters helps Opal to accept her motherless situation and to grow emotionally over a summer as she adopts a new attitude to be grateful and happy for what she has—her father, her dog, and new friends.

Books with Similar Issues or Themes

Holt, Kimberly Willis. *My Louisiana Sky.* New York: Henry Holt, 1998.
> When Tiger Ann's grandmother dies, she is left with her mentally slow parents. She is offered a chance to live a more normal life with her aunt and must make a most difficult decision: whether to leave her parents or remain as their source of emotional support.

Paterson, Katherine. *Flip-Flop Girl.* New York: Dutton, 1994.
> The death of her father brings Vinnie Matthews and her brother to a new town in Virginia. There she must adjust to a new life with the help of a friend, Lupe, who always wears bright orange flip-flops.

Peck, Richard. *A Year Down Yonder.* New York: Dial Books for Young Readers, 2000.
> Mary Alice, age fifteen, is about to spend a whole year with her Grandma Dowdel, who can fill life with lots of drama and some interesting surprises.

Rylant, Cynthia. *Missing May*. New York: Orchard Books, 1992.

      Twelve-year-old Summer is looking for a spiritual sign to go on with her life after the death of her Aunt May, the only "mother" she has known for the last six years.

Shreve, Susan. *Blister*. New York: Arthur A. Levine, 2001.

      Alyssa "Blister" Reed is angry her father has moved out and upset about having to live in a new apartment with her emotionally struggling mother following the stillbirth of a baby sister.

Author-Related Sources

Abbey, Cherie D. In vol. 10 of *Biography Today Author series: Profiles of People of Interest to Young Readers*. Detroit, MI: Omnigraphics, 2002.

Candlewick Press biography: http://www.candlewick.com/cwp/authill.asp?b=Author&m=bio&id=1989&pix=n (accessed 30 May 2004).

"Kate DiCamillo." In vol. 121 of *Something about the Author*. Farmington Hills, MI: Gale Group, 2001, 74–5.

Kate DiCamillo Web site: http://www.katedicamillo.com/ (accessed 12 May 2005).

Discussion Questions

For *Because of Winn-Dixie*

1. Why does Opal impulsively decide to claim the dog at the Winn-Dixie supermarket?

2. Why does the preacher agree to let Opal keep Winn-Dixie?

3. What do you know about Opal's personality?

4. What makes Winn-Dixie such a special dog for Opal?

5. Why does Opal at first feel more comfortable making friends with adults instead of children her own age?

6. When Gloria Dump and Opal meet, Gloria asks Opal to tell her everything about herself. What does Gloria Dump mean when she says she had to see Opal "with her heart"?

7. Why does Opal tell everything about herself to Gloria Dump, someone she has just met?

8. What does Opal wish for most?

9. Why can't Opal express her true feelings to her father?

10. Why does the thunderstorm at the end of the story cause Opal to tell her father everything she is feeling?

11. Why is Amanda's behavior aloof and unfriendly toward Opal? How does she truly feel?

12. What is the real meaning of the Littmus Lozenges in the story?

13. What do Opal and the other characters learn from their newfound friendships?

14. What does Gloria Dump mean when she tells Opal "you can't always judge people by the things they done. You got to judge them by what they are doing now"?

15. Why did the author, Kate DiCamillo, title her story *Because of Winn-Dixie*?

Chasing Vermeer

By Blue Balliett, Illustrated by Brett Helquist

New York: Scholastic Press, 2004

Reading Level: . . . . Grades 5–7
Genre: . . . . Mystery
Themes: . . . . Deception, art appreciation, problem solving, friends

Plot Summary

The new school year begins under a mysterious cloud for students Petra and Calder, their new teacher, Ms. Hussey, and several neighboring adults in the vicinity of the University of Chicago School. Three copies of a letter outlining the major art theft of a rare Vermeer painting are sent to three adults in the community, starting a chain of events for a brilliant crime scheme. Petra and Calder are classmates who live on the same block but have never been friends. They begin to talk when the publicity surrounding the ominous media coverage over the art theft seems a bit too coincidentally related to a school assignment involving a significant correspondence and a class trip to the Art Institute of Chicago. Bizarre coincidences begin to happen in both Petra and Calder's lives. Petra has a dream related to the missing painting where she visualizes the woman in the art piece, while Calder, always fascinated and intrigued by his set of pentominoes, begins to rely on their variety of probabilities to decipher a series of clues that keep popping up. As the school year progresses, a combination of intuition, problem solving, daring investigative episodes on the campus, and some old-fashioned luck result in a conclusion to the mystery and recovery of the missing painting.

Main Characterization

Petra Andalee is the oldest of five children living in a chaotic household with very little privacy. She is shy and somewhat of a loner at school with aspirations of becoming a writer.

Calder Pillay is also an outsider at school. He is an only child, with a passion for pentominoes to the point where he allows the random choosing of the letters they form to help him make choices and decisions concerning his life and the mystery he is trying to solve with Petra.

Ms. Hussey is a free-spirited teacher working with a very loose curriculum. As the recipient of one of the letters, however, she is concerned about her well-being and the potential crime with which she might be connected.

Mrs. Sharpe is an elderly, mysterious woman, appearing to be harsh and irascible, yet equally concerned about the letter she receives in the mail. She is linked to the mystery by her husband's murder several years earlier.

Vincent Watch is the third recipient of the letter, intrigued by the possibilities it might have for his own writing. He becomes a secret confidante of Mrs. Sharpe, visiting her after he closes his bookshop.

Tommy Segovia appears as a friend of Calder's through a series of coded messages. His situation with his mother and stepfather are odd additions to the storyline but serve as a way to develop the coded clues leading to the mystery's solution.

Themes

Deception and problem solving are central themes in this novel as both the thief and central adult players use a variety of ways to hide the truth while the children employ a series of mathematical and problem-solving concepts to piece together the clues to the puzzle. In addition, Calder and Petra develop a special friendship and certain respect for the value of art.

Books with Similar Issues or Themes

Raskin, Ellen. *The Westing Game*. New York: E. Dutton, 1978.
> Sixteen people gather for the reading of Samuel W. Westing's will and must figure out who among them is his murderer.

Sachar, Louis. *Holes*. New York: Farrar, Straus & Giroux, 1998.
> Three boys sent to a correctional camp in a Texas desert uncover the secret behind the mysterious buried treasure on the property.

Stanley, Diane. *The Gentleman and the Kitchen Maid*. Illustrated by Dennis Nolan. New York: Dial Books for Young Readers, 1994.
> When the subjects of two paintings across the gallery from each other fall in love and are then placed in separate rooms, they are cleverly reunited in a reproduction by an art student who has come to the museum to study the works of the Dutch masters. This is a playful introduction to the art of nineteen painters from the seventeenth century.

Van Draanen, Wendelin. *Sammy Keyes and the Art of Deception*. New York: Alfred A. Knopf, 2003.
> Super sleuth Sammy Keyes becomes involved in the art world, foils a robbery attempt and discovers the secret behind the real crime at the gallery.

Voight, Cynthia. *The Vandemark Mummy*. New York: Atheneum, 1991.
> Siblings Phineas and Althea set out to uncover the reason behind the threatened theft of a new collection of ancient Egyptian artifacts at Vandemark College, where their father is a professor and responsible for the care of the new acquisition.

Author-Related Sources

Castellitto, Linda M. "Mystery at the Museum: Blue Balliet's beguiling tale makes children think twice about art." First Person Book Page. http://www.bookpage.com/0406bp/ blue_balliett.html (accessed 31 July 2004).

Lee, Felicia R. "Chasing Art, Sixth Grader and a Dream." *New York Times,* 15 July 2004, p. E1.

Discussion Questions

For *Chasing Vermeer*

1. How does the author weave in various clues that seem disconnected yet related to solving the mystery?

2. How does the author use mathematics in a book about art and deception?

3. Why does the code that Calder and Tommy use work as part of a mathematical scheme?

4. What kind of relationship do Calder and Petra have?

5. Why is this more a story of action rather than one of character and relationships?

6. How does the concept of coincidental occurrences drive the mystery?

7. Which, if any, coincidences seemed too contrived for the story to be effective? What loopholes were left unanswered?

8. What is the significance of the frog in the story?

9. What does the author mean by the puzzle's answer, "The Lady Lives"?

The Enormous Egg

By Oliver Butterworth, Illustrated by Louis Darling

New York: Little, Brown, 1956

Reading Level: . . . . Grades 3 and 4
Genre: . . . . Science/fantasy
Themes: . . . . Freedom, responsibility, greed/self-interest

Plot Summary

Nate Twitchell, son of the local newspaper editor in Freedom, New Hampshire, is responsible for the care of the family chickens. He is amazed when one of the hens hatches an enormous egg. The egg's unusually large size proves difficult for the hen to care for alone, so Nate obliges by helping to turn it every few hours to keep it warm. Days pass, and Nate and his family realize the egg is not a normal one for a chicken and are curious to find out what will emerge. Eventually a baby triceratops that Nate names Uncle Beazley surprises everyone except Dr. Ziemer, a visiting paleontologist from the Natural History Museum in Washington, DC. Dr. Ziemer excitedly helps Nate understand the care and feeding of a dinosaur and shows him how to record the animal's progress scientifically. Nate's dilemma begins when his new pet becomes too large and expensive to keep on an average family farm, and Dr. Ziemer and the scientists offer to take him to Washington for scientific study.

Main Characterization

Nate Twitchell is an average twelve-year-old boy from a small town. He is a diligent, dedicated individual, eager to do the right thing, but also concerned about his own happiness.

Dr. Ziemer, a paleontologist, is dedicated to his science but respects the needs and concerns of his new friend, Nate.

Themes

Freedom of choice and moral responsibility are intertwined themes in this science fantasy. Nate is conscious of his role as a pet owner, which carries the responsibility of caring and feeding for the animal right from the laying of its enormous egg. He is asked to make a choice in terms of the best solution for Uncle Beazley's welfare and must put aside his desire to keep this unusual pet. Greed and self-interest are parallel themes evident in how the scientists and other various visitors arrive at the farm and try to coerce Nate into selling his pet for selfish or otherwise inappropriate reasons.

Books with Similar Issues or Themes

Coville, Bruce. *Jeremy Thatcher, Dragon Hatcher*. New York: Harcourt Brace Jovanovich, 1991.
    The shiny ball that Jeremy buys at a magic shop is really a dragon's egg, which hatches into a small dragon that begins to grow rapidly.

Griffith, Helen V. *Dinosaur Habitat.* New York: Greenwillow, 1998.

>Nathan and his younger brother are suddenly transported back in time to a dinosaur world where they must find a way to survive and return to their modern-day world.

Richler, Mordecai. *Jacob Two-Two and the Dinosaur.* New York: Alfred A. Knopf, 1987.

>The cute little lizard Jacob receives as a gift from his parents turns out really to be a Diplodocus that Jacob must hide from the Canadian government.

Yep, Laurence. *Tiger's Apprentice.* New York: HarperCollins, 2003.

>When a precious phoenix egg is stolen by a villainous magical creature trying to take over the world, Tom, a new apprentice to Mr. Hu the shape-changing man-tiger, becomes reluctantly involved in getting the talisman back to ensure peace in the world.

Zindel, Paul. *Raptor.* New York: Hyperion Books for Children, 1998.

>Zack uncovers a giant egg that hatches a baby raptor on his father's paleontologist expedition in Utah. The idea that there may be more than fossils on the site becomes a frightening reality when Zack comes face-to-face with the baby raptor's ferociously angry mother.

Author-Related Sources

Berger, Laura Standley, ed. *Twentieth-Century Children's Writers.* Detroit: St. James Press, 1995, 179.

"Oliver Butterworth." In vol. 1 of *Something about the Author.* Detroit: Gale Research, 1971, 40–1.

"Oliver Butterworth." Obituary, in vol. 66 of *Something about the Author.* Farmington Hills, MI: Gale Group, 1991, 34.

Silvey, Anita, ed. *Children's Books and Their Creators.* Boston: Houghton Mifflin, 1995, 110–11.

Discussion Questions

For The Enormous Egg

1. What moral or personal decision did Nate have to make concerning his pet, Uncle Beazley?

2. What instincts did he rely on to make these decisions?

3. What problems do Nate, his family, Dr. Ziemer, and the government officials each have in the story?

4. Could the problem of taking care of Uncle Beazley have been resolved any other way?

5. How did you feel for Nate, his family, and Dr. Ziemer?

6. How does Nate deal with the issue of responsibility and freedom of choice?

7. What did the author do to make this fantasy story seem as realistic as possible?

8. What did Nate learn from his experience with raising a dinosaur?

9. This story was written in 1956. Could it have taken place in today's world? What makes the story timeless?

10. Why was it important for the government to get involved with the solution to Nate's problem?

11. Why is it important to support research and scientific study?

12. How do television and political talk shows influence public opinion?

Feathers and Fools

By Mem Fox, Illustrated by Nicholas Wilton

New York: Harcourt Brace, 1996

Reading Level: . . . . Grade 3; discussion level: Grades 3–6
Genre: . . . . Picture book
Themes: . . . . War, jealousy, cultural differences, prejudice, ignorance

Plot Summary

A flock of swans and a pride of peacocks live side by side in a garden and begin to notice each other's differences. The first peacock points out the strangeness of the swans' ability to swim and fly and is happy that peacocks can do neither, because they would surely drown and look ridiculous. After a bit, the first peacock concludes—to the distress and anxiety of the other peacocks—that the swans' abilities give them strength and power that will force the peacocks to live by swan rules. The peacocks begin to assemble ammunition of sharpened feathers to defend their way of life, causing the swans to stockpile their own arsenal of weapons. Each species fears the other more each day; both are on edge at every movement. Eventually the first peacock panics as a swan flies overhead with a reed for her nest making, and the first shots of war are fired, ending when all birds have perished and the garden is destroyed. Time passes and two eggs left from the original inhabitants hatch, one with a swan and one with a peacock. The baby birds meet, can only see their similarities, and instantly become friends, sharing the world together.

Main Characterization

The first peacock observes his neighboring swans and cannot accept the differences. He immediately feels threatened, inciting fear, rage, jealousy, and violence in his fellow peacocks. He is stupidly narrow-minded and fairly influential.

The pride of peacocks is a group of followers, believing without evaluating and reasoning for themselves.

The flock of swans appear to be peaceful, yet when feel threatened, they choose to defend themselves, even if it means resorting to violence.

Baby swan and baby peacock represent the innocence of childhood, viewing life through an unprejudiced lens.

Themes

Jealousy and a respect for lifestyle and cultural differences are the main theme of this book, illustrated through the birds and the differing abilities of each species. Ignorance leading to fear is also prevalent as the first peacock demonstrates his viewpoint and succeeds in exaggerating the issue that flying and swimming will lead to superiority. Prejudice is a subtheme as the species develop a dislike and disdain for each other and cannot work through their differences.

Books with Similar Issues or Themes

Bunting, Eve. *Gleam and Glow.* Illustrated by Peter Sylvada. San Diego, CA: Harcourt Children's Books, 2001.
> Viktor must leave his home with his family in war-torn Bosnia to live in a refugee camp. Upon his return, he finds that, amid the destruction, his two pet fish have multiplied and filled the pond with gold.

Garland, Sherry. *The Lotus Seed.* Illustrated by Tatsuro Kiuchi. New York: Harcourt, Brace, Jovanovich, 1993.
> Fleeing the Vietnamese Civil War, a young girl saves a lotus seed to remember the brave emperor and her homeland. Years later her grandson takes the seed, plants it, and a beautiful flower blooms, representing life and hope.

Gregory, Valiska. *When Stories Fell Like Shooting Stars.* New York: Simon & Schuster, 1996.
> Two parallel fables, one focusing on greed and power leading to war, the other on cooperation and goodwill.

Popov, Nikolai. *Why?* New York: North South Books, 1996.
> A wordless story of how a mouse attacks a frog that is peacefully sitting in a meadow, forcing the frog to defend itself. The story shows how their argument escalates with each counterattack until both are annihilated.

Seuss, Dr. *The Butter Battle Book.* New York: Random House, 1984.
> The Yooks and the Snooks disagree on how to eat their buttered bread and begin to create a series of complicated weapons to make their individual points forcibly.

Tsuchiya, Yukio. *Faithful Elephants: A True Story of Animals, People and War.* Boston: Houghton Mifflin, 1988.
> During World War II, the zookeepers at the Ueno Zoo in Tokyo were forced to kill all the animals, fearing a bombing raid would cause their escape and wild run through the city. Reluctantly, three beloved elephants had to be starved to death as the only viable solution.

Author-Related Sources

Berger, Laura Standley, ed. *Twentieth-Century Children's Writers.* Detroit, MI: St. James Press, 1995, 364–5.

Holtze, Sally Holmes, ed. *Sixth Book of Junior Authors and Illustrators.* New York: H. W. Wilson, 1989, 88–9.

"Mem Fox." In vol. 80 of *Children's Literature Review.* Farmington Hills, MI: Gale Group, 2002, 8–51.

"Mem Fox." In vol. 103 of *Something about the Author.* Farmington Hills, MI: Gale Group, 1999, 50–8.

Mem Fox Web site: http://www.memfox.net/ (accessed 30 May 2004).

Silvey, Anita, ed. *Essential Guide to Children's Books and Their Creators.* Boston: Houghton Mifflin, 2002, 161–2.

Discussion Questions

For *Feathers and Fools*

1. What influence does the first peacock have on the pride of peacocks?

2. Why is the first peacock's opinion so powerful?

3. What could the swans have done to protect themselves, other than go to war?

4. Who arc the aggressors in the story?

5. What does the title "Feathers and Fools" mean?

6. What is the author trying to say through her story?

7. What do you think the story symbolizes in today's world?

From the Mixed-Up Files of Mrs. Basil E. Frankweiler

Written and Illustrated by E. L. Konigsburg

New York: Atheneum Books for Young Readers, 1967

Reading Level: . . . . Grades 4–6

Genre: . . . . Contemporary life/adventure

Themes: . . . . Self-esteem, running away, setting goals, art appreciation

Awards: . . . . Newbery Medal

Plot Summary

This classic 1968 Newbery winner presents issues and a sense of adventure that still ring today. Dissatisfied with her boring suburban life, twelve-year-old Claudia Kincaid convinces her miserly brother, Jaime, to run away and hide out in New York City's Metropolitan Museum of Art. Claudia's sense of order and structure enables her to plan their trip and weeklong clandestine stay at the museum with every detail, from sleeping arrangements, to baths, to evading the early-morning and late-night staff. Within a few hours of their museum arrival, the two siblings discover a special sculpture exhibit of the *Angel,* believed to have been created by the famous Michelangelo. The museum has no proof, but Claudia is determined to do her own research and provide the information to the proper authorities. Told through the written correspondence of the former owner of the statue, Mrs. Basil E. Frankweiler, to her lawyer, Saxonberg, this mystery/adventure, portrayed through the antics of some very crafty characters, allows for a fine mix of childhood innocence, humor, and suspense. The two children eventually find their way to the Frankweiler home where the truth about the statue and its former mysterious owner is revealed before they are driven home to their worried parents.

Main Characterization

Claudia Kincaid is a bright, resourceful twelve-year-old girl who feels the need to be recognized for a special achievement or accomplishment. Her ingenious ability to survive in a large metropolitan city and evade adult attention is paralleled by her childhood innocence and belief that she can make a difference in the adult world of art.

Jaime Kincaid, Claudia's younger brother, is a young penny pincher who agrees to go with Claudia out of his own sense of adventure, intrigue, and loyalty to his sister. His down-to-earth attitude toward spending and the realization that the comforts of a real home outweigh the precarious life of a runaway balance his sister's urgent need to persist in her crazy ideas.

Mrs. Basil E. Frankweiler is the narrator and a shadowy eighty-year-old character. Her appearance in the story serves as a conclusive, satisfying ending to the distress Claudia feels in solving the mystery of the *Angel* statue and contributes a respectable adult presence in the children's weeklong adventure.

Themes

Self-worth and making a difference are themes developed through Claudia's need to leave her comfortable home for the thrill of a museum adventure. Persistence and pursuit of a goal are other themes, expressed as the children each try to accomplish their objectives—Claudia to solve the mystery of the statue and Jaime to get himself and his sister home. An introduction to art and art appreciation is another facet of this story that can be explored in numerous ways. Coupling the discussion with some art appreciation books mentioned later can expand on this theme.

Books with Similar Issues or Themes

Balliet, Blue. *Chasing Vermeer*. Illustrated by Brett Helquist. New York: Scholastic Press, 2004.
    Art lovers, eleven years old, and new friends, Petra and Calder become involved in a series of puzzles and twist of events as they try to solve the mystery of a missing painting by Vermeer.

Funke, Cornelia Caroline. *The Thief Lord*. New York: Scholastic, 2003.
    Two orphan boys, Prosper and Bo, are on the run from their cruel aunt and uncle when they meet a thirteen year old known as the "Thief Lord" and become part of an underworld gang that survives on petty crime.

Levin, Betty. *Shoddy Cove*. New York: Greenwillow, 2003.
    Two runaway children hide in a living museum that was once a stop on the Underground Railroad and uncover the mystery behind an 1830s murder.

Roberts, Willo Davis. *To Grandmother's House We Go*. New York: Atheneum, 1990.
    Three children run away to their grandmother, a woman whom they have never met and who harbors a family mystery, to avoid being split up in foster care.

Slepian, Jan. *The Mind Reader*. New York: Philomel Books, 1997.
    Connie Leondar knows all of his vaudeville-performer father's mind-reading tricks, but when he goes on stage for his father, Connie discovers he has true psychic abilities. He decides to run away with the help of ten-year-old Annie rather than continue his act, which all too often reveals a dark truth.

Snyder, Zilpha Keatley. *The Runaways*. New York: Delacorte Press, 1999.
    Dani O'Donnell decides to run away to California from her new home in the desert town of Rattler Springs. Two other children join her, nine-year-old Stormy and a very strange girl named Pixie.

Art Appreciation Books

Ambrosek, Renee. *E.L. Konigsburg*. New York: Rosen, 2005.

Brown, Laurene Krasny, and Marc Brown. *Visiting the Art Museum*. New York: Dutton, 1986.

The Metropolitan Museum of Art, New York. *Museum ABC*. New York: Little, Brown, 2002.

Richmond, Robin. *Introducing Michelangelo*. Boston: Little, Brown, 1992.

Stanley, Diane. *Michelangelo*. New York: HarperCollins, 2000.

Weitzman, Jacqueline Preiss. *You Can't Take a Balloon into the Metropolitan Museum*. Illustrated by Robin Preiss Glasser. New York: Dial Books for Young Readers, 1998.

Author-Related Sources

Berger, Laura Standley, ed. *Twentieth-Century Children's Writers*, 4th edition. Detroit, MI: St. James Press, 1995, 533–4.

"E. L. Konigsburg." In vol. 126 of *Something about the Author.* Farmington Hills, MI: Gale Group, 2002, 127–33.

"E. L. Konigsburg." In vol. 81 of *Children's Literature Review.* Farmington Hills MI: Gale Group, 2002, 122–79.

Hanks, Dorrel Thomas. *E. L. Konigsburg.* New York: Twayne, 1992.

Hopkins, Lee Bennett. *More Books by More People: Interviews with Sixty-Five Authors of Books for Children.* New York: Citation Press, 1974, 234–8.

Marcus, Leonard S., ed. *Author Talk: Conversations with Judy Blume et al.* New York: Simon & Schuster, 2000, 49–57.

Scholastic Authors Web site: E. L. Konigsburg, http://www2.scholastic.com/teachers/ authorsandbooks/authorstudies/authorhome.jhtml?authorID=644&collateralID=5205& displayName=Biography (accessed 30 May 2004).

Silvey, Anita, ed. *Children's Books and Their Creators.* Boston: Houghton Mifflin, 1995, 377–8.

Discussion Questions

For *From the Mixed-Up Files of Mrs. Basil E. Frankweiler*

1. Why does Claudia run away, and how does it change her life?

2. Why does Jaime agree to go with her, and how does running away affect him?

3. Why does Claudia feel the need to be different?

4. Why is it important to Claudia to find out who created the *Angel?*

5. What do you think of Mrs. Frankweiler?

6. Why does Mrs. Frankweiler sell the statue and keep the sketch?

7. What is the significance of "secrets" in the story?

8. Does Claudia really want an adventure or a secret? Why?

9. How does Mrs. Frankweiler feel about Claudia and Jaime?

10. How do Jaime and Claudia feel about Mrs. Frankweiler?

11. How does art change Claudia's and Jaime's lives?

Henry Hikes to Fitchburg

By D. B. Johnson

Boston: Houghton Mifflin, 2000

Reading Level: . . . . Grades 2–3

Discussion Level: . . . . Grades 3–4

Genre: . . . . Picture Book

Themes: . . . . Setting goals, materialism versus nature, persistence, mutual respect

Awards: . . . . Boston Globe-Horn Book, New York Times Best Illustrated Book, Ezra Jack Keats New Writer Award

Plot Summary

This illustrated book is based on a passage from Henry David Thoreau's *Walden*. Two friends take different approaches to the idea of traveling the twenty-five miles to Fitchburg. Henry, thinking it faster and preferring to enjoy the outdoors while taking advantage of all its beauty, decides to walk. His friend, thinking it would be better and easier to ride the train, undertakes several jobs to earn the ninety cents to purchase a ticket. They arrive at the appointed place within hours of each other, having experienced very different journeys. Whether riding the train or walking is faster or better is debatable but, in the end, the two friends leave the discussion unsaid.

Main Characterization

Henry's character, based on the author and philosopher Thoreau, is portrayed as an individual interested in the natural world around him taking his time to stop and explore a bird's nest or honeycomb, enjoy a swim in a pond, and taste the delicious treat of fresh blackberries.

Henry's friend appears to be an industrious, hardworking, and practical person.

Themes

The book illustrates how goals can be approached from different perspectives and how people can show respect for each other's opinions through the parallel description of each character's day. Other themes include how persistence and hard work will help one to achieve a goal. Finally, the concept that materialism is not as significant as appreciation of and respect for nature is also represented.

Books with Similar Issues or Themes

Burleigh, Robert. *A Man Named Thoreau*. Illustrated by Lloyd Bloom. New York: Atheneum, 1985.
    A short biography highlighting the writer's unique personality, his home on Walden Pond, and his love of nature.

Cherry, Lynne. *The Great Kapok Tree: A Tale of the Amazon Rain Forest*. New York: Harcourt, Brace, 1990.
> The animals of the rainforest whisper their message of conservation to a man with an ax napping beneath a kapok tree.

Murphy, Jim. *Into the Deep Forest with Henry David Thoreau*. Illustrated by Kate Kiesler. New York: Clarion Books, 1995.
> A compilation from Thoreau's journal entries following his three trips into the wilderness of Maine.

San Souci, Daniel. *Country Road*. New York: Delacorte Press, 1993.
> A father and son appreciate the flora and fauna, despite the progressive development surrounding them, as they take a walk along an old road.

Thoreau, Henry David. *Henry David's House*. Edited by Steven Schnur. Illustrated by Peter Fiore. Watertown, MA: Charlesbridge, 2002.
> Thoreau's words describe his belief in the simplicity of life coupled with a respect for nature.

Author-Related Sources

D. B. Johnson Web site: http://www.henryhikes.com/henryclimbs/frames.html (accessed 2 March 2005).

Discussion Questions

For *Henry Hikes to Fitchburg*

1. How do Henry and his friend each achieve their goal of reaching Fitchburg?

2. Who works harder and why do you think so?

3. What does each character learn along the way to Fitchburg?

4. How does illustrator D. B. Johnson use his artwork to tell each character's story?

5. How does Johnson use the colors in his drawings to describe what each character is doing?

6. Describe each character's personality.

7. Which do you think was the better way to get to Fitchburg? Why?

Jip, His Story

By Katherine Paterson

New York: Lodestar Books, 1996

Reading Level: . . . . Grades 5–7

Genre: . . . . Historical fiction/suspense

Themes: . . . . Friendship, freedom, identity, death

Awards: . . . . ALA Notable Children's Book, School Library Journal Best Book, Scott O'Dell Historical Fiction Award, Booklist Editors Choice Award, YALSA Best Books for Young Adults

Plot Summary

It's 1855, and Jip has only known one home: a poor farm in Vermont that provides shelter for abandoned children, simpletons, and the unfortunate in exchange for work. Arriving there at age three after falling off a wagon on West Hill Road, the villagers assume that gypsies left the boy behind. Jip's companions include a simpleminded man named Sheldon and old, gentle, mentally disturbed Put, known as "the lunatic" because of his uncontrollable fits. Locking Put in a cage, built by Jip and Sheldon, is the only way Mr. Lyman, the farm manager, can ensure the safety of the rest of the villagers during Put's periods of insanity. Most of the time, however, Put behaves normally, talking and joking with Jip and providing a fatherly friendship that is lacking in the boy's life. Jip also has a friend named Lucy, the daughter of a widowed woman living on the farm with her other small children. Jip plays an important role on the farm, being the only bright, able-bodied male doing the physical work in addition to acting as mentor to the slow-witted Sheldon. Jip's unique ability to understand and work with animals translates to his work with Put, allowing Jip to calm him and care for him after the violent episodes that are beyond anyone's control. Put is also able to help Jip by tutoring him in his schoolwork, helping him to catch up with encouragement from the new teacher in the village. But Jip has an ominous surprise awaiting him when a stranger appears looking for information, eventually revealing that Jip is the son of a runaway slave woman and is being sought under the Fugitive Slave Act. Dealing with friend and foe alike, Jip must make some difficult choices to escape to a new life of freedom and must deal with some of the consequences of losing Put, the only true friend he has known.

Main Characterization

Jip is a boy of about twelve years who is particularly good with animals, does his assigned chores regularly, and displays responsibility for taking care of some of the less able residents of the poor farm. In particular, he spends a good deal of time coaching Sheldon, a man who is slow with the mental capacity of a young boy, and caring for Put, physically cleaning him up and helping him recover from his mental fits. Jip's light skin color conceals his true heritage, and his faith in the adults and authority figures with whom he has lived with and worked for is mostly shattered when a price for his capture becomes more appealing than aiding his escape.

Sheldon's childlike behavior does not allow him the ability to understand his dangerous job in the quarry, resulting in his very unfortunate accidental death. Put, short for Putnam, on the other hand is a bright somewhat educated man whose psychological illness prevents him from leading a normal life. He is accepting of his caged existence, feeling that he and everyone else are protected from the lunacy that periodically overtakes him. He manages to provide a positive role model for Jip, giving him advice and listening to his concerns. Lucy Wilkins is the only peer friendship that Jip has. Lucy is at first contrary, angry with her predicament of living on the poor farm after losing her drunken father. She eventually grows to respect and even help Jip to understand the importance of schooling, telling him that he is quite bright and capable of learning if he takes the opportunity to attend classes. Teacher, revealed in the end as Lyddie Worthen, the protagonist in Paterson's previous novel *Lyddie*, together with her husband-to-be Luke Stevens, a Quaker, serve as the most encouraging and honest adult figures in Jip's life, giving him the hope and means with which to escape through their Underground Railroad contacts.

Themes

Identity and how it defines a person's status in society is a theme that develops later in the story. From the beginning, Jip is viewed as an abandoned white child, possibly descending from a gypsy family. He lives a free, albeit poor, life. When his true identity—a child born to a slave woman—is revealed, everything changes in the eyes of all the people he knows, from his true friends who understand the need to help him escape to his enemies and acquaintances who will take advantage of a law to gain access to some bounty money. Friendship is tenderly portrayed through Jip's relationship with Sheldon and passionately expressed through the heartrending decision he must make to leave Put behind. Death is an underlying theme as well; Jip is fully aware of the fatal consequences around Sheldon's new job and the foolish choice of trying to run and hide with his old friend Put.

Books with Similar Issues or Themes

Avi. *Crispin: The Cross of Lead*. New York: Hyperion Books for Children, 2002.
> In fourteenth-century medieval England, a thirteen-year-old boy is falsely accused of theft and murder and declared a "wolf's head." He must constantly be on the run to avoid being killed on sight.

Carbone, Elisa Lynn. *Storm Warriors*. New York: Knopf Books for Young Readers, 2001.
> While living on the Outer Banks of North Carolina in the late 1800s, twelve-year-old Nathan encounters a group of African American storm warriors, men of the U.S. Lifesaving Service on Pea Island who rescue sailors from sinking ships. The storm warriors coach Nathan in lifesaving skills, but his dream of one day joining their group is unrealistic in the post–Civil War, racist South.

McKissack, Pat. *Run Away Home*. New York: Scholastic Press, 1997.
> Despite facing the threat of the white supremacist Knights of the Southern Order, the African American Crossman family protect a runaway Apache boy after he escapes from the reservation train.

Pryor, Bonnie. *Joseph, 1861 A Rumble of War*. Illustrated by Bert Dodson. New York: Morrow Junior Books, 1999.
> Ten-year-old Joseph Byers is torn between the opposing views of his father, a slaveholder, and his stepfather, an abolitionist.

Reeder, Carolyn. *Shades of Gray*. New York: Macmillan, 1989.
> In post–Civil War Virginia, a twelve-year-old Confederate supporter named Will Page is forced to leave his city home and adapt to farm life with his uncle, a man who refused to fight the Yankees and is now allowing a traveling northerner to stay with them.

Author-Related Sources

Berger, Laura Standley, ed. *Twentieth-Century Children's Writers*. Detroit, MI: St. James Press, 1995, 740–2.

Cary, Alice. *Katherine Paterson*. Santa Barbara, CA: The Learning Works, 1997.

Hipple, Ted, ed. In vol. 2 of *Writers for Young Adults*. New York: Scribner's, 1997, 443–54.

"Katherine Paterson." In vol. 50 of *Children's Literature Review*. Farmington Hills, MI: Gale Group, 1999, 165–207.

"Katherine Paterson." In vol. 133 of *Something about the Author*. Farmington Hills, MI: Gale Group, 2002, 134–44.

Katherine Paterson Official Web site:http://www.terabithia.com/ (accessed 30 May, 2004).

Paterson, Katherine. *Gates of Excellence: On Reading and Writing Books for Children*. New York: Dutton/Lodester, 1981.

Paterson, Katherine. *A Sense of Wonder: On Reading and Writing Books for Children*. New York: Plume, 1995.

Schmidt, Gary D. *Katherine Paterson*. New York: Twayne, 1984.

Discussion Questions

For *Jip, His Story*

1. What kind of person is Jip?

2. Why does Jip get along so well with both Sheldon and Put?

3. How does Jip feel about his true identity?

4. How do Jip's friends help to change his life?

5. Why do some of Jip's friends or companions behave more like his foes?

6. Why is Jip so troubled when he realizes that he needs to escape the fugitive slave hunters?

7. What is most important to Jip? Does he feel it is better to run freely to ensure escape or attempt to leave with Put?

8. Working with the Underground Railroad was against the Fugitive Slave Bill of 1850. What do you think about Teacher and Luke Stevens helping Jip to hide and run away, thus breaking the law?

9. Why does Jip decide to return and fight in the Civil War after he had achieved his freedom?

10. How do you think Jip's story ends?

Love That Dog

By Sharon Creech

New York: HarperCollins, 2001

Reading Level: . . . . Grades 3–6

Themes: . . . . Confidence, self-esteem, appreciation for poetry and literature, writing

Genre: . . . . Realistic fiction in poetry form, diaries

Awards: . . . . School Library Journal Best Books, ALA Notable Children's Book, Michigan Mitten Award

Plot Summary

The school year in a particular classroom is described through a diary of sorts, written in free verse by a student named Jack. Jack's lack of confidence leads him to express in his journal a dislike for poetry and his extreme reluctance to write any poems. As the year progresses, the patient and understanding teacher, Miss Stretchberry, introduces various poets using their poems as inspiration and examples. By December, Jack begins to accept and even like some of what he hears, reflecting his thoughts in his own writing. He agrees to display his work on the board, first as an anonymous author and then with his name. A poem "Love That Boy" by Walter Dean Myers reminds Jack about his beloved dog, Sky. By May, Jack is ready and confident to share his innermost feelings of sadness and guilt about the death of his dog through a long free-verse poem. After an author visit by Myers himself, Jack creates his own memorial poem for Sky, titled "Love That Dog," ending the school year with a sense of closure for his loss and renewed self assurance.

Main Characterization

Jack is the central figure in this story, which is told in his own voice as he grows emotionally throughout the school year aided by his writing and reading of poetry. The death of his dog over the summer overshadows his excitement about and enthusiasm for a new school year. The introduction of poetry has given Jack a reason to feel even more negative and unsure of himself. Miss Stretchberry, the teacher, is a silent character. Her presence in the story is indicated through Jack's voice and responses. Her actions, as described by Jack, indicate patience and understanding, as well as encouragement of his ideas.

Themes

Confidence, or the lack of it, is a major issue in Jack's young life as he struggles to accept the death of his dog and reconcile with his grief and guilt, accepting the fact that he was unable to prevent the accident that caused Sky's death. Another theme is the idea that poetry is an unpleasant and incomprehensible form of literature that boys in particular will not like. Through the clever journal and free-verse style, Creech has allowed her young male character to hesitantly explore poetry, develop an understanding and appreciation for it, and finally feel successful at writing his own poetic thoughts.

Books with Similar Issues or Themes

Alexander, Lloyd. *The Gawgon and the Boy.* New York: Dutton Children's Books, 2001.
> Eleven-year-old David is too ill to attend school and must be tutored by his old Aunt (nicknamed "Gawgon"), whose ability to combine fantasy and humor with his normal studies gives him the confidence to pursue his dreams.

Bauer, Joan. *Stand Tall.* New York: G. P. Putnam's Sons, 2002.
> Twelve-year-old Tree, named for his extreme height, learns to accept himself with the help of his friends, outspoken Sophie and a wounded Vietnam vet.

Cleary, Beverly. *Strider.* New York: Morrow Junior Books, 1991.
> Still struggling with his parents' divorce, fourteen-year-old Strider develops a strong bond with an abandoned dog he brings home from the beach and finds the confidence to begin a new life at his school.

Codell, Esme Raji. *Sahara Special.* New York: Hyperion Books for Children, 2003.
> A troubled fifth-grade girl is inspired to pursue her talented writing by a special, creative teacher who recognizes her positive attributes even amid her negative behavior.

Gantos, Jack. *Heads or Tails.* New York: Farrar, Straus & Giroux, 1994.
> Sixth-grader Jack keeps a diary about his good and bad days, knowing that life can go either way—just like flipping a coin.

Woodson, Jacqueline. *Locomotion.* New York: G. P. Putnam's Sons, 2003.
> Encouraged by his teacher, eleven-year-old Lonnie Collins Motion copes with his grief after the death of his parents by keeping a journal of his poetry.

Author-Related Sources

Hipple, Ted, ed. *Writers for Young Adults.* New York: Charles S. Scribner's Sons, 2000, 29–36.

Interview with Sharon Creech http://www.bookwire.com/bookwire/MeettheAuthor/Interview_Sharon_Creech.htm (accessed 30 May 2004).

"Sharon Creech." In vol. 89 of *Children's Literature Review.* Farmington Hills, MI: Gale Group, 2003, 22–52.

"Sharon Creech." In vol. 139 of *Something about the Author.* Farmington Hills, MI: Gale Group, 2002, 67–73.

Sharon Creech Web site: <http://www.sharoncreech.com/novels/01.asp> (accessed 30 May 2004).

Silvey, Anita, ed. *Essential Guide to Children's Books and Their Creators.* Boston: Houghton Mifflin, 2002, 109–10.

Discussion Questions

For *Love That Dog*

1. What kind of boy is Jack?

2. What kind of teacher is Miss Stretchberry?

3. What did you learn about Jack's life?

4. How did writing help Jack express his feelings?

5. Why didn't Jack want to sign his poems when they were displayed on the board?

6. What did Jack learn about himself by the end of the story?

7. This is a story told as a journal in poetry form. Why do you think the author wrote her book this way?

8. What do you think about reading a whole novel in poetry form?

9. Let's read some of the poems by the other poets in the back of the book. How did they influence Jack?

10. What was your favorite poem in Jack's journal? Why?

Maniac Magee

By Jerry Spinelli

Boston: Little, Brown, 1990

Reading Level: . . . . Grades 4–6

Genre: . . . . Realistic/legendary fiction

Themes: . . . . Racism, survival, idealism

Awards: . . . . Newbery Medal, ALA Notable Children's Book, Boston Globe Horn Book Award, Young Reader's Choice Award

Plot Summary

Eleven-year-old Jeffrey Lionel Magee, orphaned at age three, runs away from his loveless and dysfunctional home with his aunt and uncle and begins a life of homelessness in his search for family and stability. His nomadic wandering brings him to the racially divided town of Two Mills, Pennsylvania—first to the all-white West End. His boldness allows him to appear uninvited for dinner at the home of a large family, the Pickwells; outsmart a bully, John McNab, at a little league baseball game; and subsequently escape physical consequences from McNab's pals, a group known as the Cobras. The chase abruptly stops as Jeffrey, dubbed "Maniac" by kids witnessing his quick and daring moves, crosses over to the all-black East End of town. Equally unwelcome by the group of boys led by Mars Bar Thompson, Jeffrey meets Amanda Beale walking to school, carrying her personal library of books in a suitcase. His persistence and unique persuasive charm eventually lead to an invitation to her home, where he moves in and is welcomed into the black family. But the racial prejudice that is so pervasive on both sides of the town cruelly leads to public chastising of the family, and Maniac again chooses to run away rather than have his new family hurt both emotionally and physically. His wandering again takes him to the park and zoo where he is found by old Earl Grayson, an unsuccessful baseball player now working as a park attendant. As winter progresses, the two forge a relationship based on loneliness and their common love for baseball stories and reading. Shortly after Christmas, Grayson quietly dies in his sleep, leaving Jeffrey with only one choice: to run away again and continue his homeless life. In his next makeshift home, an abandoned cabin in Valley Forge, Jeffrey comes across Piper and Russell, two little runaway boys. Feeling responsibility to help them return to their family, he convinces them to join him for pizza, back in Two Mills at the Cobbler's Corner grocery, where he once helped to make the store profitable with his legendary knot untying ability. The two little boys also happen to be the younger brothers of John McNab, which brings Jeffrey back to the white side of town and into an abusive, motherless, and neglectful home headed by John's alcoholic father. Although Jeffrey does not attend school, he takes it upon himself to encourage Piper and Russell to go and stays with this very difficult family, promising the boys to perform extraordinary feats for them in exchange for their school attendance. The most disturbing thing about the McNab household, however, is how everyone is prepared to fight the rebels or enemy, explained to Jeffrey as the blacks from the East End. Piper and Russell's birthday party invitation prompts Jeffrey to bring Mars Bar Thompson with him, hoping to dispel some of the preconceived ideas on both sides of town. Although this attempt ends in humiliation for Mars Bar, Jeffrey's support, indicated by his move to the East End, results in a respectful relationship for the two boys as Jeffrey's color-blind views continue to lead his life.

Main Characterization

Jeffrey Lionel (Maniac) Magee is a white boy who is at first unaware of racial prejudice and differences. Family and a loving household is his only quest. Interacting with both black and white people, he judges them for their actions and personalities rather than for their skin color. He has difficulty understanding the generally accepted idea that people of different races must live separately. He also behaves independently with a certain "nothing is impossible" attitude, moving in and out of baseball and football games, running farther and faster than most kids his age, and generally succeeding at things that most wouldn't even attempt, like the untying of a huge, basketball-size knot. Yet his independence is offset by his need for adult love and care. Amanda Beale is a sensible, earnest black girl who is aware of the way the town is divided yet willing to make allowances for a new friend in need, Jeffrey. John McNab is the product of an abusive home that has influenced him in his prejudicial behavior. Unable to see things as Jeffrey does, he can only relate to the residents of the East End with hatred and fear. Piper and Russell McNab are young and still innocent, yet easily impressed by both their new idol, Maniac, and of course their older brother and father. Mars Bar Thompson is also a product of his home influence, displaying prejudicial feelings toward the white people on the West End. Fear and self-defense drive his bullying behavior toward Maniac. Earl Grayson, uneducated and old, is kind hearted, yet also a product of preconceived ideas. He is truly amazed to learn Jeffrey's East End friends have lifestyles similar, if not better, to his own on the West End.

Themes

The theme of racial prejudice clearly dominates this story. Characters from both sides of town display stereotypical biased behavior and attitudes toward each other. Jeffrey's role, while appearing legendary in some of his actions, is one of a bridge and of relationship building. His lack of bigotry and his tolerance are evident in his feelings of contempt for the white McNab family when he witnesses their warped conduct toward the black community. This is also a story of survival, with Jeffrey wandering for a year from place to place, meeting both good and bad folks and escaping from some nasty situations. Jeffrey's story is also one of idealism as he strives to convince those he meets that all people are basically the same.

Books with Similar Issues or Themes

Collier, James Lincoln. *Chipper*. New York: Marshall Cavendish, 2001.
> Chipper Carey is forced to run with the Midnight Rats Gang in order to survive on the 1895 streets of New York City, even though he knows he should be leading a more respectable life, as his mother would have expected.

Fox, Paula. *Monkey Island*. New York: Orchard Books, 1991.
> Separated from his parents, homeless, and living in the park with two other men who have become his family, eleven-year-old Clay is reluctant to leave the park, even when threatened by other gang members, because of his hopes to be reunited with his Ma or Daddy someday.

Levine, Gail Carson. *Dave at Night*. New York: HarperCollins, 1999.
> Running away from the Hebrew Home for Boys—or Hell Hole for Brats—is not that simple for Dave. But sneaking out at night to visit with the musical residents of 1926 Harlem provides a nocturnal refuge filled with culture and the rich experience of the Harlem Renaissance.

Myers, Walter Dean. *Me, Mop, and the Moondance Kid*. Illustrated by Rodney Pate. New York: Delacorte Press, 1988.
> After their adoption, T. J. and his brother Moondance try to help their friend, Mop (Miss Olivia Parrish), find adoptive parents before the home for orphans, the Dominican Academy, closes and she is sent far away.

Naidoo, Beverly. *No Turning Back: A Novel of South Africa*. New York: HarperCollins, 1997.
In post-apartheid South Africa, twelve-year-old Sipho leaves his abusive home to pursue life on the streets in Johannesburg and quickly discovers that placing his trust in others may hamper his survival and well-being.

Author-Related Sources

Hipple, Ted, ed. In vol. 3 of *Writers for Young Adults*. New York: Charles S. Scribner's Sons, 1997, 193–202.

Holtze, Sally Holmes, ed. *Sixth Book of Junior Authors & Illustrators*. New York: H. W. Wilson, 1989, 284–5.

"Jerry Spinelli." In vol. 82 of *Children's Literature Review*. Farmington Hills, MI: Gale Group, 2002, 161–80.

Jerry Spinelli Web site: http://www.jerryspinelli.com/newbery_001.htm (accessed 30 May 2004).

Silvey, Anita, ed. *Children's Books and Their Creators*. Boston: Houghton Mifflin, 1995, 619–21.

Spinelli, Jerry. *Knots in My Yo-Yo String: Autobiography of a Kid*. New York: Knopf, 1998.

Discussion Questions

For *Maniac Magee*

1. What kind of person is Jeffrey Lionel Magee?

2. Why does everyone call Jeffrey "Maniac Magee"? Why doesn't Jeffrey like to be called Maniac?

3. With racial prejudice evident on both the East and West Ends of town, why does Amanda Beale, a black girl, accept Jeffrey, a white boy, as a friend and even as a family member?

4. Why does Jeffrey run away even after he seems to have found a home with the Beales?

5. What do Jeffrey and Grayson learn from each other?

6. What are some of the same things that Jeffrey is able to see in both the West and East Ends?

7. Why is Jeffrey the only one able to see the similarities on both sides of town?

8. Why did Jeffrey insist on inviting Mars Bar Thompson to the birthday party at the McNab house, even though he knew everyone would be uncomfortable?

9. Days after the party, why does Mars Bar start running with Jeffrey? What do you think this means to both of them?

10. Why does everyone seem to perceive that Jeffrey has mythical powers?

11. What do you think the author is trying to say in this story?

Martin's Mice

By Dick King-Smith, Illustrated by Jez Alborough

New York: Crown, 1988.

Reading Level: . . . . Grades 3–4
Genre: . . . . Animal fantasy
Themes: . . . . Freedom, survival, friendship
Awards: . . . . ALA Notable Children's Book

Plot Summary

Martin, a very sensitive and caring farm kitten, lives with his mother, Dulce Maude, and siblings, Robin and Lark. Catching and eating mice are the typical daily routines for these cats—but not for Martin, who has an aversion to eating mice and would rather keep them as pets. Left on his own, Martin catches Drusilla, a very pregnant mouse, and decides to keep her in an old discarded bathtub in the barn where he can protect her, bring her food and drink, and generally enjoy her as an object of his affection. Unfortunately, although Drusilla is grateful to Martin for her spared life, she feels imprisoned, losing her freedom so that she may serve as a pet for Martin. Only when Martin becomes a pet for a lady living in a city apartment does he appreciate Drusilla's circumstances and vows never to keep mice as pets again.

Main Characterization

Martin is an odd, unconventional kitten—sensitive and naïve as any young child might be. Dulce Maude, the mother cat, is tough and realistic and provides strong parental support. Drusilla, Martin's pet mouse, is experienced, polite, and gracious. She acts as a surrogate mother to Martin. Pug, the absentee father cat, is strong but provides gentle emotional support for Martin.

Themes

Freedom and having the choice to live precariously but with responsibility for one's own actions versus a safe life in a controlled environment are the basic themes here. When Drusilla has her baby mice and they grow old enough to leave the nest, Martin must try to understand that letting them go live a dangerous life on the farm is a better way for them to live. Survival is a parallel theme that runs through the story, portrayed both through the farm animals and in Martin's city-life experience. Killing for food is clearly discussed, as are the concepts of compromise and negotiation. Dulce Maude teaches her kittens to chase, capture, and kill for their basic food needs, while Drusilla is able to cajole and negotiate with Martin when it comes to saving her babies from a life of sheltered imprisonment. Family and friendship are subthemes in the story and reflect a human side to the animals that children can relate to as they analyze the feelings, thoughts, and actions of each character.

Books with Similar Issues or Themes

Avi. *Poppy*. Illustrated by Brian Floca. New York: Orchard Books, 1995.

Mr. Ocax, the great horned owl, has declared himself king of Dimwood Forest and Poppy, a deer mouse, and all his friends must follow his orders to receive protection from the porcupines.

Dickinson, Peter. *Time and the Clockmice, Etcetera*. Illustrated by Emma Chichester-Clark. New York: Delacorte Press, 1994.

The Branton Town Hall Clock cannot be repaired without the assistance of the Clock Mice that have lived within it for generations.

Jarvis, Robin. *The Dark Portal*. New York: SeaStar Books, 2000.

In this spooky animal fantasy, mice are lured into the dark underground sewer world of rats and must thwart an attempt to rule London by the evil Jupiter.

King-Smith, Dick. *The Magnus Powermouse*. Illustrated by Mary Rayner. New York: Harper & Row, 1982.

A large, overgrown mouse is mistaken for a rat and carried off by the rat catcher then becomes involved in a series of hilarious adventures.

Lawson, Robert. *Rabbit Hill*. New York: Viking Press, 1944.

When a new family moves into the house on Rabbit Hill, the animals hope their meager subsistence will improve with respect to the gardening and livelihood the humans will provide.

O'Brien, Robert. *Mrs. Frisby and the Rats of Nimh*. Illustrated by Zena Bernstein. New York: Atheneum, 1971.

Mrs. Frisby, a farm mouse, must enlist the help of the highly intelligent escaped laboratory rats to save her children from the farmer's spring plough.

Author-Related Sources

Berger, Laura Standley, ed. *Twentieth-Century Children's Writers,* 4th edition. Detroit, MI: St. James Press, 1995, 521–3.

"Dick King-Smith." In vol. 40 of *Children's Literature Review*. Farmington Hills, MI: Gale Group, 1996, 129–74.

"Dick King-Smith." In vol. 135 of *Something about the Author*. Farmington Hills, MI: Gale Group, 2003, 116–24.

Dick King-Smith Web site: http://www.randomhouse.com/kids/dickkingsmith/books/ (accessed 31 May 2004).

King-Smith, Dick. *Animal Friends: Thirty-One Love Life Stories*. Illustrated by Anita Jeram. Cambridge, MA: Candlewick, 1996.

King-Smith, Dick. *Chewing the Cud*. Illustrated by Harry Horse. New York: Crown, 2002.

King-Smith, Dick. *Puppy Love*. Illustrated by Anita Jeram. Cambridge, MA: Candlewick, 1997.

Discussion Questions

For *Martin's Mice*

1. What kind of personalities do the characters of Martin, Dulce Maude, Drusilla, and Pug have?

2. Why do you think author Dick King-Smith chose the names he did for his characters? Do they have any particular meaning?

3. How does the author use the characters' personalities to tell the story?

4. Why does Martin's father, Pug, accept Martin for what he is—a gentle, loving cat? Why does Martin's mother, Dulce Maude, criticize him for it?

5. Why do both Drusilla and Martin want to escape their imprisonment, considering that they are both well treated?

6. Even though the outside world is dangerous for Drusilla's eight baby mice, why does she want them to leave the "safety" of the bathtub?

7. Can you think of other places in the world where people may be living "in a protected environment" but feel like they are prisoners?

8. How is the theme of survival portrayed in the story?

9. What does Martin learn about friendship and having a family?

10. How many of you have a pet? How do you feel about keeping certain animals as pets?

The Other Side

By Jacqueline Woodson, Illustrated by E. B. Lewis

New York: G. P. Putnam's Sons, 2001

Reading Level: . . . . Grades 3–4

Genre: . . . . Realistic picture book

Themes: . . . . Race relations, interracial friendship, friendship

Awards: . . . . ALA Notable Children's Book, School Library Journal Best Books, Booklist Editors Choice Award

Plot Summary

The long hot summer can be lonely for a little girl without siblings or playmates. Two families, one white and one African American, live side by side divided by a long fence stretching across the two country properties. The little black girl, Clover, tells how she plays daily with siblings and friends in her yard and how her mama has warned her to never climb over the fence. The little white girl, Annie Paul, curiously looks on from her side. When the jump rope games intrigue her enough to ask about climbing over to join her neighbors, she is immediately rejected—not by the little girl telling the story, but by one of the others, Sandra. At times the two little girls see each other in town shopping with their mothers, and even though they would be interested in meeting, they remain distant, as Clover explains to the reader. They continue to live their lives separately, Annie Paul playing alone, splashing through the rain puddles and amusing herself while Clover looks out the window from inside her dry home. Finally, on a sun-filled day, Clover, feeling brave, approaches the fence, and with Annie's inviting encouragement, the two girls introduce themselves. A friendship develops as they sit together on top of the fence, circumventing the parental orders of never climbing over to the other side. Their relationship grows daily atop that fence, eventually breaking a barrier between the two neighbors as both Clover and Annie Paul join a jump rope game while Clover's mama cautiously looks on hanging wet laundry and acknowledges the new friendship.

Main Characterization

Annie Paul is a little white girl about five to seven years old, eager to make a friend. She is isolated during the summer and, forbidden to leave her property, plays alone. Undeterred by rejection, she patiently waits for the right opportunity to invite her neighbor to spend time together enjoying the world around them. Clover is a little black girl of about the same age who is intrigued by her neighbor, yet obedient to her mother's wishes of staying in her yard. Her first-person narrative clearly expresses her thoughts and her lack of understanding regarding the attitudes of the adults in her town—she is unsure why she should fear climbing the fence. Time allows her the chance to observe, and enjoying a moment of self-assurance, she takes the initiative to find out more about her young neighbor. Both girls display youthful innocence and a fresh look at living and playing together despite the preconceived notions and influences from the adults around them.

Themes

Interracial friendship is woven together in this simple story related through youthful, candid expression. Two little girls from different backgrounds find the needs of friendship and camaraderie stronger than the racial differences on which their parents focus. Daily observation of each other provides evidence that similarities are also greater than the preconceived notions and different attitudes of the adults.

Books with Similar Issues or Themes

Adoff, Arnold. *Black Is Brown Is Tan.* Illustrated by Emily Arnold McCully. New York: HarperCollins, 2002.

An interracial family celebrates the many beautiful colors of their skin tones in a poetic free verse.

Bunting, Eve. *The Blue and The Gray.* Illustrated by Ned Bittinger. New York: Scholastic, 1996.

Two boys, one African American, the other white, talk about the new homes they will be living in that are being built on the grounds of a Civil War battlefield. One of their fathers tells them that their friendship represents a testament to the struggle of the historical period.

Johnson, Angela. *The Rolling Store.* Illustrated by Peter Catalanotto. New York: Orchard Books, 1997.

Two little girls, one black and one white, prepare lemonade, fans, and cookies to sell at their summer stand. The black girl tells her neighbor friend the story of the rolling store that would come to town when her granddaddy was a boy.

Taylor, Mildred D. *The Friendship.* Illustrated by Max Ginsburg. New York: Dial Books for Young Readers, 1987.

Cassie Logan and her brothers are witnesses to a disturbing encounter between white storeowner John Wallace and the elderly former slave Mr. Tom Bee, who, with permission, addresses the storeowner by his first name and then must endure a violent outburst fueled by the racist attitudes of 1933 Mississippi.

Wiles, Deborah. *Freedom Summer.* Illustrated by Jerome Lagarrigue. New York: Atheneum Books for Young Readers, 2001.

When the 1964 Civil Rights bill becomes law, it will allow Joe's best friend, John Henry, to use the town pool with the other white residents. They are both disappointed to watch the white community fill the pool with tar.

Author-Related Sources

Berger, Laura Standley, ed. *Twentieth-Century Children's Writers.* Detroit, MI: St. James Press, 1995, 1042–3.

Hipple, Ted, ed. *Writers For Young Adults.* New York: Charles S. Scribner's Sons, 2000, 377–86.

"Jacqueline Woodson." In vol. 139 of *Something about the Author.* Farmington Hills, MI: Gale Group, 2003, 243–50.

Jacqueline Woodson's Web site: http://www.jacquelinewoodson.com/ (accessed 31 May 2004).

Murray, Barbara. *Black Authors and Illustrators of Books for Children and Young Adults,* 3rd edition. New York: Garland, 1999, 408.

Discussion Questions

for *The Other Side*

1. What is Annie Paul feeling and possibly thinking when she watches the other girls play on the other side of the fence?

2. What is Clover feeling when she watches Annie Paul play in her own yard?

3. What do Clover and Annie Paul have in common?

4. What prompted Sandra to reject Annie's request to join their jump rope play?

5. How did Clover feel about Sandra's response?

6. How do the two girls find a way to be friends despite the fence and their parents' instructions?

7. What does the artist do to show how similar the girls' lives really are?

8. What did everyone, including Clover's mama, realize by the end of the story?

9. What does the fence represent in the story?

10. At the end of the story, Annie says, "Someday somebody's going to come along and knock this old fence down." What does she mean?

Pink and Say

By Patricia Polacco

New York: Philomel Books, 1994

Reading Level: . . . . Grades 3–4

Genre: . . . . Historical fiction, Civil War period

Themes: . . . . Race relations, friendship, justified war versus sense-less brutality

Awards: . . . . ALA Notable Children's Book

Plot Summary

The destructive realities of the Civil War bring two fifteen-year-old boys together, one black, one white, in the midst of battle-torn Georgia. Pinkus Aylee, fighting on the Yankee side with the Forty-eighth Colored, comes across Sheldon Curtis, a boy from Ohio, wounded, separated from his unit, and left for dead. Pink, as he likes to be called, quickly realizes that Sheldon, called Say by friends and family, is still alive. Pink undertakes the dangerous and grueling task of carrying and dragging the fellow soldier to his nearby home so that his mother, Moe Moe Bay, can nurse him back to health. Say is welcomed with love and caring attention and learns about slavery from the perspective of these two kind individuals. But the boys' presence in this former slave's home ends in tragedy when Confederate marauders barge in, search unsuccessfully for the hiding youths, and in a vengeful retaliation shoot and kill Moe Moe Bay. The boys begin a three-day walk to join the Union troops when they are captured by the Confederate army, brought to Andersonville as prisoners of war, and duly separated. Pink and Say's emotional parting as they are pulled away from each other is particularly poignant, stressing the brotherly relationship they developed over the previous few days and their appreciation for freedom. Pink is almost immediately killed with the same cold-bloodedness his mother faced, while Say's skin color allows him to survive imprisonment and the war, and, as predicted by Moe Moe Bay, he grows to be an old man. He tells his story to his grandchildren who in succession pass it down to each generation.

Main Characterization

Pinkus Aylee is a boy who has grown beyond his chronological teenage years through experiencing the harsh cruelties of slavery and war. His maturity is evident in his concern for the danger in which he has placed his mother, returning with a white, injured northern boy, yet his mother's kind, gentle, and caring influence is also apparent. He knows and fully understands the cause he is fighting for; eager to get back to his unit, he ignores any fear he may have. As a parallel character, Sheldon Curtis has joined the army; he is illiterate and too young to fight, but he is willing to carry the staff. With so many soldiers wounded and dead, Say is given a gun and told to shoot. Scared, inexperienced, and not really understanding the conflict, he is shot and wounded while trying to run away. His relationship with Pink does more than save his life as he learns about the benefits of reading, the struggle of the southern slaves, and the justification for this war. Moe Moe Bay is a loving character, coming to terms with the destruction and danger of her wartime surroundings; her senseless murder is symbolic of the blind hate of prejudice. She is mostly a mother, providing the loving encouragement that Say needs when faced with his own fears and self-doubts.

Themes

This war story reflects a very positive interracial friendship and relationship despite the surrounding hatred. A justified cause for the fighting is also a theme that Polacco expands through the two major characters, with Pink explaining that he must return to his unit to continue "his fight" and telling Say that if they don't fight together, no one will. The merciless carnal killings of Moe Moe Bay and Pink are completely contrary to the passionate, expressive behavior of the three main characters.

Books with Similar Issues or Themes

Crist-Evans, Craig. *Moon over Tennessee: A Boy's Civil War Journal*. Wood Engravings by Bonnie Christensen. Boston: Houghton Mifflin, 1999.
> A poetic journal of a young boy's journey with his father in the Confederate army and the personally devastating loss he feels at the Battle of Gettysburg.

Fleischman, Paul. *Bull Run*. Woodcuts by David Frampton. New York: HarperCollins, 1993.
> The effects of the Civil War are recounted through the words of sixteen individuals representing whites, blacks, men, women, northern and southern folks—all from different backgrounds.

Lyon, George Ella. *Cecil's Story*. Illustrated by Peter Catalanotto. New York: Orchard Books, 1991.
> Cecil imagines what he will have to do to keep the farm productive if his father goes off to fight in the Civil War and comes home wounded.

Reeder, Carolyn. *Across the Lines*. New York: Atheneum Books for Young Readers, 1997.
> Two friends tell their personal experiences of the siege of Pittsburg in alternating viewpoints. Edward is the son of a white plantation owner, and Simon is a black slave who runs to freedom and the Union Army.

Wisler, G. Clifton. *Red Cap*. New York: Lodestar Books, 1991.
> The memorable story based on the life of Ransom J. Powell, who joined the Union Army as a drummer boy. He was captured by the Confederates and sent to Andersonville prison, where he was allowed to work as a drummer boy entertaining the other captives.

Author-Related Sources

Berger, Laura Standley, ed. *Twentieth-Century Children's Writers*. Detroit, MI: St. James Press, 1995, 759–60.

Holtze, Sally Holmes, ed. *Seventh Book of Junior Authors and Illustrators*. New York: H. W. Wilson, 1996, 253–5.

"Patricia Polacco." In vol. 40 of *Children's Literature Review*. Farmington Hills, MI: Gale Group, 1996, 175–201.

"Patricia Polacco." In vol. 123 of *Something about the Author*. Farmington Hills, MI: Gale Group, 2001, 120–3.

Patricia Polacco Web site: http://www.patriciapolacco.com/ (accessed 31 May 2004).

Polacco, Patricia. *Firetalking*. Photographs by Lawrence Migdale. Katonah NY: R.C. Owen, 1994.

Silvey, Anita, ed. *Essential Guide to Children's Books and Their Creators*. Boston: Houghton Mifflin, 2002, 361–2.

Discussion Questions

For *Pink and Say*

1. Why does Pink stop to help Say by bringing him home to his mother's house?

2. Why do the boys consider each other family?

3. Why was it so dangerous to stay with Moe Moe Bay?

4. What has the skill of reading done for Pink?

5. What does Pink mean when he tells Say about the big house: "I blessed this house because of all those beautiful books ... but I cursed it, too, for what it stood for"?

6. Why does Say think that touching the hand of President Lincoln was important?

7. What does Say learn from Pink?

8. Why does Pink want to get back to fighting with his unit?

9. Why does Pink think that it was just as much Say's fight as it was his?

10. Why is it important that Say tell his story to his children and grandchildren?

11. What do the pictures describe and point out in the story that the words alone do not?

The Real Thief

By William Steig

New York: Farrar, Straus & Giroux, 1973

Reading Level: . . . . Grades 3–5
Genre: . . . . Mystery/fantasy
Themes: . . . . Honesty, trust, responsibility, friendship, loyalty

Plot Summary

Gawain the Goose views his job as Chief Guard of the newly built Royal Treasury very seriously, even as he laments not achieving his true dream of being an architect. Nevertheless, his loyalty and love for King Basil the Bear is enough to encourage him to do his best in this important position. The king respects and has great faith in Gawain, trusting him not only with the safety of his wealth in the treasury, but with one of only two keys to the locked door; the king keeps the other. Despite every precaution taken, expensive coins, rubies, and other silver ornaments are disappearing from the vault, and it quickly becomes apparent that a thief is present. Yet there is no evidence of any kind of break in or foul play. When King Basil questions Gawain on his knowledge or involvement in the thefts, Gawain is perplexed and continually claims his innocence. But with his possession of the only other key, he is accused and charged of the crime and found guilty. Before he can be sentenced, he escapes, flying over the land to a wooded area on the other side of the lake. The king and all of Gawain's friends are shocked at his alleged criminal behavior but cannot believe in their former friend, for the evidence against him is so strong. Gawain is equally hurt by the lack of confidence and trust his friends and the king have shown. During the trial, the real thief, a very small and quiet mouse named Derek, realizes that his friend Gawain is being falsely accused, but he is too afraid to come forward with the truth. Stealing first one small ruby by digging beneath the treasury leads to more and more thievery until Derek is so overly impressed with his new possessions, he does not see the enormous trouble he has secretly caused both the king and Gawain. Weeks go by, and feeling terrible remorse for what he has done, Derek decides to first steal some more to prove Gawain's innocence and then secretly and slowly return everything to the Royal Treasury. Gawain's innocence is now clearly realized, even though the true identity of the thief has not been revealed. Guilt and the need to set things right prompt Derek to find Gawain and to confess. Together they return to the kingdom where everyone including the king asks Gawain's forgiveness for their lack of faith and trust in him. Derek, however, maintains his secret with Gawain, reasoning that he has repented worrying over the consequences of his actions, enduring a lengthy time of isolation, and learning the value of honesty and true happiness.

Main Characterization

Gawain the Goose is earnest and hardworking, grateful for his stature in the kingdom, but unhappy with the routine. His loyalty to the king and his faith and trust in his fellow citizens and friends are shattered when he cannot prove his innocence. He is able to forgive and accept Derek's shortcomings when confronted by the truth despite such strong feelings of betrayal. Derek the Mouse lacks confidence and self-esteem and wrongfully finds a way to be noticed and admired. His emotional struggle with the consequences of his actions eventually gives him the impetus to face Gawain, yet he still lacks the courage to come forth with the king and the entire community. King Basil the Bear appears to be fair, at first keeping an open mind to the situation, yet feeling regret and then genuine anger as the evidence moves against his trusted guard.

Themes

Living a responsible life and coming forth with the truth is the overall theme here as the story clearly outlines the concept of honesty. Derek is a definite thief yet cannot acknowledge or take full accountability for his actions. His guilt and remorse only allow him to find a way to correct the wrong he has done to his friend. Friendship is a strong second theme coupled with loyalty as Gawain and Derek find ways to maintain and even develop their relationship even by trusting each other to keep the thief's true identity as their secret.

Books with Similar Issues or Themes

Fleischman, Sid. *Bandit's Moon*. Illustrated by Jos. A. Smith. New York: Greenwillow, 1998.
> In the days of the California Gold Rush, Annyrose, in exchange for reading lessons and to escape the villainous O.O. Mary, teams up with the Mexican bandit Joaquin Murieta.

Fleischman, Sid. *The Whipping Boy*. Illustrated by Peter Sis. New York: Greenwillow, 1986.
> Prince Brat and Jemmy, his whipping boy, trade places and become involved with a group of outlaws. But when Jemmy is accused of abducting Prince Brat, the mistaken identities must be revealed.

Holub, Joseph. *The Robber and Me*. New York: Henry Holt, 1997.
> When orphan Boniface Schroll is sent to live with his stern uncle, the mayor of a German village, he befriends Christian Knapp, the son of a known outlaw. When a series of robberies occur and Christian's father is accused, Boniface must decide how to tell his uncle the true identity of the thief, risking his newly found home life.

King-Smith, Dick. *The Robber Boy*. Illustrated by Lynette Hemmant. New York: Alfred A. Knopf, 1991.
> Tod Golightly, descendant from a long line of highway robbers, appears to be too small and nonthreatening to make it as a thief until he forms an unlikely but effective robber band with a donkey, dog, magpie, and ferret.

Roberts, Willo Davis. *Jo and the Bandit*. New York: Atheneum, 1992.
> Traveling by stagecoach to the home of their uncle, Judge Macklin, orphans Josephine and Andrew witness a holdup. When two of the bandits appear in town, Josephine struggles with the idea of helping the younger one, Rufus, escape the law while the older one is brought to justice.

Author-Related Sources

Angell, Roger. "William Steig." *The New Yorker*, 20 October 2003, 69.

Berger, Laura Standley, ed. *Twentieth-Century Children's Writers*. Detroit, MI: St. James Press, 1995, 902–4.

Boxer, Sarah. "William Steig, 95, Dies: Tough Youths and Jealous Satyrs Scowled in His Cartoons." *New York Times*, 5 October 2003, A39.

Steig, Jeanne. "What My Husband Saw." *New York Times*, 11 October 2003, A15.

Steig, William. *When Everybody Wore a Hat*. New York: HarperCollins, 2003.

"William Steig." In vol. 15 of *Children's Literature Review*. Detroit, MI: Gale Research, 1988, 175–202.

"William Steig." In vol. 111 of *Something about the Author*. Farmington Hills, MI: Gale Group, 2000, 170–7.

William Steig Web site: http://www.williamsteig.com/index2.htm (accessed 31 May 2004).

Discussion Questions

For *The Real Thief*

1. Why does Derek the Mouse—the real thief—take the first ruby from the king's Treasury?

2. Why does he keep stealing even when he knows it is wrong?

3. If he can't share the knowledge of his stolen wealth with anyone, why does he feel so important and think that everyone else views him as special?

4. Why is Derek so sure that Gawain will be found innocent?

5. The longer Derek waits and broods over his own guilt, the more difficult it becomes for him to come forward and confess the truth. Why?

6. Why does Gawain choose to forgive Derek?

7. Why isn't it necessary for the rest of the kingdom to know the true identity of the thief?

8. Who suffers the most in this story?

9. Do you think that Derek receives a just punishment? How will keeping his role as the real thief a secret affect the rest of his life?

10. What do the king, Gawain, Derek, and others in the kingdom all learn from this episode?

Ronia, the Robber's Daughter

By Astrid Lindgren, Translated by Patricia Crampton

New York: Viking Press, 1983

Reading Level: . . . . Grades 4–6

Genre: . . . . Adventure/fantasy

Themes: . . . . Prejudice, rivalry/conflict resolution, honesty/thievery, friendship/loyalty

Awards: . . . . Mildred L. Batchelder Award, ALA Notable Children's Book

Plot Summary

In an imaginary forest, two groups of robbers compete, hijacking travelers for stolen loot and treasure. In a Romeo and Juliet–type scenario, the children of the opposing leaders, Ronia, daughter to chief Matt, and Birk, son to the rivaling chief Borka, meet in the wood one day and quickly become inseparable friends, despite the prejudice and hate that their respective fathers display for the other family and band of robbers. Matt raises Ronia to be brave and smart in the forest, to outwit the dangerous supernatural creatures such as the angry gray dwarfs or wild harpies, allowing her to thrive in the natural environment of his wood. Borka does the same for his son Birk, yet when boy and girl meet at the edge of Hell's Gap, they begin a competition by alternately jumping across it. Birk's fall in the Gap's abyss changes everything. Ronia helps the struggling Birk, who is barely standing on a stone beam just below the edge, to climb out with the aid of her braided leather rope, and the friendship begins to bond. The discovery of their companionship infuriates both fathers and causes Ronia to leave Matt's castle, setting up life in the wood while maintaining her relationship with Birk. A lot of soul searching for both Matt and Ronia take place as each must deal with feelings for the other, re-evaluating the long-standing feud the two robber families have endured. Both Birk and Ronia are torn between their newfound friendship and loyalty to their robber band. In the end, youthful camaraderie helps to address the reality both gangs face when the law threatens them, and they are forced to combine resources to survive. Paradoxically, Ronia and Birk choose to live a life with honor in Bear's Cave, hunting, fishing, and living off the land.

Main Characterization

Ronia is a feisty, tomboyish, adventurous girl who is sometimes lonely for peer-related companionship while she begins to address thoughts of independence typical of the average ten- to twelve-year-old. She is emotionally attached to her father yet strong-willed, refusing to compromise her principles as displayed when she stubbornly jumps over Hell's Gap to stand with Borka's family after her father captures Birk. Birk, an independent boy of the same age is bright and fun loving, yet also concerned about the meager supplies left to last his family and robber band through the winter. He would prefer a life of free hunting and fishing, rather than looting and thieving. Ronia's father, Matt, is highly emotional, boisterous, and overreacts to situations in almost violent, savage, and stormy ways. His high-strung behavior affects the personal decision he makes, when he rejects his own daughter after she sides with Birk's family, leaving him overwrought with grief. Borka, Birk's father, also displays the behavior of a typical outlaw; however, his leadership is lacking, evidenced by the meager supplies his band has left because of a poor season of looting. Lovis, Matt's woman and mother to Ronia, balances her support to both husband and child and provides some reason and understanding to Ronia's life. Undis, Borka's woman and mother to Birk, is a minor figure in the story, supportive of her men, nevertheless. Noodle-Pete is an old, "retired" robber in Matt's castle, who humorously contributes his thoughts and experience to both Matt and Ronia through critical commentary.

Themes

Four themes are continually present in this story and are woven together through the actions and feelings of the well-developed characters. The children of both camps have been introduced to a form of learned prejudice and are taught to hate the rival robber band without a doubt. The bitter rivalry between the two robber chiefs is ever present, yet the innocence of youth, the loyalty of a true friendship, and the idea that opinions be formed on an individual basis prevails. Another important theme is that of thievery contrasted with an honest livelihood. Both Ronia and Birk choose to live outside the robber bands' culture and environment and cooperate to create their own honest sustenance. Finally, Lindgren encompasses symbolic meaning in the setting of an imaginary forest as a refuge, a playground, and a home.

Books with Similar Issues or Themes

Colfer, Eoin. *Artemis Fowl.* New York: Hyperion, 2001.
>When a twelve-year-old criminal mastermind kidnaps a female fairy, the captain of the LEPrecon Unit, and threatens to expose the existence of the fairies underworld by demanding a ransom in gold, he is unprepared for the high level of technology and ingenuity her fellow colleagues can use to protect their secret fairy life.

Hahn, Mary Downing. *The Gentleman Outlaw and Me Eli.* New York: Clarion Books, 1996.
>Twelve year-old Eliza, disguised as a boy, teams up with Calvin Featherbone, an eighteen-year-old con artist and travels west in search of her missing father.

Karr, Kathleen. *Oh, Those Harper Girls!* New York: Farrar, Straus & Giroux, 1992.
>Five sisters agree to help their father save the cattle ranch from foreclosure by becoming stagecoach highway robbers and end up with a theatrical future on the New York stage.

Karr, Kathleen. *Skullduggery.* New York: Hyperion, 2000.
>Matthew Morrissey begins to work for Dr. Asa B. Cornwall, a phrenologist, who requires him to rob graves of famous individuals to study their skulls.

Turner, Megan Whalen. *The Thief.* New York: Greenwillow Books, 1996.
>The king enlists a known master thief, Gen, from his prison to steal an ancient treasure from the temple of the Gods.

Author-Related Sources

"Astrid Lindgren." In vol. 39 of *Children's Literature Review.* Farmington Hills, MI: Gale Group, 1996, 119–65.

"Astrid Lindgren." In vol. 38 of *Something about the Author.* Detroit, MI: Gale Research, 1985, 120–35.

"Astrid Lindgren" [obituary]. In vol. 128 of *Something about the Author.* Farmington Hills, MI: Gale Group, 2002, 155.

Hurwitz, Johanna. *Astrid Lindgren: Storyteller to the World.* Illustrated by Michael Dooling. New York: Viking Kestrel, 1989.

Metcalf, Eva-Maria. *Astrid Lindgren.* New York: Twayne, 1995.

Silvey, Anita, ed. *Essential Guide to Children's Books and Their Creators.* Boston: Houghton Mifflin, 2002, 265–6.

Discussion Questions

For *Ronia, the Robber's Daughter*

1. What kind of leader is Matt?

2. How does his personality affect his decisions?

3. What kind of leader is Borka?

4. Why does Ronia first save Birk from falling in Hell's Gap?

5. What kind of relationship do Ronia and Birk have?

6. Why do Ronia and Birk become such close friends despite the learned prejudice they have experienced with their families?

7. What do Ronia and Birk feel for each other's families?

8. How does Lovis feel about Matt and Borka's rivalry?

9. What does Noodle-Pete really think about Matt and the robber lifestyle?

10. Why does Matt feel uncomfortable telling Ronia about his work?

11. After Matt captures Birk, Ronia crosses over to Borka's keep and forces an exchange at Hell's Gap. Why does Matt have trouble with the decision he has made to reject his daughter?

12. How do things change in Matt's fort after the exchange of Birk and Ronia?

13. Why does Matt finally accept the friendship of Ronia and Birk?

14. Why do Ronia and Birk choose to live their lives differently from how their fathers live theirs?

15. What does the forest represent to Ronia and Birk?

16. What is the author trying to tell the reader in her story?

Running Out of Time

By Margaret Peterson Haddix

New York: Simon & Schuster, 1995

Reading Level: . . . . Grades 4–6

Genre: . . . . Mystery/adventure, historical/science fiction

Themes: . . . . Ethics, experimental research, survival, freedom

Awards: . . . . YALSA Best Books for Young Adults, Sequoyah
Book Award

Plot Summary

What started out as an opportunity to live life in a simpler time turns into a twisted scientific experiment to create a perfect gene pool. In 1840, Residents of the Indiana village of Clifton are in a desperate situation. With each new day, more children are contracting diphtheria, a fatal disease in preantibiotic times. In addition, a secret is harbored by the adults of the village. They have consented to live forever a nineteenth-century lifestyle within a living museum rather than as actors playing the various roles of blacksmith, preacher, teacher, and so on. All the children are being raised without the knowledge that outside the village, it is really 1996— with all the advantages of modern medicine and technology. Miles Clifton, the creator of the museum village and tourist attraction, invited twenty-five families to become part of the nineteenth-century community that tourists would view through two-way mirrors. His ulterior motive, however, is to see how many could survive diseases without modern-day medications and thus create a superior human species. When thirteen-year-old Jessie Keyser's little sister develops signs of the disease and becomes very ill, Mrs. Keyser, a nurse in her former twentieth-century life, decides to reveal the truth and enlists Jessie in a plan. Giving her some modern-day clothing and money she has kept hidden for the last fifteen years, Mrs. Keyser shows Jessie how to escape through a secret passageway that leads to the tourist section of the village and how to behave and blend in with the 1996 society. Once out, Jessie must contact Mr. Neely, a man who was originally against the concept and who will call in the authorities, organize a press conference, and bring the health department to provide medical care to the ill children. Jessie bravely undertakes the frightening task and must not only find her way to Indianapolis but also adapt very quickly to twentieth-century life, never having seen anything beyond her simple 1840 home. The villainous, evil men involved in this twistedly sick scheme are watching Jessie, aware of her escape. When she finally meets the man she thinks is Mr. Neely, she discovers to her horror that he is an impostor, part of Miles Clifton's sleazy group, placing her in mortal danger. Escaping once again, she cleverly figures out a way to call attention to the situation in Clifton Village by getting the media involved and saving all but two of the children who are so deathly ill.

Main Characterization

Jessie Keyser is a bright, curious, strong-minded thirteen-year-old girl who feels a sense of responsibility when she understands her mission will save the lives of her sister and the other children. Her cleverness and her fortitude allow her to persevere even when confronted with danger and some modern-day obstacles. Miles Clifton is a man who has taken it on himself to decide what would be good for all mankind. The creation of a superior race is a motive that he feels is justified, despite the dire consequences. In reality, the Mr. Neely whom Mrs. Keyser knew has passed away and is being impersonated by another man who is part of Clifton's vile and dangerous group of "scientists." Mr. and Mrs. Keyser represent the adults who have consented to live within the museum boundaries and are, in essence, good people who have been deceived and are now literally prisoners of Clifton's grand experiment. Most of them lack the courage to rebel or go against Miles Clifton. However, Mrs. Keyser's medical training and her sense of justice help her acknowledge the truth. She is also courageous enough to send her eldest child out alone, with little experience, in a world 150 years into the future.

Themes

Survival and the ethics involved with certain experimental research are major themes in this story. Sacrificing the weak willingly to create a stronger race is something that all the characters, both within the museum village and beyond it, have to consider in terms of the choices they will make. Some will go along with the plan to pursue their own personal survival; others like Jessie and her mother will undertake a more aggressive role to help everyone survive.

Books with Similar Issues or Themes

Defelice, Cynthia C. *The Apprenticeship of Lucas Whitaker*. New York: Farrar, Straus & Giroux, 1996.

>In the medically primitive world of the mid-1800s, Lucas has lost his entire family to tuberculosis and is willing to try any remedy including one of digging up the first dead family member, burning the person's heart, and breathing the smoke as a way to ward off the disease.

Grifalconi, Ann. *The Village That Vanished*. Illustrated by Kadir Nelson. New York: Dial Books for Young Readers, 2002.

>Having faith in the ancestors and courage, an old woman and a young girl devise a plan to help their fellow villagers escape capture by the slave traders.

Lowry, Lois. *The Giver*. New York: Houghton Mifflin, 1993.

>Twelve-year-old Jonas is granted the secret of the memories and must come to terms with the knowledge of how cruel, controlled, and constrained his utopian society really is.

McCann, Michelle R. *Luba the Angel of Bergen-Belsen*. Illustrated by Ann Marshall. Toronto: Tricycle Press, 2003.

>The true story of the Jewish nurse, Luba Tryszynska, who secretly provided shelter and food for a group of fifty Dutch children, left to die in the woods at the concentration camp.

Morpurgo, Michael. *Waiting for Anya*. New York: Viking, 1990.

>Benjamin and Jo devise a plan to help save a group of hidden children on a reclusive widow's farm in Vichy, France, during the Nazi occupation.

Author-Related Sources

"Margaret Peterson Haddix." In vol. 125 of *Something about the Author*. Farmington Hills, MI: Gale Group, 2002, 90–5.

Discussion Questions

For *Running Out of Time*

1. Why do you think the original idea of Clifton Village convinced some adults to want to give up their life in modern times?

2. Why do they agree to be part of a living museum and be watched all the time?

3. Why do the adults keep the secret of the living museum from the children?

4. Why are the adults unable to band together and confront Mr. Clifton and his men?

5. What gives Jessie the strength to pursue her mission, even when it seems she may be too weak to continue?

6. What adjustments would the residents of Clifton Village have to make to live comfortably and happily in the twentieth century?

7. What time period was Jessie happier in, 1840 or 1996? Why?

8. What is the author trying to say about humanity in her story?

9. What do you think about the ethics of creating a perfect gene pool?

10. When it comes to the theory of survival of the fittest, why is the human race different from other animal species?

Samir and Yonatan

By Daniella Carmi, Translated from the Hebrew by Yael Lotan

New York: Scholastic/Arthur A. Levine Books, 2000

Reading Level: . . . . Grades 5–7
Themes: . . . . Respect, cultural differences, tolerance, war/peace
Genre: . . . . Contemporary life, realistic fiction
Awards: . . . . Mildred L. Batchelder Award

Plot Summary

Two boys from opposite worlds in the politically ravaged environment of the Middle East are brought together in an Israeli hospital. Samir is a Palestinian needing surgery for a shattered knee, the result of a daring bicycle stunt. Yonatan is a Jewish boy recovering from hand surgery. The story is told through Samir's narrative mental thoughts as he observes the behavior of each of his ward mates. He struggles with the grief he feels for his brother's death at the hands of an Israeli soldier and can only view Tzahi in the next bed as an Israeli boy, the enemy, with an older brother in the army. Samir's initial fear and reluctance to be left in the Jews' hospital until the American surgeon can be brought in for his treatment is eventually diminished as he interacts with Israeli children in his ward, Ludmilla, Tzahi, and Razia, all with various medical situations. Yet it is Yonaton, the son of an astronomer, who eventually helps Samir deal with his uncertain feelings and grief for his brother through a magical and almost spiritual experience they share playing a space travel computer game. Yonaton's insightful reflection on how all human beings and living things are made of the same materials—water, carbon, calcium, iron, protein and "some other stuff … arranged differently"—offers Samir a fresh perspective on the world with the idea that perhaps Arabs and Jews are not all that different. In the end, Samir's stay in Israel heals more than his knee and brings him closer to an understanding of a peaceful and harmonious life amongst races and religions.

Main Characterization

Samir is a Palestinian boy, influenced by the difficult political situation that is responsible for the death of his brother. He has a preconceived image of Jews and is apprehensive yet surprised to find that people are individuals to be judged for their own merits. Yonatan is an Israeli boy, interested in astronomy, with an optimistic view of life and the world around him. He is accepting of everyone and finds solace in his extreme beliefs about the universe. He represents the idealistic view that all should live together in harmony. Tzahi is an Israeli boy with an older brother in the army. He is proud, a little daring, and possesses an inner strength that is portrayed through his brazen actions and words. Razia is a girl, a victim of domestic abuse; she is angry with more emotional than physical scars. Ludmilla is a quiet girl suffering from an eating disorder, withdrawn, yet close to the others in the ward through an unspoken understanding.

Themes

Respect and understanding of different cultures is clearly portrayed through the various relationships that develop among the four children in the hospital ward. An underlying theme of war versus peace is also present through the vague references to the Israeli army and the Palestinian lifestyle before the escalated conflict began.

Books with Similar Issues or Themes

Banks, Lynne Reid. *Broken Bridge*. New York: Morrow Junior Books, 1995.

After witnessing the murder of her visiting cousin, Glen, by a Palestinian terrorist, Israeli Nili chooses to conceal the identity of the killer as payment for sparing her life.

Clinton, Cathryn. *A Stone in My Hand*. Cambridge, MA: Candlewick Press, 2002.

When her father is killed on a public bus attacked by a terrorist's bomb in Israel, Malaak, a Palestinian girl living in Gaza, withdraws to a silent world but must soon come back to reality to try and reach her militant brother who has become involved with a group of radicals.

Levine, Anna. *Running on Eggs*. Chicago: Front Street/Cricket Books, 1999.

Two girls living in Israel, one a Jewish girl on a kibbutz, the other a Palestinian girl in a nearby village, meet on an Arab-Israeli track team and develop a friendship despite the disapproval of their families.

Miklowitz, Gloria D. *The Enemy Has a Face*. Grand Rapids, MI: Eerdmans Books for Young Readers, 2003.

Newly living in Los Angeles, Israeli Netta Hoffman is befriended by a Palestinian boy at her middle school and must confront her fears that terrorists are not responsible for her brother's mysterious disappearance.

Nye, Naomi Shihab. *Habibi*. New York: Simon & Schuster, 1997.

Liyana must adjust to her new home in Jerusalem, the birthplace of her Arab father, and learn to live with the tensions between the Israelis and Palestinians.

Discussion Questions

For *Samir and Yonatan*

1. What is Samir most concerned about and why?

2. How does Yonatan view his world and the people who live in it?

3. How are Samir and Yonatan different?

4. What do Samir and Yonatan have in common?

5. What are some of the issues presented in the story?

6. How does the author use humor to illustrate some of the issues in the story?

7. Why does Tzahi behave so boldly, especially at the end of the story?

8. How do the four children in the ward help each other?

9. How is prejudice portrayed in this story?

10. What is the author's message or purpose in writing this book?

11. How can we relate the themes in this story to life in the United States?

Sector 7

By David Wiesner

New York: Clarion Books, 1999

Discussion Level: . . . . Grades 3–6

Genre: . . . . Wordless fantasy picture book

Themes: . . . . Imagination, creativity

Awards: . . . . Caldecott Honor, ALA Notable Children's Book,
School Library Journal Best Books

Plot Summary

On a class trip to the top of the Empire State Building in New York City, a boy is first over-whelmed by a cloudy, misty wind and then befriended by a cheery, jolly-looking cloud who first teases him by taking his red mittens, scarf, and hat and then plays with him by creating funny cloud shapes for him to enjoy. Gaining his trust, the good-natured cloud takes the boy to a place in the sky called Sector 7, a kind of factory for making clouds sent out to the rest of the world. Resembling a large train station, the clouds line up to depart and arrive based on their type. The clouds approach the boy with a problem. They are being sent out in very ordinary shapes and wish that the designer would create something more interesting. The boy, an artist, begins to design cloud fish as new assignments are passed out with his drawings. This does not sit well with the Sector 7 supervisor and workers and the boy is sent back to the Empire State Building via another "cloud taxi." Returning to his class-mates, the boy's floating appearance is strangely noticed but what is more remarkable are all the fish floating above the skyline of Manhattan.

Main Characterization

This story is told in pictures through the fantastical experience of a boy as he is first taken by surprise by the playful, teasing behavior of the cloud and then, feeling adventurous, cheerfully ac-companies him to Sector 7. The boy's creativity, inventiveness, and imagination are evident in the cloud drawings he designs. His whimsical vision is offset by the rigidity of the supervisor and the boy's unwavering attitude toward creating different cloud shapes. Reading the pictures carefully al-lows for varied interpretations of the characters moods, needs, interests, and way of thinking. Not all the workers are opposed to the new aquatic designs as indicated by their amused expressions.

Themes

Having the willingness and courage to be mentally adventurous in producing creative, imagi-native work is the major theme of this inventive, wordless story. In addition, the book offers the op-portunity to vocalize a variety of interpretations based on visual information provided.

Books with Similar Issues or Themes

Burningham, John. *Cloudland*. New York: Crown, 1996.
> After Albert accidentally falls from a cliff, the cloud children magically intervene and make him light enough to float and join them in a playful time of jumping, painting, swimming, and racing in the sky until he begins to miss his parents as the Cloud Queen and the man in the moon help him return home.

Rohmann, Eric. *Time Flies*. New York: Crown, 1994.
> A bird flying around a dinosaur exhibit at the museum gets caught in a dreamlike flight back in time to where the live dinosaur views him as potential prey.

Sis, Peter. *An Ocean World*. New York: Greenwillow, 1992.
> A whale born in captivity is released in the ocean and must explore and discover her natural habitat.

Spier, Peter. *Dreams*. New York: Doubleday, 1986.
> Two children spend a glorious day outside gazing at the sky imagining the cloud shapes as dragons, horses, trains, and race cars.

Van Allsburg, Chris. *Ben's Dream*. Boston: Houghton Mifflin, 1982.
> Ben falls asleep while studying on a soggy, rainy day and imagines his house floating past all the monuments of the world.

Wiesner, David. *Free Fall*. New York: Lothrop, Lee & Shepard, 1988.
> Falling asleep with his geography book, a boy dreams of many magical places until he falls freely, waking to a new day.

Author-Related Sources

"David Wiesner." In vol. 84 of *Children's Literature Review*. Farmington Hills, MI: Gale Group, 2003, 138–62

"David Wiesner." In vol. 139 of *Something about the Author*. Farmington Hills, MI: Gale Group, 2003, 221–9.

David Wiesner, The Art of Storytelling (Web site): http://www.houghtonmifflinbooks.com/authors/wiesner/home.html (accessed 7 June 2004).

Holtze, Sally Holmes, ed. *Seventh Book of Junior Authors and Illustrators*. New York: H. W. Wilson, 1996, 338–9.

Silvey, Anita, ed. *Essential Guide to Children's Books and Their Creators*. Boston: Houghton Mifflin, 2002, 470–1.

Discussion Questions

For *Sector 7*

1. Why does the friendly cloud choose to bring the boy wearing the red scarf, mittens, and hat back to Sector 7?

2. What clues does the artist place in the pictures to tell us what interests the boy?

3. What kind of people does the boy meet in Sector 7?

4. Why does the supervisor get angry with the boy and the other clouds?

5. What are the clouds trying to convey to the boy?

6. How does the boy's visit make a difference to the clouds and people working in Sector 7?

7. How does the class trip make a difference in the boy's life?

8. Is the boy's visit to Sector 7 in his imagination or a dream?

9. What is the author/illustrator trying to say in his story?

10. Why is this a story even though it is told without words?

11. What does this story mean to you?

A Single Shard

by Linda Sue Park

New York: Clarion Books, 2001

Reading Level: . . . . Grades 6–8

Genre: . . . . Historical fiction/medieval Korea

Themes: . . . . Tenacity and perseverance, honesty, trust, pride versus foolishness, respect, loyalty

Awards: . . . . Newbery Medal, School Library Journal Best Books, Booklist Editors' Choice Award, YALSA Best Books for Young Adults, ALA Notable Children's Book

Plot Summary

In a potter's village in medieval Korea, thirteen-year-old Tree-ear has lived his orphaned life under a bridge with a surrogate father, the one-legged and homeless Crane-man. The village of Ch'ulp'o is a center where celadon ceramic ware is created, fostering Tree-ear's ambition to become a potter. The boy most admires Min, one of the most skilled and artistic potters in the trade. From a distance, Tree-ear watches Min work each day. The boy's ragged existence, however, does not afford him any respect from the well-known and talented craftsman, and when Tree-ear boldly approaches his shop to look more closely at his work and accidentally breaks a piece, Min confronts him as a common thief. Tree-ear timidly and most respectfully explains that he would never steal, but instead wanted only to examine the valued artwork. At first degrading and belittling the boy for his careless intrusion, Min reluctantly agrees to allow Tree-ear to pay for the damage by working nine days, triple the amount of time necessary to make the delicate piece. Overjoyed and thinking that he will now learn how to spin a wheel and create a vase, Tree-ear soon realizes that his work for the potter entails some backbreaking, blistering chores—chopping and carrying wood over a great distance for the kiln fires, digging for clay, and collecting seashells to use as stilts in the kiln. Exhausted and bruised from his physically challenging duties, Tree-ear is disappointed that his day never includes time with the potter to learn how to make the vase he envisions in his dreams. Still, at the end of the nine days of repayment, Tree-ear convinces Min to take him on as an unpaid assistant, hoping that their continued relationship will eventually provide the opportunity to learn. A national competition to receive a royal commission changes both Min and Tree-ear's lives and brings the two closer. Min's craftsmanship is admired by the royal emissary, yet the older and reluctant master potter needs encouragement and some bold action from Tree-ear to help him create a final example of his work for the ultimate judging in the nearby town of Shongdo. Road bandits attack Tree-ear, who is carrying the precious celadon ware for his master, and the pottery is shattered. Feeling the weight of responsibility, Tree-ear resolves to continue on his mission with a single shard he has recovered, enough to impress the emissary of the potter's quality and accomplished artistry, thus gaining the most important and lifelong commission for the grateful Min.

Main Characterization

Tree-ear, named after the stray mushroom that grows on dead or fallen tree trunks, is a thirteen-year-old boy living a homeless life with an elderly crippled man. Orphaned at the age of two, he was brought to the seaside city of Chu'ulp'o where he was left with Crane-man until the monks at the temple could recover from a fever but ultimately remained under his care and affection. He is an earnest, hardworking young man, eager to learn the potter's trade and art and willing to do anything to succeed in his ambitions. His underlying need for family and positive role models is fulfilled by his relationships with Crane-man, Min, and Ajima, Min's wife.

Crane-man is a humble, honest old man, born with one deformed leg, who has managed to live with the benefit of one good leg but was unfortunate to have outlived all his relatives. No longer able to work, he has been forced into a homeless situation under the bridge. His philosophies on life present a moralistic view to Tree-ear as he teaches him kindness, the value of honest work, and tenacious self-reliance.

Min is a middle-aged potter who is extremely gifted in his craft but views life through bitter eyes. He is sad and resentful after the death of his only son and initially assesses Tree-ear as a hindrance to his work. His perfectionist expectations slow his ability to produce an abundance of work, limiting his earnings each year.

Ajima is Min's wife, also sad but kind-hearted in the way she understands Tree-ear's circumstances, subtly provides extra food and clothing, and eventually adopts him in place of the son she has lost.

Kang is a rival potter in the village who is not as proficient as Min but has developed a new way to create ceramic inlay and initially wins a partial royal commission. His minor role in the story serves as the impetus for Tree-ear's bold initiatives in helping his master win the commission.

Themes

Tenacity and perseverance are themes that are represented by both Crane-man's willingness to live his unfortunate life as best he can, and by Tree-ear's persistence in pursuing an apprenticeship in ceramics as well as providing an opportunity for Min to achieve his lifelong dream of a royal commission. Honesty and the virtue of hard work are displayed in Crane-man's philosophy and teachings. His homelessness does not permit him the excuse to beg or steal. At the same time, his pride can be overshadowed by foolishness, as when he refuses to take any food from Ajima and is finally convinced that pulling weeds in her garden will provide a service in exchange for the daily meal. Trust and having faith recurs in both Min's attitude toward Tree-ear, allowing him first to work as an assistant and then to accept the boy's confident help in presenting his work to the emissary. Tree-ear never loses his trust and faith in the idea that he will one day learn the art of ceramics and, more specifically, that his master's brilliant work can be valued even in a single, broken shard. Respect and loyalty for his elders and role models despite the circumstances of events in his life are a constant within the historical context of the story.

Books with Similar Issues or Themes

Crossley-Holland, Kevin. *The Seeing Stone*. New York: Arthur A. Levine Books, 2000.

> A boy living in twelfth-century England yearns to become a knight and is given a black stone by his father's friend, Merlin, that allows him to view the past and the stories of King Arthur, his namesake.

McCaughrean, Geraldine. *The Kite Rider*. New York: HarperCollins, 2001.

> Haoyou is given an opportunity to learn to perform as a kite rider in the traveling Jade Circus in thirteenth-century China, leaving his impoverished home and widowed mother.

Namioka, Lensey. *Island of Ogres*. New York: Harper & Row, 1989.
> In sixteenth-century Japan, unemployed samurai Kajiro stumbles on the residence of the island's commander, falls in love with his sister-in-law, and solves a mystery full of intrigue and adventure that prevents the overthrow of the island's ruler.

Paterson, Katherine. *The Master Puppeteer*. New York: Crowell, 1975.
> A thirteen-year-old boy, Jiro, becomes an apprentice to a puppeteer who becomes involved with a mysterious thief in eighteenth-century Japan.

Yep, Laurence. *The Serpent's Children*. New York: Harper & Row, 1984.
> Cassia struggles to keep her family together despite the cruel effects of the Manchu and British domination in nineteenth century China.

Author-Related Sources

"Linda Sue Park." In vol. 84 of *Children's Literature Review*. Detroit, MI: Gale Group, 2003, 18–33.

"Linda Sue Park." In vol. 127 of *Something about the Author*. Detroit, MI: Gale Group, 2002, 166–7.

Linda Sue Park's Web site: http://www.lindasuepark.com/bio.html (accessed 7 June 2004).

Silvey, Anita, ed. *Essential Guide to Children's Books and Their Creators*. Boston: Houghton Mifflin, 2002, 337.

Discussion Questions

For *A Single Shard*

1. Why did Crane-man continue to care for Tree-ear even after the monks came back to take him to the monastery?

2. Crane-man often tells Tree-ear, "Work gives a man dignity, stealing takes it away." What has Tree-ear learned from Crane-man about living a homeless life?

3. How did Tree-ear make Crane-man's life better?

4. Why did Min continue to allow Tree-ear to work for him after the original nine days of repayment?

5. Why does Min treat Tree-ear in such a degrading way? Why does Tree-ear work so hard for him despite the humiliating treatment?

6. When Ajima begins to fill Tree-ear's bowl with extra food, why does Tree-ear feel it is wrong to tell her about Crane-man?

7. Why does Crane-man first refuse Ajima's offer of pulling weeds for food and then finally accept?

8. Why does Min refuse to teach Tree-ear anything about the potter's craft, even after a year of Tree-ear's service?

9. When Tree-ear spies on Kang and discovers his method of creating inlay ceramics, why does he first keep it to himself? Why does he eventually explain it to Min?

10. How did Tree-ear feel after the robbers smashed the precious vases he was carrying for Min to Shongdo?

11. Why did he decide to continue on to the judging with only one piece of the broken vases?

12. How did Tree-ear change Min's life?

13. What did Min and Tree-ear learn from each other?

14. Why did Min finally come to accept Tree-ear as his wife did, like a new son? Why did they choose to give him the name Hyung-pil?

15. What is the meaning of the title the author gives to this book, "A Single Shard"?

Smoky Night

By Eve Bunting, Illustrated by David Diaz

San Diego, CA: Harcourt, Brace, 1994.

Reading Level: . . . . Grades 3–5

Genre: . . . . Realistic picture book

Themes: . . . . Race relations, interpersonal relationships, friendship, respect for others, right versus wrong

Awards: . . . . Caldecott Medal, ALA Notable Children's Book

Plot Summary

Daniel and his mother are experiencing one of the most frightening nights of their lives. The street they live on is under siege, with rioters and looters destroying everything in sight through vandalism, theft, or fire. Mama explains the riot as something that happens when people get angry enough that they become indifferent to right and wrong behavior. Daniel watches from his window as store windows are smashed, television sets are hauled away, and food cartons are stolen from the Korean grocer, Mrs. Kim. Daniel explains how his cat Jasmine and Mrs. Kim's cat fight all the time and why Mama will not buy from Mrs. Kim's store, preferring to patronize a store owned by African Americans instead. Mama tells Daniel to stay in her bedroom for this scary, noisy night, but soon smoke and fire begin to envelope their building, and everyone must evacuate. Finding shelter in a nearby church, Daniel, his mother, and a group of ethnically diverse neighbors (Hispanic, African American, and Asian) confront their prejudices head on when Daniel's beloved cat is found by a fireman, huddled together with its supposed enemy, the carrot-colored cat belonging to Mrs. Kim. As Mama expresses amazement at the cats' newfound friendship, Daniel innocently remarks that not knowing each other before might be the reason for their previous mutual dislike. Insightfully realizing the significance of Daniel's statement, an embarrassing silence quickly spurs Mama to introduce herself to Mrs. Kim, inviting her and her cat over for milk and friendship.

Main Characterization

Daniel is a young boy, probably between ages six and ten. His youthful innocence makes him blind to the realities of racial prejudice, allowing him to see things clearly as right and wrong. Even as his mother tries to explain the rioting, he does not understand or accept what he witnesses. Mama, on the other hand, is much more jaded and has developed a sense of stoic resistance to people of other backgrounds, as evidenced by her unwillingness to shop in a Korean store, but nevertheless, she does her best to protect Daniel from both physical and emotional harm. The two cats in the story are of different colors—one orange and one yellow. They represent the idea that different colors, races, and groups can get along with each other and even be respectful when the common need for coexistence is met.

74

Themes

The Los Angeles Riots of 1992 inspired this author to place all the issues surrounding that unfortunate event in perspective for a young child. Race relations, interpersonal relationships, friendship, respect for others, and right versus wrong are both subtly and more overtly evident as Daniel recounts the rioters' actions and the reasons for them as defined by his mother that night. Bunting cleverly employs the symbolic use of animal characters, as the two cats with different colored fur, owned by people of different races, create a new relationship in the midst of the chaos, thereby encouraging the adults involved to view each other beyond their prejudices.

Books with Similar Issues or Themes

McKissack, Pat. *Goin' Someplace Special*. New York: Atheneum Books for Young Readers, 2001.
>In her segregated 1950s town, Tricia Ann convinces her grandmother to let her take the bus downtown to the only integrated building, the public library, and the doorway to freedom.

Pinkwater, Jill. *Tails of the Bronx*. New York: Macmillan, 1991.
>The racially mixed children of Burnridge Avenue work together to solve a mystery of disappearing cats and garbage as they are introduced to the survival world of the homeless.

Polacco, Patricia. *Chicken Sunday*. New York: Philomel Books, 1992.
>Three children, two black and one white, make decorated eggs in the Ukrainian style to sell in Mr. Kodinski's shop. They hope to raise money and buy their African American grandmother, Miss Eula, an Easter hat in return for her delicious Sunday fried chicken dinners.

Taylor, Mildred. *The Well*. New York: Dial Books for Young Readers, 1995.
>David Logan has difficulty sharing his family's well, the only one still providing water, with the town's belligerent white teenager, Charlie Hammer, who is capable of inciting racial violence.

Woodson, Jacqueline. *The Other Side*. New York: G. P. Putnam's Sons, 2001.
>Two little girls, one black, one white, become friends across the fence that separates their two properties, despite their parents' reservations.

Author-Related Sources

Berger, Laura Standley, ed. *Twentieth-Century Young Adult Writers*. Detroit, MI: St. James Press, 1994, 81–4.

Bunting, Eve. *Once Upon a Time*. Katonah, New York: R. C. Owen, 1995.

"Eve Bunting." In vol. 110 of *Something about the Author*. Farmington Hills, MI: Gale Group, 2000, 25–34.

"Eve Bunting." In vol. 82 of *Children's Literature Review*. Farmington Hills, MI: Gale Group, 2003, 1–53.

Hipple, Ted, ed. In vol. 1 of *Writers for Young Adults*. New York: Charles S. Scribner's Sons, 1997, 183–9.

Discussion Questions

For *Smoky Night*

1. How does Daniel feel as he watches the rioting and looting from his apartment window?

2. What does his mother mean when she explains the riot stating, "It can happen when people get angry. They want to smash and destroy. They don't care anymore what's right and what's wrong"?

3. How does Daniel's mother feel about the rioting?

4. Why does Mama feel she should not buy food from Mrs. Kim's store?

5. How does the riot change the neighbors' attitudes toward one another?

6. How does Daniel's comment about the cats not knowing each other change his mother's and neighbors' thinking?

7. What do the people learn from the cats? Why is it important to get along with everyone?

8. Why is the artwork in this book just as important in telling the story as the words?

9. How does the artist use colors and lines to show the scary portions of the riot and the people's reactions to it?

10. What types of art supplies other than paint does the artist use to create his pictures?

11. What does the artist do in his paintings to make it seem more realistic?

12. Is Daniel's story one of sadness and fear or one of hope and courage? Why?

13. How do the paintings show that the story has a positive ending?

The Watertower

By Gary Crew, Illustrated by Steven Woolman

Brooklyn, New York: Crocodile Books, 1997

Reading/Discussion Level: . . . . Grades 5–7

Genre: . . . . Picture book/fantasy

Themes: . . . . Friendship, trust, taking risks

Awards: . . . . School Library Journal Best Books, Australian Children's Book of the Year

Plot Summary

Two good friends, Spike Trotter and Bubba D'Angelo, take a daring swim on a bone-dry, scorching hot day in the town's watertower, despite parental warnings about the dangers of such play. The boys' display of bravado is tempered a bit as Bubba follows Spike down the ladder into the murky, dark water and begins to feel an eeriness and discomfort, then loses sight of his friend. Ascending to the top, Bubba realizes his shorts are missing; not wanting to face his mother's disparagement and physical punishment, he accepts Spike's offer to sneak back into Bubba's room and return with another pair of pants. Bubba's wait in the sun becomes unbearable, forcing him to descend once again, part way, down the tower. Upon climbing out the second time, he emerges a different boy. He is changed both physically and emotionally, with an altered personality that Spike immediately recognizes as strange. Bubba appears to be bolder, and he looks different—there's a bizarre look in his eye that seems to be common among the other town residents. His hand now also has a kind of tattoo mark—the circular symbol that appears on the watertower.

Main Characterization

Spike Trotter is a bit of a risk taker, portrayed as brave and somewhat daring, but also displaying a sensitivity to and understanding of Bubba's needs and concerns. His quick, instinctive assessment that Bubba is behaving oddly and out of his normal character is indicative of the sudden, subtle, and eerie transformation that has taken place. Bubba D'Angelo is a follower, cautiously brave but wary and uncomfortable about waiting too long for his friend to return with his pants. The eerie sounds, smell, and movement in the watertower become frightening to him. The transformation after his second descent seems unnatural and perhaps almost alien induced.

Themes

Friendship and trust are the dominant themes in this story with an unexplained and open-ended conclusion. The two boys have a close relationship that is definitely affected by Bubba's experience in the watertower. Daring—taking risks versus fear and uncertainty—is an alternating theme set in a twilight zone-like environment.

Books with Similar Issues or Themes

For this particular selection, a collection of short stories involving supernatural overtones are suggested.

Coville, Bruce. *Odder Than Ever*. San Diego, CA: Harcourt, Brace, Jovanovich, 1999.
Nine stories ranging from chilling horror to humorously fractured fairy lore are included in this collection.

Duncan, Lois, editor. *Night Terrors*. New York: Simon & Schuster Books for Young Readers, 1996.
Authors such as Norma Fox Mazer, Chris Lynch, and Richard Peck contribute eleven original stories with supernatural and psychological overtones.

Gorog, Judith. *Three Dreams and a Nightmare and Other Tales of the Dark*. New York: Philomel Books, 1988.
Fourteen stories involving the supernatural and occult.

Pearce, Philippa. *Familiar and Haunting*. New York: Greenwillow, 2002.
This collection includes thirty-seven realistic and supernatural tales with unsettling plots, situations, and conclusions.

Read If You Dare: Twelve Twisted Tales from the Editors of Read Magazine. Brookfield, CT: Millbrook Press, 1997.
Twelve stories involving fate and destiny with some twisted and bizarre outcomes.

Richardson, Jean, editor. *Beware! Beware! Chilling Tales*. New York: Viking Kestrel, 1989.
Nine stories of sinister and strange happenings.

Author-Related Sources

Berger, Laura Standley, ed. *Twentieth-Century Young Adult Writers*. Detroit, MI: St. James Press, 1994, 155–6.

"Gary Crew." In vol. 42 of *Children's Literature Review*. Farmington Hills, MI: Gale Group, 1997, 45–62.

"Gary Crew." In vol. 110 of *Something about the Author*. Farmington Hills, MI: Gale Group, 2000, 71–6.

Gary Crew Web site: http://www.home.gil.com.au/~cbcqld/crew/crew.htm (accessed 8 June 2004).

Discussion Questions

For *The Watertower*

1. What kind of relationship do Spike and Bubba have?

2. Why do they choose to go swimming in the watertower?

3. What is at the bottom of the watertower tank?

4. What does Bubba see or experience at the end of the story?

5. How does Bubba's physical appearance change at the end of the story?

6. How do the illustrations tell the story with the author's words?

7. What does the artist, Steven Woolman, do to describe the town where Spike and Bubba live?

8. How do the colors of the illustrations help you to understand what kind of day it is and how the boys are feeling?

9. What is a possible meaning of the circular symbol throughout the story, and how does the artist use it in different ways in his pictures?

10. What indications are there in the story and in the pictures that this may be a science fiction book?

11. How do you think this story might end?

Wingwalker

By Rosemary Wells, Illustrated by Brian Selznick

New York: Hyperion Books, 2002

Reading Level: . . . . Grades 3–4
Genre: . . . . Historical fiction, Depression/Dust Bowl era
Themes: . . . . Confidence, ambition, courage, faith and trust

Plot Summary

Small for his age, second-grader Reuben attends the 1933 Oklahoma Air Races with his family and holds the winning raffle ticket for a ride on the two-seater plane called *Gypsy Moth.* Frightened to go, he is first teased by his jealous cousin, Mary Ellen. Then, unwilling to disappoint his gently encouraging father, he bravely weathers the pilot's heart-stopping and stomach-lurching air stunts, returning to the ground with little recollection of the experience. Reuben's first flight, however, serves as an introduction to the new life his family will undertake as his unemployed dancing-teacher father answers a job advertisement for a traveling fair that will have him walk and later dance on the wing of Dixie Belle's airplane know as *The Land of Cotton.* The newfound circus life not only offers employment for Reuben's father as stunt performer and his mother as county fair canteen cook, it also brings new friendships and learning opportunities for Reuben with Otto the Fat Man, Josephine the Tattoo Lady, Buck the Fire Eater, and Frank Dingo the Human Snake. Reuben shares a genuine concern with his mother about his father's safety during those daredevil dancing flights and learns to appreciate everyone's unique talents and abilities. His greatest realization however, is learning to trust his father's talent, ability, and faith in the future by joining him aboard the wing for the last performance of the season.

Main Characterization

Reuben, an eight year-old boy, is called "shrimp-boats" because of his small stature by his fellow classmates. He has some large fears about his father's safety and his family's well-being in a world lacking steady employment and a stable lifestyle. His father is an optimistic man providing constant encouragement as a balance to his mother's legitimate concerns for safety and realistic expectations. Reuben's young life is surrounded by children who either make fun of or bully him, such as his cousin, Mary Ellen Hockerbee, who is eager to bring attention to any of Reuben's inadequacies. The adults he meets in the traveling fair provide an awakening to how others can find a solution to negative or difficult circumstances in their lives and therefore create their own happiness. Otto the Fat Man teaches him magic, Josephine shares her reason for painting her physically marked body with tattoos, Buck gives lessons in juggling, and Frank provides encouragement telling Reuben to have faith and trust in his father by holding his hand.

Themes

Living life with confidence, faith, and trust are themes developed within the characters and their interrelationships. Both Reuben and his mother express their concern for the future, both when the depression brings unemployment and when the prospect of a new job for his father involves a daily stunt performance on the wing of a flying airplane. Reuben's father trusts his ability and looks to the future; this, along with Reuben's interaction with the four circus performers, counters his fears. Each performer's story, recounting his or her reason for joining the circus to achieve either a better or more interesting life, leaves an impression on Reuben. He realizes that, like his father who took a chance using his ability and talent for a new kind of job, success is possible for those brave enough to try new ventures. Reuben also gains enough courage and trust in the end to join his father in a last performance on top of the wing, really enjoying this second, much more daring flight aboard a plane.

Books with Similar Issues or Themes

Adler, David A. *The Babe & I*. Illustrated by Terry Widener. San Diego: Harcourt Brace, 1999.
    A boy helps his unemployed father by selling newspapers outside Yankee Stadium in 1932 and actually meets the famous ball player, selling him a paper and receiving a huge tip.

Birchman, David Francis. *A Green Horn Blowing*. Illustrated by Thomas B. Allen. New York: Lothrop, Lee, & Shepard, 1997.
    During the Depression, a boy learns to make music with a trombolina, a horn-looking squash, from a transient worker on his aunt's berry farm.

Haseley, Dennis. *The Amazing Thinking Machine*. New York: Dial Books, 2002.
    During the Depression, eight-year-old Patrick and his brother Roy build a sort of answer machine out of an old typewriter and spare parts to raise money from the neighborhood kids and help their mother make ends meet while their unemployed father has left looking for work.

Horvath, Polly. *The Happy Yellow Car*. New York: Farrar, Straus & Giroux, 1994.
    A comic novel set in Depression-era Missouri. The Grunt family is surprised by Mr. Grunt's purchase of a yellow car with the hidden money Mrs. Grunt is saving to send their very bright Betty to college.

Ryan, Pam Muñoz. *Esperanza Rising*. New York: Scholastic Press, 2000.
    Just before the Great Depression, Esperanza must leave her comfortably well-off home with her family in Mexico to work as a migrant on the farms in southern California.

Author-Related Sources

Berger, Laura Standley, ed. *Twentieth-Century Children's Writers*. Detroit, MI: St. James Press, 1995, 1009–10.

"Rosemary Wells." In vol. 69 of *Children's Literature Review*. Farmington Hills, MI: Gale Group, 2001, 149–83.

"Rosemary Wells." In vol. 114 of *Something about the Author*. Farmington Hills, MI: Gale Group, 2000, 224–32.

Silvey, Anita, ed. *Essential Guide to Children's Books and Their Creators*. Boston: Houghton Mifflin, 2002, 463–6.

The World of Rosemary Wells (Web site): http://www.rosemarywells.com/ (accessed 8 June 2004).

Discussion Questions

For *Wingwalker*

1. How does Reuben feel the day he wins the raffle ticket to ride the airplane?

2. What are some of the general concerns that Reuben has?

3. Why does Reuben feel that his cousin Mary Ellen is scarier than the new people he meets at the traveling fair?

4. What do the other performers teach Reuben?

5. How do Reuben and his mother feel about his father's stunt performances?

6. Why does Reuben's father feel it is so important for Reuben to join him on the wing during a flying performance?

7. What gives Reuben the courage to trust his father?

8. Why does Reuben finally go up with his father for the last performance?

9. How does Reuben feel way up there with his father?

10. Before they take the last performing flight, Reuben's father says, "We never know what's around the next bend in the river, do we?" What does he mean?

11. What does the traveling circus fair represent to Reuben, his parents, and the other performers?

The Wish Giver: Three Tales of Coven Tree

By Bill Brittain, Illustrated by Andrew Glass

New York: HarperCollins, 1983

Reading Level: .... Grades 3–5

Themes: .... Cause and effect, wishing

Genre: .... Fantasy

Awards: .... Newbery Honor, ALA Notable Children's Book

Plot Summary

Four residents of Coven Tree are involved in separate situations that are ultimately connected through the magic of a wish giver they meet at the annual Church social. A funny little man, Thaddeus Blinn, stands outside his tent and entices each with the promise of granting them any wish they desire for the price of fifty cents. Polly Kemp longs to be accepted by the popular crowd in school. Rowena Jervis is in love with a traveling salesman and hopes to be courted and wed by him. Adam Fiske works hard carrying water several times per day on his parent's drought-parched farm and prays for a way to irrigate the land. The narrator, general store owner Stewart Meade, goes by the name of Stew Meat and is curiously attracted to the tent, but really has no reason to believe or make any wishes. Each pays fifty cents and receives a white card with a red circle on it. The four take home their cards, and with the exception of Stew Meat who puts his away as a memento of fifty cents foolishly spent, they make their wishes within the next couple of days—with disastrous results. Polly's feisty, surly behavior with everyone she meets is the real reason for her unpopularity, and when she makes her wish that people pay attention to her and smile when they see her, she cannot talk normally and begins to croak like a frog "jug-a-rum." Rowena is frustrated that her salesman, Henry Piper, will leave after three days of doing business with her father and wishes that he put down roots in Coven Tree and never leave again. Henry turns into a tree and becomes part of the wooded area behind Rowena's house. Adam is so tired of carrying water to help his father earn a meager living that he wishes for water all over the farm and is surprised when water begins gushing out nonstop from beneath the earth, completely flooding both farm and house. The three children have gotten their wishes granted in ways they never intended and conclude that Stew Meat and his unused wish can undo all three wishes, bringing life back to the way it was before the church social.

Main Characterization

Thaddeus Blinn, the Wish Giver, is a quirky, small man with a mission or motive behind his good intentions of granting wishes. Polly Kemp is an eleven-year-old girl who speaks her mind without regard to people's feelings. Her unpopularity is misunderstood, and she wants to be accepted by the well-to-do girls in school who are only interested in society and fashion. Her invitation to a tea party enlightens her and helps her to realize what is truly important in leading her own life. Rowena Jervis is fifteen years old and dreamy about love in general. She is naïve and taken in by Henry Piper's sweet-talking act believing his interest in her is genuine. She feels some guilt for her wishing but quickly realizes Henry's true motives. Adam Fiske is a hard worker but wants to be able to have time for things that interest him. He is sincere and concerned for his parents, and he feels remorse for what his wish has done to the family's home. Stew Meat is the adult voice of reason, unbelieving yet willing to help when called upon.

Themes

Cause and effect is the major theme throughout all three scenarios. Each wisher strives for a better situation and sets in motion uncontrollable results. Life is what one makes of it, but taking responsibility for one's thoughts and actions is present in all three children's attitudes and reasons for undoing their wishes.

Books with Similar Issues or Themes

Alexander, Lloyd. *The Cat Who Wished to Be a Man*. New York: E. P. Dutton, 1973.
> Granted the gift of speech by his master, Lionel the cat wishes to become a man and must use his feline abilities to tolerate both the good and bad qualities of humanity.

Billingsley, Franny. *Well Wished*. New York: Atheneum Books for Young Readers, 1997.
> Knowing that wishes are dangerous and often go wrong, Nuria tries to outsmart the wishing well in a time of dire need.

Eager, Edward. *The Well-Wishers*. San Diego: Harcourt, Brace, 1960.
> In this classic sequel to *Tales of Magic*, the old wishing well comes to life again, involving the children in a new series of adventures.

Hearne, Betsy. *Wishes, Kisses and Pigs*. New York: Margaret K. McElderry Books, 2001.
> Louise must figure out how to undo her wish, which has turned her brother into a pig, without provoking another dangerous result.

Nesbit, E. *Melisande*. Illustrated by P. J. Lynch. San Diego: Harcourt Brace Jovanovich, 1989.
> Melisande uses the one wish her father the king has saved to undo the curse she received at birth that left her forever bald; now she must endure the endless growth of her hair.

Author-Related Sources

Berger, Laura Standley, ed. *Twentieth-Century Children's Writers*. Detroit, MI: St. James Press, 1995, 148–9.

"Bill Brittain." In vol. 76 of *Something about the Author*. Farmington Hills, MI: Gale Group, 1994, 20–4.

Discussion Questions

For *The Wish Giver: Three Tales of Coven Tree*

1. What kind of person is each character—Polly, Adam, and Rowena?

2. What do Polly, Adam, and Rowena each hope to accomplish with their wishes?

3. How does believing affect the lives of Polly, Adam, and Rowena?

4. What does wishing do for Polly, Adam, and Rowena?

5. Why do all of the wishes have the results that they do?

6. What kind of person is Thaddeus Blinn?

7. Stew Meat says, "The Wish Giver could make dreams come true, but only on his own terms, of course." What were the Wish Giver's terms?

8. Why does Thaddeus Blinn grant every wish the way he does—that is, so it will cause misery and trouble?

9. Why does Thaddeus Blinn grant only one wish?

10. Adam's father said, "wishing that things were better is something all people do." What is the author trying to say with these words?

11. How do the lives of Polly, Adam, and Rowena change after their wishes are undone?

12. What does the old saying "be careful what you wish for" mean?

Yang the Youngest and His Terrible Ear

By Lensey Namioka, Illustrated by Kees De Kiefte

Boston: Little, Brown, 1992

Reading Level: . . . . Grades 3–4
Genre: . . . . Realistic fiction
Themes: . . . . Success, cultural differences, individuality, immigration, friendship

Plot Summary

Nine-year-old Yingtao Yang is the youngest of four children in his musically talented Chinese immigrant family living in Seattle, Washington. While his siblings all play a string instrument competently, Yingtao is tone deaf and cannot hear the mistakes he makes. Unwilling to believe a member of this family has not been given the gift of music, Mr. Yang continually pressures his son to try harder, practice better, until he can play as well as the rest. Expectations reach a peak as the family works toward a recital performance that will hopefully attract more music students to take Mr. Yang's private lessons. Music isn't Yingtao's only problem. Yet adjusting to American life, learning English, doing well in school, and making friends are all overshadowed by the responsibility to help his father develop a successful student clientele with an impressive recital performance. Yingtao intuitively knows he will never be good in music, but he is more successful at school making a best friend, Matthew, and discovering his true interest—baseball. Ironically, Matthew is musically talented with the violin, and the Yang family encourages him to join their practice sessions even though Matthew's parents do not see the value in it. A clever, although somewhat deceitful, solution is devised by Yingtao, his older sister Mary, and Matthew for a musically successful performance on the day of the recital. Matthew will play Yingtao's part behind a screen while Yingtao will only pretend to play during the string quartet portion. Both parents and children resolve their differences when the true violinist is revealed, and Matthew and Yingtao are finally supported in their respective interests of music and baseball.

Main Characterization

Yingtao is a nine-year-old boy adjusting to his new American life. He very much wants to be accepted into the world of his new classroom peers and also gain the respect and admiration of his family members for his talent and achievements. Pleasing his family is much more difficult because of his lack of musical ability, causing feelings of inadequacy. His newfound friendship with Matthew gives him the courage to find and develop his interest in baseball and to express his individuality to his family. Matthew is the American counterpart to Yingtao, growing up in a household that does not see great value in his musical interest, but has a rather stereotypical view that boys should play sports. Although Matthew would love to develop his talent in playing the violin, he is expected to participate in little league instead.

Themes

Feeling successful by finding one's talent and developing it is the main theme in this story. Yingtao and Matthew help each other to awaken their parents' views about allowing the boys to express their individuality that may differ from family expectations. Yingtao's story is also one of immigration, noting cultural differences through humorous idiomatic dialogue that Yingtao misunderstands and Matthew then explains. Differences in family names (siblings in the Yang family are called Eldest, Second Eldest, and so on), in how simple family dinners are held, and in the acceptability of children earning part-time money are all examples outlined through Matthew and Yingtao's relationship. Their friendship provides them with the strength to develop their respective identities.

Books with Similar Issues or Themes

Estes, Eleanor. *The Lost Umbrella of Kim Chu*. Illustrated by Jacqueline Ayer. New York: Margaret A. McElderry/Atheneum, 1978.
> Nine-year-old Kim must search out of her New York City Chinatown neighborhood for her father's prize umbrella, which she borrowed without permission to protect her books and was taken from the stand at the library.

Lord, Bette Bao. *In the Year of the Boar and Jackie Robinson*. Illustrated by Marc Simont. New York: Harper & Row, 1984.
> Chinese immigrant Shirley Temple Wong adjusts to her new life in Brooklyn and learns about baseball and the Brooklyn Dodgers.

Marsden, Carolyn. *The Gold-Threaded Dress*. Cambridge, MA: Candlewick Press, 2002.
> Thai-American fourth grader Oy struggles to fit in with the popular girls in her predominantly Mexican-American neighborhood and school.

Yep, Laurence. *The Amah*. New York: G. P. Putnam's Sons, 1999.
> When Amy Chin's mother is engaged as a Chinese nanny to Stephanie, wealthy daughter of a widow, Amy must neglect her beloved ballet lessons to help babysit her own brothers and begins to feel resentment and jealousy toward her mother's charge.

Author-Related Sources

Berger, Laura Standley, ed. *Twentieth-Century Young Adult Writers*. Detroit, MI: St. James Press, 1994, 480–1.

Holtze, Sally Holmes, ed. *Seventh Book of Junior Authors and Illustrators*. New York: H. W. Wilson, 1996, 236–7.

"Lensey Namioka." In vol. 48 of *Children's Literature Review*. Farmington Hills, MI: Gale Group, 1998, 58–69.

"Lensey Namioka." In vol. 89 of *Something about the Author*. Farmington Hills, MI: Gale Group, 1997, 149–52.

"Lensey Namioka, Autobiography." In vol. 116 of *Something about the Author*. Farmington Hills, MI: Gale Group, 2000, 110–12.

Lensey Namioka Web site: http://www.lensey.com/index.html (accessed 8 June 2004).

Silvey, Anita, ed. *Essential Guide to Children's Books and Their Creators*. Boston: Houghton Mifflin, 2002, 320.

Discussion Questions

For *Yang the Youngest and His Terrible Ear*

1. Why is music such an important part of Yingtao's family life?

2. Why is it difficult for Yingtao's father, and even his brother and sisters, to accept Yingtao's lack of musical ability?

3. Why does Yingtao have trouble telling his father that he really loves baseball?

4. How does Matthew make Yingtao's life better in his new home?

5. How is Yingtao's family life different from Matthew's? How is it the same?

6. How does the author use language or certain sayings to make us understand Yingtao's difficulty with English?

7. Why is it acceptable for Matthew to earn money outside of school, but unacceptable for Yingtao?

8. What makes both Matthew and Yingtao feel successful?

9. How does Yingtao feel about having Matthew play his part in the recital behind a screen? Why does he agree to the scheme?

10. Why does Yingtao's sister purposefully reveal Matthew by knocking down the screen at the end of the recital?

11. What do Yingtao and Matthew learn from each other?

12. What do all the parents and children understand after the recital?

Chapter 3

Mother-Daughter Series

The tremendous popularity of the Mother-Daughter book discussion groups introduced by Shireen Dodson in her books *The Mother-Daughter Book Club* (HarperCollins, 1997) and *100 Books for Girls to Grow On* (HarperCollins, 1998) sparked a new interest in promoting multigenerational discussion groups in libraries, church groups, and other individual settings. Discussion groups provide a venue for girls between the ages of ten and fourteen to form a positive, mutually respectful relationship with their mothers at a most psychologically difficult and sometimes volatile, almost always tense period in their upbringing. Books are often the best way to open a new line of communication among friends and family and can introduce concepts, ideas, opinions, thoughts, concerns, and issues that lie dormant when normal home life conversation is minimal or forced. These discussions can ultimately create a new form of bonding between girls and their moms, touching on topics that can bring forth a unique female perspective.

Through today's media, girls are exposed to myriad female role models, some positive, some not. Adding female literary characters to their experience can introduce another view of feminine behavior, morality, and social responsibility. Clinical social worker Jeanette Gadeberg states in her 1995 book *Raising Strong Daughters* (Fairview Press) that providing good books with both biographies of innovative, ground-breaking women and fictional heroines who are and have done important things to shape and change the world will help girls "build bridges between women of the past and the woman she wants to become" (p. 178).

What topics interest girls? What do they like to read about and why? The Smartgirl.Org Teen Read Week online survey for 2003 had a 60 percent female response with results that included reading about characters similar to the reader, characters and people who do amazing things, fantasy portrayals, hard issues such as poverty and crime, and people with very different lifestyles and situations than the reader.

Historically these interests are not very different from what girls and young women yearned for and tried to find in the reading material they chose. Kelly Schrum in her essay " 'That Cosmopolitan Feeling': Teenage Girls and Literacy, 1920–1970," writes that the classic series characters in the Nancy Drew and Bobbsey Twins books resulted in "intense pleasure and powerful memories surrounding female heroines" and that girls "demonstrated their passion for reading, especially about themselves" through magazines (p. 107).

Similarly, in her article "Reading Like a Woman," Anne G. Berggren points out women's needs to feel a personal connection with the characters by identifying with their personalities and psyches. Historical novels are a way to acquire knowledge through someone else's experiences. In addition, maintaining a balance between aggressive, assertive behavior and sympathetic cognizance is equally important. In her 1994 Horn Book article "Creative Reading: Books in the Classroom," Susan Moran concluded from studying what her female eighth-grade students recorded in their reading journals that girls "value the strength of the female protagonists ... and they rejoice when these characters prevail, but prefer that triumph not come at the cost of sensitivity and compassion" (p. 497).

Keeping these views in mind, selections for this chapter include the following:

- Coming of age novels such as Jean Thesman's *The Ornament Tree* or Joan Bauer's *Squashed*

- Novels with a liberated viewpoint such as *Ella Enchanted* or *Caddie Woodlawn*

- Stories with strong female protagonists such as *Catherine, Called Birdy* or *Gooney Bird Greene*

- An assortment of historical time periods from medieval England to post–World War II

- A variety of cultural backgrounds including some not as well known like the Peruvian jungle in *Go and Come Back* or the character Nhamo in *A Girl Named Disaster*

- Girls succeeding in traditional male roles such as Aerin, a dragon slayer, in *Hero and the Crown*

- Heroines from a variety of environments both rural and urban such as *Our Only May Amelia* and *Ruby Electric*

So let the girls discover their own female perspectives and a new, willing way to connect with mom through what they like to do best—talk—while you provide an impetus for getting together.

References

Bauermeister, Erica, and Holly Smith. *Let's Hear It for the Girls: 375 Great Books for Readers*. New York: Penguin Books, 1997.

Berggren, Anne G. "Reading Like A Woman." In *Reading Sites: Social Difference and Reader Response*, ed. Patrocinio P. Schweickart and Elizabeth A. Flynn. New York: The Modern Language Association of America, 2004, 166–88.

Cooper-Mullin, Alison. *Once upon a Heroine: 450 Books for Girls to Love*. Chicago: Contemporary Books, 1998.

Dodson, Shireen. *100 Books for Girls to Grow On*. New York: HarperCollins, 1998.

Gadeberg, Jeanette. *Raising Strong Daughters*. Minneapolis, MN: Fairview Press, 1995, 178.

Moran, Susan. "Creative Reading: Books in the Classroom." *The Horn Book Magazine*, July 1994: 497–505.

O'Dean, Kathleen. *Great Books for Girls*. New York: Ballantine Books, 2002.

Schrum, Kelly, " 'That Cosmopolitan Feeling': Teenage Girls and Literacy, 1920–1970." In *Girls and Literacy in America: Historical Perspectives to the Present*. Edited by Jane Greer. Santa Barbara, CA: ABC-CLIO, 2003, 103–20.

Smartgirl.org Web site: http://www.smartgirl.org/reports/2734196.html (accessed 5 September 2004).

Caddie Woodlawn

By Carol Ryrie Brink, Illustrated by Trina Schart Hyman

New York: Macmillan, 1973 (first published in 1935)

Reading Level: . . . . Grades 4–6
Genre: . . . . Historical fiction
Themes: . . . . Female strength, gender roles, pioneer life, maturation
Awards: . . . . Newbery Medal

Plot Summary

Wisconsin pioneer life in 1864 brings adventure, sorrow, and maturity to eleven-year-old Caddie Woodlawn. Allowed to run free with her two brothers, Tom and Warren, Caddie behaves more like a tomboy than a well-groomed young lady. And while her father's experiment bolsters her physical strength and health, her mother is concerned about the inappropriateness of such uncharacteristically boyish behavior. Caddie is one of the eldest of seven children, bonding more with her older and younger brother than with her sisters. A visit from her Boston cousin, Annabelle, a recent finishing-school graduate, forces Caddie to think about her rowdy way of living and reevaluate her life as a young woman. The year provides a glimpse into pioneer farm life through a variety of episodic chapters recounting stories filled with daring childhood pranks, one-room schoolhouse occurrences, visitations from the traveling preacher or circuit rider, and dealings with the neighboring Indian tribe countered against the family's more civilized Eastern and English ancestry. When the family has an opportunity to move to England as part of an inheritance Caddie's father is offered, a certain amount of suspense and agitation is created within each member of Caddie's family as they must weigh wealth over familiar surroundings and a simpler life.

Main Characterization

Caddie Woodlawn is a typical for her age and time period. She is bold, daring, brave, and a risk taker, sometimes against her better judgment. Always interested in keeping up with the boys, she will put herself into precarious situations without thinking through the circumstances or consequences. However, her forthright courage allows her to ride alone at night to warn her family's Indian friends of an impending attack by some of the town's men, too fearful and prejudicial to accept the tribe's peaceful coexistence. In addition, Caddie is generous and wise beyond her years as she uses her saved silver dollar to buy happiness for some unfortunate young mixed-race children whose Indian mother is forced out of town. Her prankish behavior toward city-bred cousin Annabelle and resulting punishment are a turning point in her life, helping her realize the full potential of her responsibility as a person and woman.

Tom and Warren Woodlawn, two years older and younger than Caddie respectively, provide both brotherly camaraderie and friendship that Caddie has yet to experience with another girl.

Hetty Woodlawn is younger than Tom, Warren, and Caddie and considered a pesky tag-along, tattletale until Caddie's soul searching at the end of the book brings her closer to a female and sisterly companionship.

Father, descendant from a wealthy aristocratic English family, is happier living the simpler, pioneer life. He is advanced in his thinking with his advice to Caddie that girls can be both strong and feminine by bearing the responsibility to live life wisely with a gentle and understanding heart.

Mother, raised in Boston, represents the typical pioneer wife, trusting and following her husband's choices and direction, as she allows Caddie to run with the boys for her first twelve years of life.

Themes

Gender roles, what is and isn't appropriate behavior for a girl in the Civil War–era pioneer life is the crux of this story as Carrie's escapades, successes, and failures are outlined in each chapter. Her well-developed character shines with a certain strength and fortitude that shape her thinking and attitude on life in this most important year of her upbringing.

Books with Similar Issues or Themes

Cushman, Karen. *The Ballad of Lucy Whipple*. New York: Clarion Books, 1996.
>Uprooted from her comfortable New England city life and brought to the upheaval of a California gold-mining town, Lucy Whipple recounts her unhappiness in a humorous first-person narrative peppered with letters sent home to her grandparents in Massachusetts.

Fritz, Jean. *The Cabin Faced West*. New York: Coward-McCann, 1958.
>Ann Hamilton adjusts to her new life in the early wilderness of Western Pennsylvania where it seems there are only boys, babies, and lots of hard farm work.

Holm, Jennifer L. *Boston Jane: An Adventure*. New York: HarperCollins, 2001.
Holm, Jennifer L. *Boston Jane: Wilderness Days*. New York: HarperCollins, 2002.
>Jane Peck, well bred and educated, learns to survive and thrive in her new rustic nineteenth-century environment as the only young white woman in the Pacific Northwest settlement of Shoalwater Bay, after her promised fiancé never appears.

Karr, Kathleen. *The Petticoat Party: Go West, Young Women!* New York: HarperCollins, 1996.
Karr, Kathleen. *The Petticoat Party: Phoebe's Folly*. New York: HarperCollins, 1996.
Karr, Kathleen. *The Petticoat Party: Oregon, Sweet* Oregon. New York: HarperCollins, 1997.
>Westward expansion series humorously describes a practically female-only wagon train en route to Oregon with a feisty, daring young twelve-year-old protagonist named Phoebe Brown, her feminist seventeen-year-old sister, Amelia, and fifteen year-old fellow travelers, the Kennan twins.

Whelan, Gloria. *Once on This Island*. New York: HarperCollins, 1995.
>The summer of 1812, as war begins between the United States and England, twelve-year-old Mary O'Shea is left to protect her home with her older brother and sister on Mackinac Island when their father joins the American army based in Detroit.

Author-Related Sources

Berger, Laura Standley, ed. *Twentieth-Century Children's Writers*. Detroit, MI: St. James Press, 1995, 145–6.

Bingham, Jane, ed. *Writers for Children: Critical Studies of Major Authors Since the Seventeenth Century*. New York: Charles S. Scribner's Sons, 1988, 85-90.

"Carol Ryrie Brink." In vol. 30 of *Children's Literature Review*. Farmington Hills, MI: Gale Group, 1993, 1–17. Detroit, MI: New York:

"Carol Ryrie Brink." In vol. 100 of *Something about the Author*. Farmington Hills, MI: Gale Group, 1999, 32–5.

Hopkins, Lee Bennett, ed. *More Books by More People: Interviews with Sixty-Five Authors of Books for Children*. New York: Citation Press, 1974, 53–9.

Silvey, Anita, ed. *Children's Books and Their Creators*. Boston: Houghton Mifflin, 1995, 84–5.

Discussion Questions

For *Caddie Woodlawn*

1. In this historical story, what parallels can you see between Caddie's life and that of an American girl today?

2. What is Caddie's stature among the boys?

3. How do the adults around Caddie treat her and why?

4. What makes Caddie confident enough to trust her Indian neighbors?

5. Why does Caddie choose to become an "ambassador to the enemy"?

6. What does Cousin Annabelle's visit bring to the story and to Caddie's life?

7. Why do you think Caddie is treated differently from her brothers after the three of them treat Annabelle so meanly?

8. What does Caddie's father really mean when he tells her, "I want you to be a woman with a wise and understanding heart, healthy in body and honest in mind"?

9. What do you think Caddie's father would want for his sons?

10. Why did the family vote to stay in America over the opportunity to live a rich, wealthy life in England?

Catherine, Called Birdy

By Karen Cushman

New York: Clarion Books, 1994

Reading Level: 6–8
Genre: . . . . Historical fiction
Themes: . . . . Women's role, independence
Awards: . . . . Newbery Honor, Golden Kite Award

Plot Summary

Life for a young girl of fourteen, daughter to a knight in the medieval era of 1290 England, is one of subservience and docility. For Catherine, nicknamed Birdy, it is a boring, unchallenging existence controlled by men. In the old English style of the period, Birdy recounts her fourteenth year in a journal noting religious dates, feasts, observances and her daily, weekly, and monthly battle to avoid an arranged marriage by her father, "the beast," to any man capable of producing a mutually acceptable economic arrangement. Her mother has given her permission to write this account in the hopes that it will provide a way for her to mature, but Birdy portrays herself the opposite of the well-behaved good girl as she outwardly questions all the unpleasant and menial tasks required of a lady—spinning, sewing, soap making, and the overall lack of choices one has in her future. Birdy is clever and devious, systematically foiling each new prospective husband's attempt to strike a bargain with her father. She is continually incensed at the idea that she will be "sold" into marriage, a position of "spinning, bearing children, and weeping," releasing her worries, anger, fears, and feelings of injustice through her diary entries. She wonders why a boy is permitted to achieve his goals while a girl must remain the object of her father's and husband's affairs. Paradoxically, Birdy envies the common folk who have the luxury of falling in love and choosing their marriage partners. After several failed attempts at finding a marriage proposal for Birdy, her father succeeds in closing a deal with a "shaggy-bearded pig" that owns a manor next to property owned by Birdy's mother, making perfect economic sense. This betrothal is the worst yet as the man is a brute with a murderous, vicious demeanor—and he's old enough to be Birdy's father with a son, Stephen, closer to her age. Birdy is consumed with figuring a way out of this contract but is spared not by her plans or pleas to her father but by the fortunate death of her intended husband. Seeking to honor the contract his father made, Stephen offers to wed Birdy, resulting at least in a more suitable match for the girl.

Main Characterization

Catherine (Birdy) daughter of the Lady Aislinn and the Lord Rollo, is a feisty, sometimes rebellious girl who wishes she had the opportunities afforded her brothers and is desperate to save herself from an arranged, unreasonable, and abusive marriage. Relying on her craftiness and bold, unladylike behavior, she manages to save herself from a variety of suitors but continually finds herself punished and locked in her chambers. Physical punishment is also the norm in this era as her father, whom she hates and shows little respect for, will think nothing of using his hand to strike a blow when he feels his orders are unheard and unheeded. We see an assortment of other characters through Birdy's eyes as she writes about them. There are her brothers, Edward, who is away at a monastery, as well as Robert and Thomas. In addition, there is her nursemaid Morwenna and an aunt, Madame Joanna, who provides some of the most realistic advice for Birdy when she is trying to understand and accept her status and predicament of her impending marriage.

Themes

Birdy's female status in her medieval world limits her ability to choose her own destiny, interests, and even vocation. As a noble lady, she is expected to be submissive, deferential, and obedient, learning the activities deemed proper for her status in society. Conflicting with this theme of an expected women's role is one of independence as characterized by Birdy's outlandish behavior and way of thinking.

Books with Similar Issues or Themes

Konigsburg, E. L. *A Proud Taste for Scarlet and Miniver.* New York: Atheneum, 1973.
>A clever fictionalized account of the life of Eleanor of Aquitaine as told by three of her contemporaries while they wait in heaven for Henry II's divine admittance.

Springer, Nancy. *Rowan Hood, Outlaw Girls of Sherwood Forest.* New York: Philomel Books, 2001.
>Disguised as a boy, thirteen-year-old Rowan sets out to find the murderer of her father, the legendary Robin Hood.

Temple, Frances. *The Ramsay Scallop.* New York: HarperCollins, 1994.
>Elenor and the Lord Thomas are sent on a religious pilgrimage before their marriage as a last chance for discovery and adventure.

Williams, Laura. *The Executioner's Daughter.* New York: Henry Holt, 2000.
>Lily lives in fifteenth-century England, is interested in the practice of healing, but must assist her father, the town's executioner, filling her mother's role after she takes ill.

Informational Books on the Middle Ages

Dean, Ruth, and Melissa Thomson. *Women of the Middle Ages.* Farmington Hills, MI: Lucent Books, 2003.
A historical perspective on the contributions of women during this period.

Krull, Kathleen. *Lives of Extraordinary Women: Rulers, Rebels (and What the Neighbors Thought).* New York: Harcourt, 2000.
>A unique view of famous strong women including several from the Middle Ages such as Eleanor of Aquitaine and Joan of Arc.

Leon, Vicki. *Outrageous Women of the Middle Ages.* New York: Wiley, 1998.
>A lively account of fourteen outspoken and courageous women from Europe, Africa, and the Far East including brief excerpts of historical and religious information for their respective countries.

Author-Related Sources

Hipple, Ted, ed. *Writers for Young Adults.* New York: Charles S. Scribner's Sons, 2000, 37–46.

Holtze, Sally Holmes, ed. *Seventh Book of Junior Authors and Illustrators.* New York: H. W. Wilson, 1996, 72–3.

"Karen Cushman." In vol. 55 of *Children's Literature Review.* Farmington Hills, MI: Gale Group, 1998, 55–75.

"Karen Cushman." In vol. 147 of *Something about the Author.* Farmington Hills, MI: Gale Group, 2004, 30–6.

Marcus, Leonard S., ed. *Author Talk: Conversations with Judy Blume et al.* New York: Simon & Schuster, 2000, 16–21.

Discussion Questions

For *Catherine, Called Birdy*

1. What was life like in medieval England for the noble class?

2. What expectations were there for girls and women in general?

3. Why was marriage so important in the eyes of Birdy's parents?

4. What kind of person was Catherine, and why was she nicknamed Birdy?

5. Birdy's diary entry of November 23 (page 42) has her mother giving her advice. "Song maker, Birdy? Don't stretch your legs longer than your stockings or your toes will stick out." What was her mother trying to say and why?

6. Similarly in Birdy's diary entry of February 22 (page 84) her aunt Madame Joanna tells her, "I flap my wings at times, choose my fights carefully, get things done, understand my limitations, trust in God and a few people, and here I am, I survive, and sometimes even enjoy." What was Madame Joanna trying to say to Birdy?

7. How does Birdy's independent nature cause her problems and also help her to cope?

8. What is Birdy's attitude toward religion?

9. What does Birdy learn from the Jewish travelers?

10. What is the most difficult part of living the life of a relatively wealthy nobleman in medieval England? Was life better or worse for men or women?

The Clock

By James Lincoln Collier and Christopher Collier, Illustrated by Kelly Maddox

New York: Delacorte Press, 1992

Reading Level: . . . . Grades 6–8

Genre: . . . . Historical fiction

Themes: . . . . Women's roles/expectations, women's rights, vengeance, abuse, child labor

Plot Summary

Fifteen-year-old Annie Steele has ambitions of studying and becoming a school teacher, but in her 1810 Connecticut home, helping to supplement the farm living and pay for her father's impulsive buying forces her out of school and into the wool mill to work as a spinner. Brother George and Ma sympathize and want to support Annie in her desires but are obligated to abide by Pa's choices. Mr. Steele is infatuated with any new mechanical advancement and continually makes irresponsible purchases, even though the farm proceeds can barely support the family's normal needs. His latest acquisition is a clock that he will use to run the farm by mechanical time rather than sun time. All this has created anxiety and resentment in Annie, who is concerned about working in a mostly male environment and losing time she would rather spend earning her teaching diploma. Hetty Brown, neighbor and friend, also works as a spinner and helps Annie adjust to her new situation. Annie's longtime childhood friend, Robert, is the tally boy at the mill and has discovered that the overseer, Mr. Hoggart, is stealing wool. When Annie is docked for being late one morning and decides to plead her infraction to Mr. Hoggart, she is threatened by his drunken "friendly" advances, yet cannot make her father understand that Mr. Hoggart's behavior toward her is inappropriate. In addition, Robert's knowledge of Mr. Hoggart's pilfering and stealing results in his increasingly abusive treatment of Robert, leading to his death and to Annie's vengeance by exposing the truth to the owner of the mill.

Main Characterization

Annie Steele is a fifteen-year-old girl who aspires to live beyond the expected role of wife and mother. She struggles to maintain her dream to study and pursue a career while obeying her father's orders to help pay his debts by working at the mill. Her female status precludes her ambitions, intelligence, and rights as her position in society is deemed inferior or subservient. Yet she is courageous and determined to bring justice to Robert's untimely and unnecessary death as caused by Mr. Hoggart's deliberate mistreatment.

Pa (Mr. Steele) is a farmer with a futuristic vision of the world. He tries to invest in certain items such as a rare merino sheep and a new clock, hoping to make more money when he resells, but his enterprising ways never materialize and place him in greater debt. He relies on his children to work off the farm to earn the extra cash, thus placing a greater burden on the family for his unwise choices.

Ma (Mrs. Steele) is very supportive of her daughter, eager for her to accomplish her goals, yet submissive to her husband as is expected of the time period.

George Steele is Annie's brother, who cuts firewood for extra money and ultimately comes to her rescue as she uncovers the wool hidden by the furiously angry Mr. Hoggart.

Robert Bronson is the tally boy who cannot do hard labor because of his bad foot. After learning of Mr. Hoggart's dishonesty, he is made to do more physically demanding work at the mill. He is wise and proud, willing to work as he is told to make his wages, yet he loses his life because he feels he cannot refuse any assignment even when he knows the physical requirements are beyond his ability.

Hetty Brown is a sweet girl of only eight years, who has been hired to work as a spinner in the mill. She is an optimist, always seeing the bright side of a situation. Her encouragement to Annie is tempered by her docile acceptance of what society expects from women in general.

Tom Thrush is one of the orphan boys working at the mill who becomes Annie's secret partner in exposing Mr. Hoggart. His bravado is more for show, however, as Annie's daring plans frighten him and he is beaten and abused by the overseer.

Mr. Hoggart is well respected in the town but harbors a secret, abusive past in his former position in another town. He is a thief and a drunkard and will take advantage of the girls or anyone else including his employer. Most of the boys and girls who work at the mill are terrified of him.

Themes

The ability to choose to set goals outside the expected role for women is the crux of this story as Annie is forced to work according to her father's arrangements rather than set and achieve her own goals in life. Annie's obedient nature conflicts with her feelings of injustice as she seeks revenge for Robert's death, taking numerous risks and placing her own life and well-being in danger. Her rights as a female are violated even by her father, who first makes decisions for her about her future and then refuses to take action when Annie confronts him about Mr. Hoggart's inappropriate advances, citing Mr. Hoggart's good reputation.

Books with Similar Issues or Themes

Bartoletti, Susan Campbell. *Kids on Strike!* Boston: Houghton Mifflin, 1999.

This book highlights the role children played in America's labor strikes to gain better wages and conditions and change child labor laws during the nineteenth and early twentieth centuries.

Beatty, Patricia. *Be Ever Hopeful, Hannalee.* New York: Morrow Junior Books, 1988.

During the Civil War, Hannalee leaves her job in the North at a Yankee mill to return to Atlanta and start a new life with her family, working in a dry-goods store.

Blos, Joan. *A Gathering of Days: A New England Girl's Journal, 1830–1832: A Novel.* New York: Scribner, 1979.

In nineteenth-century New Hampshire, Catherine recounts a year of living on the farm with her remarried father and without her best friend.

Freedman, Russell. *Kids at Work; Lewis Hine and the Crusade against Child Labor.* New York: Clarion Books, 1994.

A history of the investigative reporter and photographer Lewis Hine and the campaign to end child labor in the United States.

McCully, Emily. *The Bobbin Girl.* New York: Dial Books, 1996.

Ten-year-old Rebecca supplements the family's farm income by working as a bobbin girl and must decide whether to support a strike by her fellow women workers who are fighting for better wages and working conditions.

Paterson, Katerine. *Lyddie.* New York: Lodestar Books, 1991.

Seeking to earn more money to save her family farm, Lyddie goes to work in a cloth mill in Lowell, Massachusetts, and gains a level of independence by earning her own money and striving to attend college.

Author-Related Sources

Berger, Laura Standley, ed. *Twentieth-Century Young Adult Writers*. Detroit, MI: St. James Press, 1994, 141–4.

Hipple, Ted, ed. In vol. 1 of *Writers for Young Adults*. New York: Charles S. Scribner's Sons, 1997, 257–9.

"James Lincoln Collier." In vol. 3 of *Children's Literature Review*. Detroit, MI: Gale Research, 1978, 44–50.

"James Lincoln Collier." In vol. 70 of *Something about the Author*. Farmington Hills, MI: Gale Group, 1993, 39–43.

Silvey, Anita, ed. *Children's Books and Their Creators*. Boston: Houghton Mifflin, 1995, 155–6.

Discussion Questions

For *The Clock*

1. What is Annie's ambition?

2. What could Annie do to try to achieve her goals?

3. What does the clock represent to Annie and her father?

4. What expectations do Annie's father and men in general have concerning work and education for women?

5. How were children expected to behave and contribute during this time period?

6. How are women treated in this story?

7. How does Annie deal with her feelings of sorrow and revenge for Robert's death?

8. At the end of the story, Annie asks George to explain the reason there has been so much change in their lives. How does change affect the lives of Annie and her family?

9. Changes in life are inevitable. How do we deal with them in our everyday lives?

Ella Enchanted

By Gail Carson Levine

New York: HarperCollins, 1997

Reading Level: . . . . Grades 4–6

Genre: . . . . Fantasy

Themes: . . . . Independence, behavior – good versus obedient, love and loyalty

Awards: . . . . Newbery Honor

Plot Summary

The traditional Cinderella fairytale is retold here using a magical curse to drive the plot and characterization of Ella, the heroine. The well-intentioned Lucinda gives Ella a gift: the "good" curse of obedience resulting in her obeying everyone's commands. Although this may appear as a way to create a docile child, Ella becomes more rebellious and independent as she gets older, wishing to break the curse and live her life her way. Following her mother's unfortunate death, Ella's well-meaning father sends her to finishing school with two neighboring ill-mannered girls, Hattie and Olive, who begin to make Ella's life a demanding ordeal. Unable to refuse an order, obeying Hattie's continuously tormenting and demeaning commands, Ella gives up her mother's keepsake necklace and money. Ella's rebellious nature and need to find Lucinda to rescind the curse of obedience motivates her enough to run away from the school and seek out her father and Lucinda, hoping to take charge of her life. Along the way, Ella encounters the various dangers of an enchanted forest complete with elves, ogres, giants, and magical creatures. She is rescued by the Prince Charmont from eight hungry ogres, reunites with her father only to learn his business ventures have failed and that he is preparing to marry a rich woman to solve his financial troubles. Ella is also protected by her fairy godmother, Mandy, who serves as the family cook and is her nurturing confidante. Mandy provides Ella with a magical storybook that she keeps with her at all times giving her information, advice, and encouragement as she progresses on her quest to undo the curse. When her father marries the Dame Olga, mother of the odious sisters Hattie and Olive, Ella falls under their demanding thumb once more. In the meantime, a romantic correspondence develops between Ella and the Prince Char, giving Ella more concern about the curse of obedience. Her relationship with the prince can only place him and the Kingdom of Kyrria in utmost danger, for her obedience could cause rogue states and statesmen to take advantage. Love, loyalty, and a fierce desire to be independent and protective of her prince and country undo the curse to a happy conclusion.

Main Characterization

Ella is a smart, feisty, strong character who has a good heart yet is trapped in a curse that forces her to do things against her will or better judgment. Her independent nature brings out a rebellious feature in her personality that allows her to see life in all its irony and absurdity.

Mandy is a mother figure to Ella, giving her the emotional encouragement to prevail against the unforeseen results of Lucinda's unsuspecting gift.

Prince Char is described as a "toiling prince," one with a good, kind heart who gives of himself to his subjects.

Dame Olga is the selfish and greedy stepmother, whose interests lie in her two daughters, the malicious and conniving Hattie and the simple and timid Olive.

Themes

Ella is challenged to be a good daughter, friend, and companion while living within the constraints of a magical gift gone awry. The gift of obedience works against the concept of goodness and kindness. Following orders, whether right or wrong, does not allow her to think and do for herself, make considered decisions, and live her life as she would like. Love and loyalty both to her father and to the prince work as unifying strengths to conquer the challenge she faces.

Books with Similar Issues or Themes

Billingsley, Franny. *The Folk Keeper*. New York: Atheneum Books for Young Readers, 1999.
> Corinna, working as a folk keeper, controlling the folk who live beneath the ground of the foundling home, is summoned by the lord of a seaside estate to learn of her secret half-seal heritage and the powers that come with it.

Haddix, Margaret Peterson. *Just Ella*. New York: Simon & Schuster, 1999.
> Following her romantic courtship and marriage, Ella must face the reality of a boring life in the castle with a dull, uninteresting husband and take steps to escape to a better life. A feminist approach to the traditional Cinderella story.

Kaye, M. M. *The Ordinary Princess*. New York: Doubleday, 1984.
> When the seventh princess born to Queen Rhodesia is given the gift of ordinariness by the most powerful fairy godmother, she becomes unfit to marry any prince in the kingdom and resolves to run away and lead an independent life.

McKinley, Robin. *Spindle's End*. New York: G. P. Putnam's Sons, 2000.
> Cursed by the evil fairy Pernicia to one day prick her finger and fall into a poisoned sleep, Rosie is rescued by a young good fairy, Katriona, to live her life away from the kingdom, unaware of her heritage and doomed fate.

Tarnowska, Wafa. *The Seven Wise Princesses*. Illustrated by Nilesh Mistry. New York: Barefoot Books, 2000.
> Based on the medieval Persian epic, this is the story of King Bahram who leads his kingdom based on the separate wise stories told to him by seven princesses.

Author-Related Sources

Gail Carson Levine Homepage: http://www.harperchildrens.com/authorintro/index.asp?authorid=12385 (accessed 18 August 2004).

"Gail Carson Levine." In vol. 85 of *Children's Literature Review*. Farmington Hills, MI: Gale Group, 2003, 111–15.

"Gail Carson Levine." In vol. 98 of *Something about the Author*. Farmington Hills, MI: Gale Group, 1998, 97–8.

Discussion Questions

For *Ella Enchanted*

1. What kind of a personality does Ella have?

2. Is Ella a good girl or an obedient girl? What is the difference?

3. How does the curse of obedience affect Ella's life and the people she encounters?

4. How does Mandy, Ella's fairy godmother, help Ella with her predicament without using her magical powers?

5. What does the book of fairytales Mandy gives to Ella represent in the story?

6. When Ella meets Lucinda, she is told to "be happy to be blessed with such a lovely quality." How does this affect the original curse?

7. Why is Ella's curse of obedience so dangerous to the prince and the land of Kyrria?

8. Why is Ella finally able to undo the curse herself?

9. How does the author use the original fairy tale of Cinderella as a base for her book *Ella Enchanted*? How is the story of *Ella Enchanted* different from the original fairy tale?

10. How can the concept of being good and obedient work together with an independent personality?

11. Why is it important to have some independence in your life?

A Girl Named Disaster

By Nancy Farmer

New York: Orchard Books, 1996

Reading Level: . . . . Grades 6–8
Genre: . . . . Adventure/cultural fiction
Themes: . . . . Survival, loneliness, controlling one's destiny, courage
Awards: . . . . Newbery Honor, National Book Award Finalist

Plot Summary

In post–colonial Portuguese Mozambique, eleven-year-old Nhamo is an orphan living with her Aunt's family in their Shona village. Treated more like a servant than a relative, Nhamo feels unloved and resented by everyone except her grandmother, Ambuya. In the Shona culture, religion and supernatural beliefs are tied together under a system that stresses the natural order. Anything that falls out of this such as the birth of a child out of wedlock or the birth of twins must be put right or disaster will occur. Nhamo's name translates to "little disaster" because she was born to parents who may have had a Catholic wedding but did not have a proper Shona marriage arrangement. In addition, her father is known as the alleged murderer of Gore Mtoko, which shames the rest of her Shona family. When an outbreak of cholera kills many in the village, the elders seek the advice of the witch finder (the *muvuki*) who tells them that the village's fortune will change by avenging the murder of Gore and marrying Nhamo to his cruel and abusive brother, Zororo. This sparks fear and bold planning in Nhamo's grandmother, who is a former resident of a civilized culture in Zimbabwe. She encourages her granddaughter to escape by canoe, a two-day journey against the current, to her former town, Mtoroshanga, to find and live with her father's family. Having no other choice, Nhamo sets out with a supply of food in the only boat available, one abandoned by the deceased fisherman, Crocodile Guts. Nhamo's journey does not go well; the rowing is very difficult and her sense of direction gets confused. Instead of going south, she gets lost and is swept upstream much farther north than she realizes and begins a survival period lasting months, foraging for food, avoiding the dangers of the wild, and struggling to maintain her human sanity amid the spiritual and real creatures she encounters. After a long period on a large island, Nhamo succeeds in reaching Efifi, a town on the border in Zimbabwe, where she is finally rescued by a group of scientists, cared for, and brought to her family. But the happy anticipated reunion is not to be, as Nhamo is never accepted by anyone except her very old great-grandfather who explains the past to her. Her adopted family of scientists rescues her once again as they encourage her to open a secret bank account with the gold her grandmother gave her at the beginning of her journey and to continue her formal schooling so that she can make her own choices concerning her future without the threat of a life of forced servitude or an unfavorable arranged marriage.

Main Characterization

Nhamo is an intelligent girl whose faith in her religion brings her emotional strength and perseverance during her arduous journey and ordeal. Her long period of isolation from any human encounter forces her to spend a lot of time reasoning out and thinking through a variety of situations that will move her to her destination and out of danger. She is very determined in her slow, painstaking work of creating shelters, food traps, and other necessary survival tools. Nhamo learns a great deal about the habitat and behavior of animals and about living in the wild and off the land. Her emotional well-being is also fragile at times, however, as her extreme isolation leads to loneliness and fear, alternating between optimism and despair. Two things keep her going: her belief in the spiritual world and a careful relationship with a clan of baboons that has taken up residence near her campsite. The spirits of her mother, fisherman Crocodile Guts, and her former ancestors bring continual emotional company, advice and encouragement, while the need for physical contact is constantly present in her dangerously close relationship to the baboons.

Ambuya is Nhamo's grandmother and ally, more educated than the Shona villagers and aware of the religious superstitions that can ruin the life of a child.

Mother is a spiritual character in Nhamo's mind whose tragic death by a leopard has haunted the villagers and caused more trouble for Nhamo and her grandmother.

Crocodile Guts, victim of the cholera, is another spiritual ally of sorts to Nhamo as she struggles to travel with his leaky boat.

Water spirits (*njuzu*) come to Nhamo in her dreams and both terrify and help her cope with her survival struggle.

The baboon family is the closest contact Nhamo has with humanlike behavior. Her extreme isolation and loneliness force her to relate cautiously with them as she names them and gets almost close enough to be groomed or touched, realizing that physical contact is what she misses most.

Themes

Nhamo's story is one of danger, excitement, and courage to overcome unusually difficult emotional and physical obstacles to survive. Encouraged by her grandmother and the spirits of her mother and ancestors, she forges ahead, taking control of her destiny. This theme is carried through to the end of the story as Nhamo's scientist friends help her control her future with advice on finances and school. Loneliness and the need for continual human contact is another theme, addressed through Nhamo's communication with both the spiritual and animal world.

Books with Similar Issues or Themes

George, Jean Craighead. *Julie of the Wolves*. New York: Harper & Row, 1972.
> Miyax, a thirteen-year-old Eskimo girl, runs away from her husband's parents' home. She becomes lost in the Alaskan tundra and survives with a pack of wolves that accept her into their world.

O'Brien, Robert C. *Z for Zacharia*. New York: Atheneum, 1975.
> Ann, sixteen, has lived the last year as the only survivor in her town following a nuclear holocaust. She must now face the intrusion of a scientist who is slowly making his way into her territory and appears to be threatening.

O'Dell, Scott. *Island of the Blue Dolphins*. Illustrated by Ted Lewin. Boston: Houghton Mifflin, 1990.
> Karana, an Indian girl, survives eighteen solitary years on an isolated island off the coast of California through her resourceful strength and courage.

Paulsen, Gary. *Hatchet*. New York: Bradbury Press, 1987.
> Thirteen-year-old Brian survives fifty-four days in the Canadian wilderness alone after the single-engine plane he is on crashes.

Taylor, Theodore. *The Cay*. New York: Doubleday, 1989.
> Phillip is marooned on an island during World War II after his boat is torpedoed, leaving him blind with the only other survivor, a West Indian older man.

Spirit and African Pourquoi Stories

Bryan, Ashley. *Ashley Bryan's African Tales, Uh-huh.* New York: Atheneum, 1998.

Hamilton, Virginia. *The Dark Way: Stories from the Spirit World.* San Diego, CA: Harcourt, Brace, Jovanovich, 1990.

Author-Related Resources

Holtze, Sally Holmes, ed. *Seventh Book of Junior Authors and Illustrators.* New York: H. W. Wilson, 1996, 98–100.

"Nancy Farmer." In vol. 117 of *Something about the Author.* Farmington Hills, MI: Gale Group, 2000, 56–9.

Discussion Questions

For *A Girl Named Disaster*

1. Why does Nhamo's grandmother encourage Nhamo to leave the Shona village and go against her mother's relatives?

2. How does Nhamo's grandmother act differently from her other two daughters, Nhamo's Aunt Chipo and Aunt Shuvai?

3. What was the most difficult part of Nhamo's journey?

4. What does Nhamo's relationship with the baboon family indicate about her life on the island?

5. How does Nhamo's creativity help her survive by herself in the wild?

6. Why is Nhamo's storytelling an important part of her life and of this book?

7. What role do religion and faith play in Nhamo's life?

8. How does Nhamo take control of her own destiny?

9. Would you consider this story to be a fantasy or one of adventure and survival?

Go and Come Back

By Joan Abelove

New York: DK, 1998

Reading Level: . . . . Grades 6–8

Genre: . . . . Realistic fiction

Themes: . . . . Cultural differences, acceptance, tolerance, values

Awards: . . . . School Library Journal Best Books, ALA Notable Children's Book

Plot Summary

When two anthropologists in their twenties, Joanna and Margarita, arrive in the Isabo village of Poincushmana in the Peruvian jungle to observe the lifestyle of its inhabitants, young Alicia tells her views about the "two old ladies," regarding them as so different from her own culture. Labeling them "stingy, stupid, but fun to watch," Alicia judges them negatively because they do not do things correctly— the Isabo way—and is critical of the women's "civilized" Western needs, marking their behavior as inappropriate according to her tribe's acceptable practices. The anthropologists have brought enough supplies to last them several months, but Alicia immediately considers the women to be stingy because they are unwilling to give their supplies away to the villagers who believe in using what they have, such as meat, liquor, and batteries, when they are available without saving for future use. Alicia and the other villagers also think the anthropologists are ignorant or stupid because they do not follow or understand their customs. Alicia becomes interested in "educating" Joanna and Margarita and slowly begins to explain things when the opportunity arises, such as the proper way to bathe in the river, accepted sexual practices, why and how babies are made, how to share their supplies, and so on. The other villagers see an opportunity to take advantage of the women, who are busy taking numerous notes both on paper and through tape recordings, by trading their old, worn, less useful personal items for shiny new beads. As the relationship between Alicia, Joanna, and Margarita becomes a bit stronger, we see and understand the Isabo culture and its traditions and practices through the eyes of a native. Everything, from the concept of work, to bathing, eating, caring for babies, and so on, seems primitive to us, yet for the tribe, it is the strange civilized ways of the anthropologists that are wrong and uneducated. Misunderstandings from both perspectives make one culture strange, shameful, or improper to the other. While Joanna and Margarita have learned much from Alicia and the others to complete their research and book, Alicia is content in knowing that she has helped them to learn to behave properly, as is the Isabo way. The story is based on events that took place in the 1970s and on the experience of two anthropologists.

Main Characterization

Alicia is a young teenage girl somewhere between the age of twelve and fourteen. She is logical, opinionated, caring, and independent. She has her own personal concerns, refusing to acknowledge her marriage to a man much older than she while at the same time adopting an abandoned Peruvian baby. After a bout with dysentery, the baby dies, and Alicia mourns her death, yet accepts it, as is the Isabo way. Alicia lives her life with a certain curiosity and ambition. Completely isolated in her own culture and jungle village, she is only vaguely aware of the outside modern world through occasional brief visits of Peruvian citizens and missionaries. Still, when exposed to Joanna and Margarita's way of life, she cannot accept it as the correct way to behave, particularly within the context of her village. At the end of the story, when Joanna invites her to take a brief ride on her outgoing airplane, Alicia eagerly accepts and is in awe of the view of the larger world surrounding her village, symbolically comprehending the idea that her village can appear different from another's perspective.

Elena is Alicia's friend and peer, sometimes giving her advice, other times laughing at and criticizing the anthropologists with Alicia as they secretly observe their guests.

Joanna is an anthropologist who is able to understand and accept the Isabo's cultural traditions, practices, and behavior in a way that is ultimately respectful. She is gentler and more sensitive than her coworker Margarita and develops a personal relationship with Alicia that extends into a caring, if not loving, affinity. The death of Cami, Alicia's baby, affects her much more than even Alicia.

Margarita, the other anthropologist, is stronger than Joanna and a bit harsh with the villagers, although fearful of them at times as well. She is nonetheless able to develop an understanding of their culture in her own way for her research. She does not become as emotionally invested in a relationship with Alicia or any of the other villagers as Joanna does.

Themes

This novel clearly brings to light the idea that respect and tolerance for cultural differences is important. Abelove has taken the unique narrative approach of telling the story through the eyes of a young Isabo girl to point out how attitudes from various groups with their own agenda can lead to misunderstanding and cultural intolerance. Both the native Indians and the missionaries in the story have difficulty understanding each others' ways, even trying unsuccessfully to force certain practices that do not seem sensible for the culture's needs. As the book comes to a close, Joanna has come to accept Alicia's "teachings" and can value them within the context of the villagers' lifestyle.

Books with Similar Issues or Themes

Cameron, Ann. *Colibri*. New York: Farrar, Straus & Giroux, 2003.
> Living a nomadic life moving from town to town in present-day Guatemala with "Uncle," the man who claims to have rescued her from abandonment, Colibri (Spanish for "hummingbird") must find the courage to escape his abuse and mistreatment and try to reunite with her Mayan family.

Castaneda, Omar S. *Among the Volcanoes*. New York: Lodestar Books, 1991.
> Isabel Pacay, eldest daughter of a Mayan family, longs to break from the tradition of marrying young, wishing instead to attend school and become a teacher. When her mother becomes ill and an American medical researcher in the village offers Western medical treatment, she must decide whether defying the local healer will help her mother.

Farmer, Nancy. *A Girl Named Disaster*. New York: Orchard Books, 1996.
> Nhamo, an orphan living with her Aunt's family in Mozambique, runs away to avoid an arranged marriage and becomes lost in the jungle, alone for a period of months.

Mikaelsen, Ben. *Tree Girl*. New York: HarperCollins, 2004.
> Witnessing a massacre from the safety of the tree she loves to climb, Guatemalan Gabriela spends months alone, avoiding more violence from the soldiers who killed her family and eventually seeks refuge across the border in Mexico where her sister Alicia lives.

Author-Related Sources

"Joan Abelove." In vol. 110 of *Something about the Author*. Farmington Hills, MI: Gale Group, 2000, 1–3.

Discussion Questions

For *Go and Come Back*

1. What are some of the differences between the culture of the Isabo people and that of the American women?

2. Why does Alicia view Joanna and Margarita as "stingy, stupid, but fun to watch"?

3. Why does Alicia call the visitors "old ladies"?

4. Why does Alicia feel she needs to educate the "two old ladies"?

5. At one point Joanna says, "there is so much we don't know." What does she mean by that?

6. How is the concept of work different for Alicia, Joanna, and Margarita?

7. Why are the villagers and the anthropologists unable to trust each other completely, even after living together?

8. How does this experience change Joanna and Margarita? What similarities in the two cultures do they ultimately realize?

9. Why are the anthropologists more successful in developing a relationship with the villagers than the missionaries?

10. How does this experience change Alicia and her fellow villagers?

11. What does the author mean by her title "Go and Come Back"?

Gooney Bird Greene

By Lois Lowry, Illustrated by Middy Thomas

Boston: Houghton Mifflin, 2002

Reading Level: . . . . Grades 3–4

Genre: . . . . Contemporary/realistic fiction

Themes: . . . . Self-esteem, confidence, individuality, truth versus the perception of truth

Awards: . . . . ALA Notable Children's Book

Plot Summary

One month after the beginning of the school year, a new girl arrives in Mrs. Pidgeon's class ready to learn and participate, offering a new perspective on her classmates' view of the world. Gooney Bird Greene, as her parents named her, is a bit eccentric for an eight or nine year old; she wears unique and oddly matched clothing and likes to be completely and immediately involved in everything. She begins to talk about her life, telling very unusual stories. At first, the patient Mrs. Pidgeon uses Gooney Bird's creative and intriguing stories as a way to complement the class story-writing lessons, but she tells Gooney Bird that she must be truthful when she talks about her life. In the following days, Gooney Bird takes the floor and tells stories about how she got her name; how her family moved from China and she arrived on a flying carpet; her experience with the prince, the palace, and a set of diamond earrings; how directing a symphony orchestra made her late for school; and how her cat named Catman was consumed by a cow. Gooney Bird diligently and ethically claims all her stories are absolutely true, and she does have logical explanations for all her statements, making the point that language is used in different ways and can imply multiple meanings. Both the teacher and the other children appreciate Gooney Bird's way of looking at and describing her life with "invisible stories" that are interesting and almost unbelievable, but absolutely true.

Main Characterization

Gooney Bird Greene is a confident, assertive girl who uses her status as a new student to her advantage. Although her behavior is intriguing, her individuality does not prevent her from displaying a healthy respect for her classmates or her new teacher. Her creative way of recounting her experiences while proving everything to be truthful affords her the ability to be respected and admired by the other children.

Mrs. Pidgeon is a patient, respectful teacher who allows her students the time to learn and benefit from knowing a clever girl like Gooney Bird.

Themes

Gooney Bird's individuality is a predominant theme in this story, which stresses self-esteem and confidence. In addition, a clever use of language works around a concept of telling the truth versus perceiving the truth because there are hidden meanings to Gooney Bird's fictitious-sounding but authentic anecdotes.

Books with Similar Issues or Themes

Conford, Ellen. *Annabel the Actress Starring in Just a Little Extra*. Illustrated by Renee W. Andriani. New York: Simon & Schuster, 2000.
> Confident and audacious Annabel finds a way to land a part as an extra in a movie being filmed in her town.

Conford, Ellen. *Jenny Archer, Author*. Illustrated by Diane Palmisciano. Boston: Little, Brown, 1989.
> After writing an embellished account of her life for an autobiography assignment, Jenny rewrites her story realistically to gain appreciation from her teacher.

Greenwald, Sheila. *Rosy Cole Discovers America*. Boston: Little, Brown, 1992.
> Investigating family ancestry as part of a "USA is US" project at school, Rosy must find a truthful way to make her relatives appear interesting and daring.

McDonald, Megan. *Judy Moody*. Illustrated by Peter Reynolds. Cambridge, MA: Candlewick Press, 1999.
> On the first day of third grade, Judy Moody can't wait to tell about her new pet Venus flytrap and how she ate a shark over the summer in the "Me" collage she is supposed to create for her new class.

Park, Barbara. Junie B. Jones series. Illustrated by Denise Brunkus. New York: Random House, 1992.
> This unlikely heroine and her hilarious escapades told in her creative and ungrammatical English will keep you laughing all the way.

Author-Related Sources

Berger, Laura Standley, ed. *Twentieth-Century Young Adult Writers*. Detroit, MI: St. James Press, 1994, 408–10.

Daniel, Susanna. *Lois Lowry*. New York: Rosen Central, 2003.

Hipple, Ted, ed. Vol. 2 of *Writers for Young Adults*. New York: Charles S. Scribner's Sons, 1997, 269–70.

"Lois Lowry." In vol. 72 of *Children's Literature Review*. Farmington Hills, MI: Gale Group, 2002, 192–206.

"Lois Lowry." In vol. 127 of *Something about the Author*. Farmington Hills, MI: Gale Group, 2002, 134–50.

Lowry, Lois. *Looking Back: A Book of Memories*. Boston: Houghton Mifflin, 1998.

Marcus, Leonard S., ed. *Author Talk: Conversations with Judy Blume et al*. New York: Simon & Schuster, 2000, 58–63.

Markham, Lois. *Lois Lowry*. Santa Barbara, CA: Learning Works, 1995.

Silvey, Anita, ed. *Children's Books and Their Creators*. Boston: Houghton Mifflin, 1995, 419–21.

Discussion Questions

For *Gooney Bird Greene*

1. What kind of person is Gooney Bird Greene?

2. What is important to Gooney Bird?

3. Why does everyone like Gooney Bird?

4. What concerns does Mrs. Pidgeon have when Gooney Bird tells her stories?

5. Why are Gooney Bird's stories so interesting and intriguing?

6. What do the class and Mrs. Pidgeon learn from the way Gooney Bird tells stories about her life?

7. What does Gooney Bird mean by telling "invisible stories" that are absolutely true?

8. Which of Gooney Bird's stories do you like the most and why?

9. What invisible story can you tell about your life?

The Hero and the Crown

By Robin McKinley

New York: Greenwillow Books, 1985

Reading Level: . . . . Grades 6–8
Genre: . . . . Fantasy/adventure
Themes: . . . . Women's role, courage, good versus evil, heroism
Awards: . . . . Newbery Medal, ALA Notable Children's Book

Plot Summary

Aerin, daughter to King Arlbeth of Damar, is mistrusted and disliked by the kingdom, and in particular by her cousin Galanna, for her questionable lineage, for Aerin has witch's blood. Her mother, a witch from the north, died in childbirth; the rumor is she died in despair, having given birth to a girl instead of a boy. Unable to ascend to the throne and wanting to gain acceptance in her father's court, Aerin takes on the alternate role of dragon slayer. She teams up with Talat, her father's lame horse, whom she nurses back to health. She learns to fight with a sword and discovers the magic power of kenet, a fire-protective ointment. Successfully killing her first dragon, Aerin sets out to protect Damar from the evil, grotesque, fire-breathing Maur and is almost mortally wounded in the battle. Rescued by a mage, Luthe, she is taught to use the magical powers she has inherited from her mother and takes on the responsibility of conquering her mother's brother Agsded, who is in possession of the Hero's Crown. It is Agsded who is the true villain and threat to the future of the kingdom of Damar. She manages to kill her uncle with the poisonous surka plant, brings the Hero's Crown to her father, and eventually gains the respect of her citizenry, marrying Tor, the descendant to the throne and her childhood friend. Aerin not only accomplishes the difficult task of saving her country from evil, but also discovers a strength and purpose to her life, proving her determination to succeed in spite of what is expected of her gender.

Main Characterization

Aerin is a young woman of seventeen who is not only limited by her female status, but also disliked for her mother's unorthodox relationship with her father. She finds a way to break from tradition and be recognized by training herself to be a soldier in the war against dragons. She is brave, courageous, persistent, and resourceful, doubting herself only when she doesn't understand her relation to a witch's family. She is unable to accept the rumors and disapproving whispers that surround her in her father's kingdom and chooses to withdraw and separate herself from the daily routines and rituals by spending time alone with nature and her father's lame horse. She ultimately proves worthy of her regal status, although ascending to her place as queen only through her marriage to Tor. She must also accept the help of another powerful male, Luthe, to reach her goals and become respected by the court and kingdom.

Tor, the only male descendant to the throne, is in love with his cousin, Aerin, and supports her as confidante, mentor, and his only friend in the court. Eventually he helps her claim her rightful place as queen through their marriage.

115

Luthe is an old magician who rescues Aerin from certain death after her battle with the powerful dragon Maur. He teaches her to use her inherited powers and gives her the mental strength to take on her unique challenge.

Agsded is a villainous master wizard and a deadly threat to the kingdom. He can only be defeated by his last remaining blood relation, Aerin.

Arlbeth, king of Damar, is a caring father and leader, proud of his daughter's surprising achievement as dragon killer.

Themes

The need to break away from the "acceptable" female vocation or purpose in life is the main theme in this novel. Aerin is the king's only child. The royal court rejects her because of her mother's questionable nonroyal status and witch's blood, and she is denied her birthright as the next monarch. Her indignation drives her to find a way to pursue an alternative path that eventually brings her respect and favorable recognition. Conquering evil through heroic courage and determination makes Aerin a strong female role model.

Books with Similar Issues or Themes

McKinley, Robin. *The Blue Sword*. New York: Greenwillow Books, 1982.
> Crewe, an orphan girl, leaves her homeland following her father's death and becomes involved with the Free Hillfolk, the last of the Damarians, battling the North in the king's army. A sequel to *The Hero and the Crown*.

Pierce, Tamora. *Wild Magic*. New York: Atheneum, 1992.
> Daine's magical skill with horses enables her to train as a mage, battling dragons and other monsters when the fate of the kingdom is at risk.

Pullman, Philip. *The Golden Compass*. New York: Alfred A. Knopf, 1995.
> Lyra Belacqua becomes involved in the struggle to prevent her friend Roger from becoming part of a scientific experiment involving scores of kidnapped children that separates humans from their daemons.

Wrede, Patricia C. *Searching for Dragons*. New York: Harcourt Brace Jovanovich, 1991.
> Princess Cimorene and King Mendanbar must rescue Kazul, dragon leader, while discovering each other romantically. Part of the Enchanted Forest Chronicles.

Yep, Laurence. *Dragon War*. New York: HarperCollins, 1992.
> The dragon princess, Shimmer—together with her allies, Monkey, a Chinese trickster hero, and Thorn, the human prince—fights to save the dragon cauldron from the immortal Boneless King.

Author-Related Sources

Berger, Laura Standley, ed. *Twentieth-Century Young Adult Writers*. Detroit, MI: St. James Press, 1994, 442–4.

"Robin McKinley." In vol. 81 of *Children's Literature Review*. Farmington Hills, MI: Gale Group, 2002, 180–90.

"Robin McKinley." In vol. 89 of *Something about the Author*. Farmington Hills, MI: Gale Group, 1997, 137–41.

Robin McKinley Web site: http://www.robinmckinley.com/ (accessed 28 September 2004).

Silvey, Anita, ed. *Children's Books and Their Creators*. Boston: Houghton Mifflin, 1995, 446–7.

Discussion Questions

For *The Hero and the Crown*

1. Why do the people of her father's kingdom distrust Aerin?

2. Why does Aerin choose to fight dragons?

3. What does her father, the king, think of Aerin's ability and willingness to search and kill dragons?

4. What is the significance of the Hero's Crown? Why is it Aerin's quest alone?

5. What does Aerin learn from Luthe?

6. What does Luthe mean when he tells Aerin that there is a price to pay for immortality?

7. How do Aerin's adventures killing both the dragon Maur and her uncle Agsded affect her life?

8. Aerin has inherited a certain power or gift called Kelar that bestows magical abilities. What else does Aerin have that helps her succeed?

9. How does Aerin interpret success?

10. What is Aerin's true strength as a heroine?

Ida B . . . and Her Plans to Maximize Fun, Avoid Disaster, and (Possibly) Save the World

By Katherine Hannigan

New York: Greenwillow Books, 2004

Reading Level: . . . . Grades 4–6

Genre: . . . . Contemporary fiction, realistic fiction

Themes: . . . . Family love, emotional strength, loneliness, friendship, individuality

Plot Summary

Ten-year-old Ida B Applewood lives a contented, individual life on her parents' orchard. Her friends consist of the brook and her favorite apple trees, which have names and personalities she has devised, such as "the punk Paulie T.," the gentle and knowing Viola, and "old tree" at the top of the hill. Home-schooled and accustomed to a life around adults and her imaginary conversations with her orchard "friends," Ida B's perfect world is shattered when her mother's cancer treatments force her father to sell part of the orchard, cut down some of her best tree friends, and enroll Ida B at what she perceives as the loathsome and conformist public school. Ida B's happy carefree spirit and loving heart have always carried her through life; she has always believed that making and following good plans will lead her where she wants to be. In this case, Ida B loses control and must obey her parents' decision. Feeling her life is drastically changing, Ida B's plan is to let her newly hardened heart feel nothing but anger so that she can protect herself from any hurt feelings. She enters the fourth-grade public school class determined to keep her behavior just under the impertinent line until her parents come to their senses and her life returns to the blissful times she once knew. But Ida B's plan does not go as she has envisioned it; her new teacher, Ms. Washington, patiently and quietly gives Ida B the emotional fortitude to learn to like school, to make some friends in her peer group, and to come to terms with her obstinate relationship with her parents. As Ida B's mother recuperates and school life becomes unexpectedly interesting and fun, Ida B's sense of values and responsibility cause her to apologize to her parents for her behavior and to some of the children whom she has treated meanly. But her "avenue of atonement" as she calls it, is not complete until she has a cathartic conversation with her trees and the brook, apologizing for abandoning them and for not listening to their wisdom. Ida B's life has changed in more ways than just attending school.

Main Characterization

Ida B is a creative, thoughtful, optimistic girl with an attitude about life that is well beyond her years. Her somewhat solitary, free-spirited childhood is augmented by her imaginary relationship with nature, the brook, and the trees. Through her imagined conversations, we are allowed to see Ida B's thoughts on life. When her world changes and she must attend school, Ida B protects herself from her fears by building a protective wall around her emotions only to realize that her happiness is dependent on her attitude.

Themes

Ida B's individuality is supported by her parents' initial decision to home-school her. Her unique attitude on life gives her emotional strength to work through her problems. The importance of friendship and family love are also stressed, as is the theme of loneliness. Ida B feels very much alone throughout her difficult transition, even shutting herself off from her nature friends in the orchard.

Books with Similar Issues or Themes

Bauer, Joan. *Squashed.* New York: Delacorte Press, 1992.
> Sixteen-year-old Ellie Morgan learns a lot about life, competition, and the importance of friendship during the year she raises the winning three-hundred-pound pumpkin for the annual Harvest Fair.

Creech, Sharon. *Chasing Redbird.* New York: HarperCollins, 1997.
> Thirteen-year-old Zinny Taylor discovers truths about her family and life as she clears away a neglected, overgrown trail on her family's Kentucky farm.

Lisle, Janet Taylor. *Forest.* New York: Orchard Books, 1993.
> Caught between animal and human behaviors and fears, twelve-year-old Amber Padgett's innocent climb up the giant white oak in her backyard sparks a battle of misconstrued malice and invasion between the tree's squirrel inhabitants and Amber's family.

Author-Related Sources

Katherine Hannigan Biography: http://www.pippinproperties.com/authill/hannigan/index.htm (accessed 1 January 2005).

Katherine Hannigan Interview: http://www.bookbrowse.com/index.cfm?page=author&author ID=1055&view=interview (accessed 1 January 2005).

Discussion Questions

For *Ida B . . . and Her Plans to Maximize Fun,
Avoid Disaster, and (Possibly) Save the World*

1. What do Ida B's conversations with her tree friends tell you about her out-look on life?

2. Why does Ida B make her heart change to one of stone and coldness?

3. What positive changes occur in Ida B's life amid her unhappiness and the difficult times surrounding her mother's illness?

4. What does Ida B gain from her year in fourth grade?

5. How is Ida B able to maintain her individual way of thinking, yet get along in her new school situation?

6. Which life is better for Ida B, the one before her mother was sick when she lived her own way or the one she creates after attending school?

7. Why does Ida B feel she will not have completed her "avenue of atone-ment" until she talks to her nature friends, the brook and the trees?

8. What does Ida B mean when she tells her father "I think the earth takes care of us" after he tells her to remember that "we are the caretakers of the earth"?

In the Year of the Boar and Jackie Robinson

By Bette Bao Lord, Illustrated by Marc Simont

New York: Harper & Row, 1984

Reading Level: . . . . Grades 4–6
Genre: . . . . Realistic fiction
Themes: . . . . Immigration, friendship, belonging, assimilation
Awards: . . . . ALA Notable Children's Book

Plot Summary

Shirley Temple Wong, known to her Chinese family as "Bandit," has an exciting, wondrous first year in 1947 Brooklyn, as she blossoms into an assimilated American child. Ten-year-old Shirley tells her story in twelve chapters beginning with the Chinese New Year in January and continuing monthly throughout the year. Much to the chagrin of the elders in her family, who do not want them to leave China, Shirley and her mother are reunited with her father in New York to begin a new life complete with strange American customs, a foreign language, and mechanical conveniences such as washing machines that immediately amaze and confound Shirley's sense of confidence. Shirley's adjustment is difficult at first, entering school in the middle of the term with no knowledge of English and no friends. She refers to herself as a ghost disappearing within the body of the class, ignored by the other children even as she struggles to behave and act as they do. When a poetry assignment is given to everyone in the class, and the teacher excuses Shirley for her lack of English, a determined Shirley goes home and memorizes a Disney record complete with all of the sounds and intonations of the Donald Duck, Mickey Mouse, and Chip and Dale characters. Although the class laughs and the teacher is impressed by her efforts, Shirley feels humiliated despite her parent's constant reminders of her good fortune and status in both the Chinese and American worlds. Private piano lessons with the landlady are introduced as a way to lift Shirley from her low mood. After a physical encounter with the female class bully sends her home with two black eyes, her refusal to divulge the name of the culprit offers an opportunity to develop a friendship. Shirley is then accepted by the schoolyard stickball crowd, and her loneliness finally abates. The game of baseball becomes the key to Shirley's successful transition as she learns to understand and play the game and becomes a huge Dodgers' fan, cheering for Jackie Robinson along with her fellow Brooklynites. As the year draws to a close, assimilation is nearly complete when Shirley and her family, so busy with their new lifestyle, almost forget their own customs in time to celebrate the mid-autumn Festival of the Full Moon.

Main Characterization

Shirley Temple Wong is a ten-year-old girl trying to meet the expectations of her immigrant Chinese parents while she struggles to learn quickly the ways of her new American surroundings. She is both resilient and fragile as her initial confidence is challenged when she finds that adjusting to a new culture is harder than she had anticipated. When she insists on participating in the poetry assignment and works to imitate the only recitation she can duplicate, a Disney record, she demonstrates her longing to be like everyone else in the class. Shirley's parents are loving yet cannot completely understand her unhappiness and need for friendship and peer acceptance. Their solution, in the form of piano lessons, returns to Shirley a certain amount of confidence as she encourages her piano teacher/landlady to visit family while the Wongs watch the house.

Mabel is a classic bully who tests Shirley's resolve, then eventually respects her for not tattling and becomes a kind of mentor in schoolyard games.

Emily, the new girl in the fall, becomes Shirley's best friend, validating the serious, studious characteristics that Shirley would like to maintain.

Jackie Robinson personifies the symbolic use of baseball as representing the opportunity each individual has to achieve success in America.

Themes

Shirley's desire to make new friends and belong to a core group in a new school are made difficult by her immigrant status, foreign customs, language, and appearance. Everything in her new country is so different and strange, yet she works hard to participate equally until she is eventually accepted and becomes part of both the core group as well as her larger American neighborhood. The friendships she cultivates depend strongly on her assimilating within the new American culture, playing games, and celebrating triumphs and holidays at school.

Books with Similar Issues or Themes

Ada, Alma Flor. *My Name Is Maria Isabel*. New York: Atheneum, 1993.

> Puerto Rican–born Maria does not want to be called by her American name, Mary, and finds a way to help her teacher understand her reasons to be addressed by her given name, of Maria Isabel, through a class writing assignment.

Hest, Amy. *When Jessie Came across the Sea*. Cambridge, MA: Candlewick Press, 1997.

> Given the opportunity to leave her European shtetl with a ticket to the promised land from her rabbi, thirteen-year-old Jessie emigrates to America, uses her skills as a lace maker to work in a dress shop, and earns enough money to send for her grandmother, all the while adjusting to her new life in a new world.

Levitin, Sonia. *Silver Days*. New York: Atheneum, 1989.

> Lisa recounts the "silver days" between 1940 and 1943 when her family is adjusting to their new life in New York City after being uprooted from their comfortable life in Germany.

Namioka, Lensey. *Yang the Third and Her Impossible Family*. Boston: Little, Brown, 1995.

> Yingmei Yang, now known as Mary, sees her way to assimilating and fitting in with her new American friends by adopting a kitten from classmate Holly Hanson and keeping it secretly in her home, one filled with musical instruments and Chinese customs.

Sheth, Kashmira. *Blue Jasmine*. New York: Hyperion Books for Children, 2004.

> Twelve-year-old Seema Trivedi moves from an upper-middle-class life in India to a Midwestern suburban American town and struggles to adapt to new foods, culture, seasons, and language while maintaining her Indian identity.

Author-Related Sources

"Bette Bao Lord." In vol. 58 of *Something about the Author*. Farmington Hills, MI: Gale Group, 1990, 121–3.

Holtze, Sally Holmes, ed. *Sixth Book of Junior Authors and Illustrators*. New York: H. W. Wilson, 1989, 176–8.

Discussion Questions

For *In the Year of the Boar and Jackie Robinson*

1. How does Shirley feel about leaving China and coming to live in the United States?

2. What is most important to Shirley in her new school and home?

3. What is most important to Shirley's parents?

4. Why does Shirley refer to herself as a "hungry ghost"?

5. How does Shirley's relationship with Mabel finally help her to fit in?

6. How does baseball help Shirley to make her life better in her new country?

7. What does baseball represent to Shirley and her teacher, Mrs. Rappaport?

8. How does Shirley become a little ambassador for China and her school?

9. Why does Emily choose Shirley to represent the school during the Jackie Robinson assembly visit?

10. In what ways have the lives of Shirley and her family changed by the end of the year?

Jacob Have I Loved

By Katherine Paterson

New York: HarperCollins, 1980

Reading Level: . . . . Grades 6–8
Genre: . . . . Historical fiction, realistic fiction
Themes: . . . . Jealousy, sibling rivalry, coming of age, ambition, poverty
Awards: . . . . Newbery Medal

Plot Summary

Born one minute apart, twins Caroline and Louise are as different as night and day. Louise, dubbed "Wheeze" by her younger twin, feels overshadowed by Caroline's delicate physical stature that brings coddling and sympathetic attention from their parents and neighbors on the 1940s Chesapeake Bay fishing island. Ambitious to work as a waterman, Louise spends most of her spare time crabbing with her friend Call. Together, they become acquainted with Captain Wallace, who has been away from the island for the last fifty years, and help him fix up the neglected and abandoned house of his childhood. Unlike Call who is eager to offer free assistance and is impressed with the captain's jokes, Louise resents the lack of compensation and is a bit miffed at losing Call's complete attention. When Caroline is offered a scholarship to attend a music school on the mainland and develop her singing talent, Louise is jealous and begins to question her island life and whether leaving is a possible and practical choice. The war changes Louise's relationship with Call as he leaves to join the service. Left to question her goals and desires, Louise spends the next couple of years working with her father. Call's return and impending engagement to her sister Caroline force Louise to face her own reality and her wish to become a doctor. Louise instead pursues the acceptable route for women of the time, a medical career as a nurse and midwife and finally leaves the island to work in rural Appalachia. Her new life brings love, marriage, and a family of her own.

Main Characterization

Sara Louise Bradshaw is the eldest twin who spends a good portion of her life torn between resentment and love toward her younger twin, Caroline. She misunderstands the fact that her parents don't worry about her as a lack of love, when in fact, her independent strength of character is what allows her parents to worry less about her and encourage her to pursue her goals. Her childhood friendship with a neighbor boy, Call Burnett, is the only peer companionship Louise develops, leaving her quite lonely after he leaves for military service. Her father is glad to have her help with his fishing business as a substitute for the sons he never had. Louise feels trapped and dreams of escaping the island to a place with mountains. Her confusion is exacerbated by her grandmother's cantankerous, hurtful, and irrational, almost insane, behavior, stressing biblical images of Jacob and Esau as a comparison to the twin sisters.

Caroline, the younger twin sister, is characterized as weaker, having had a difficult birth, but she clearly enjoys playing the role of the prettier, more feminine twin who everyone cherishes.

Call grows from a very literal-thinking boy who has never experienced life off the island to a sincere young man returning from war, seeing Louise more as a sister than a childhood friend.

Themes

Jealousy coupled with sibling rivalry are key to understanding Louise and Caroline's relationship and status on the fishing island. In addition, Louise's soulful search for her happiness on and off the island dovetails with a coming of age theme. Poverty is another issue shown through the lives of the island residents and portrayed more strongly through Call's family situation, forcing him to join the service as a means of support.

Books with Similar Issues or Themes

Hamilton, Virginia. *Cousins*. New York: Philomel Books, 1990.
　　Cammy's jealousy of and anger at her perfect and patronizing cousin is tempered during a tragic accident that brings grief and a new perspective to her life.

Hunter, Mollie. *Cat, herself*. New York: Harper & Row, 1985.
　　Cat McPhie struggles to break away from her wandering tinker Scottish family and live her life her own way.

Sleator, William. *Singularity*. New York: E. P. Dutton, 1985.
　　Twin boys, Harry and Barry, have opposite personalities that cause friction and competition. Their lives are altered and transformed when they come across another world that changes time and their place in the universe.

Jacob and Esau References

Brunelli, Roberto. *A Family Treasury of Bible Stories*. New York: H. N. Abrams, 1997.

Segal, Lore, and Leonard Baskin. *The Book of Adam to Moses*. New York: Alfred Knopf, 1987.

Author-Related Sources

Berger, Laura Standley, ed. *Twentieth-Century Children's Writers*. Detroit, MI: St. James Press, 1995, 740–1.

Cary, Alice. *Katherine Paterson*. Santa Barbara, CA: The Learning Works, 1997.

Hipple, Ted, ed. Vol. 2 of *Writers for Young Adults*. New York: Charles S. Scribner's Sons, 1997, 443–54.

"Katherine Paterson." In vol. 50 of *Children's Literature Review*. Farmington Hills, MI: Gale Group, 1999, 165–207.

"Katherine Paterson." In vol. 133 of *Something about the Author*. Farmington Hills, MI: Gale Group, 2002, 134–44.

Katherine Paterson Official Web site: http://www.terabithia.com/ (accessed 30 May 2004).

Paterson, Katherine. *Gates of Excellence: On Reading and Writing Books for Children*. New York: Dutton/Lodester, 1981.

Paterson, Katherine. *A Sense of Wonder: On Reading and Writing Books for Children*. New York: Plume, 1995.

Schmidt, Gary D. *Katherine Paterson*. New York: Twayne, 1984.

Silvey, Anita, ed. *Children's Books and Their Creators*. Boston: Houghton Mifflin, 1995, 507–9.

Discussion Questions

For *Jacob Have I Loved*

1. What kind of relationship do the twin sisters have?

2. What causes Louise's feelings of inferiority and resentment toward her younger sister?

3. What does Louise have to do to find her own identity and create her own goals?

4. What role does Call play in Louise's life?

5. How does the grandmother's behavior complicate the lives of Louise and her family?

6. What role does religion play in Louise's life?

7. Looking at the bible story of Jacob and Esau, how does it compare with the story of Louise and Caroline?

8. How do the twins that Louise delivers at the end of the story help her to realize she has achieved her dreams?

9. Why did the author choose the title "Jacob Have I Loved" for this story?

Lydia, Queen of Palestine

By Uri Orlev, Translated from the Hebrew by Hillel Halkin

Boston: Houghton Mifflin, 1993

Reading Level: 4-6

Genre: . . . . Historical fiction

Themes: . . . . Holocaust, divorce, independence, self-esteem/iden-
tity, communal living

Plot Summary

Lydia is a Romanian Jewish girl living in pre–World War II Europe with her divorced mother amid an increasingly perilous and politically charged situation. Concerns for their safe passage out of the pre-Nazi environment lead her journalist father to Palestine with intentions of arranging future similar escape routes for Lydia and her mother. The war, lack of money, and a misunderstanding between her parents force Lydia and her mother to move several times, consequently losing contact with her father and his transport papers. Eventually, Lydia's mother arranges for her to leave Europe with an organized group of Jewish children who will be cared for on a kibbutz. Lydia is kept in the dark about her parents' divorce and relationship, only catching glimpses of her mother's unhappiness and her father's association with another woman. Lydia recounts her thoughts, feelings, concerns, and fears through a spunky first-person narrative describing her play with dolls, imaginative fairy-tale scenarios, and ambitions to marry a prince. Her relocation to Palestine is difficult not only because she is separated from both parents, but also because her individuality and self-assurance get in the way of her adjusting to the kibbutz philosophy of communal life and socialist sharing of supplies, clothing, food, and work. Reuniting with her father and new stepmother is painful at first, as Lydia rebels against any kind of effort to include her in their life. Similarly, the long-awaited arrival of her mother proves to be both joyous and shocking as Lydia learns of her mother's marriage and her new stepfather. In the end, loyalty to both her mother and father bring a renewed appreciation for family as Lydia realizes her fortunate circumstances with two sets of parents who love her and have succeeded in creating new lives in a new country.

Main Characterization

Lydia is a very smart, feisty ten-year-old girl who deals with the difficult realities of her broken home, an impending war, and anti-Semitism with a crafty, devilish, and funny personality. Her independent almost bullish attitude gives her a quality that is still childishly real as she terrorizes the adults around her through tantrums and maliciously executed plans. Her unhappiness is played out through her imaginative games, dreaming, and fantasies of how to get rid of "that woman," her father's mistress, and how she will marry Prince Michael, move to Palestine, and live a life of royalty. She hates being compared to any relative, least of all her father, and wants just to be herself. Her strong personality and confidence help her to fair well on her trip to Palestine, using her meatball supply of food in an enterprising way to bargain for good seats on the train and treats such as ice cream and pastries at the various stops along the way.

Mama is ashamed of her divorce and keeps it a secret from Lydia, but she cannot control her anger enough to not allow the child to hear about "that woman." She takes charge of both their lives by working to develop relationships and connections that will lead to passage out of the country to Palestine.

127

Papa is a less visible character, described through Lydia's eyes as she struggles to justify his absence and lack of family interest. His disappearance to Palestine is misunderstood, yet he proves to be genuinely interested in being a good father to Lydia as he welcomes her to his new home.

"That woman" (Lili) is a mysterious yet hated person in Lydia's life. A doll that represents Lili allows Lydia to play out her wishful fantasies and vent her violent frustrations.

Ruti is the best friend whom Lydia comes to rely on in Palestine, symbolically adopting her parents as surrogates when her relationship with her assigned foster family and mother is tense and strained.

Hannah is Lydia's English teacher on the kibbutz. Her influence through her husband's British military appointment helps to reunite Lydia with her father. Hannah becomes the adult confidante that Lydia needs to sort out her feelings concerning her defiance toward her parents and stepparents, her overall maturation, and her acceptance of life's uncontrollable situations.

Themes

Set in pre–World War II Europe, the Holocaust theme serves only as background to a story of divorce and a child's coping skills. Lydia is mostly unaware of her Jewish heritage until the political situation places her and her family in danger. More important, this story is one of a very independent character who fiercely protects her identity as a confident individual. Lydia's play indicates her aspirations to succeed and be recognized, and although her experience in the communal living of a kibbutz conflicts with her self-assurance, it nevertheless helps her to protest successfully against certain situations that infringe on her privacy.

Books with Similar Issues or Themes

Bergman, Tamar. *The Boy from Over There*. Translated from the Hebrew by Hillel Halkin. Boston: Houghton Mifflin, 1988.
>   At the end of World War II, Rina and Avramik are living on a kibbutz, waiting to be reunited with their parents. They try to adjust to kibbutz life as Israel's War of Independence is about to begin.

Mazer, Norma Fox. *Good Night, Maman*. New York: Harcourt Brace & Company, 1999.
>   Twelve-year-old Karen Levi and her brother Marc are fortunate to obtain passage to a refugee site in Oswego, New York, fleeing Nazi-occupied Paris and leaving their mother behind.

Semel, Nava. *Becoming Gershonah*. Translated by Seymour Simekes. New York: Viking, 1990.
>   Twelve-year-old Gershonah comes of age surrounded by Holocaust-scarred relatives and a new relationship with her grandfather in 1958 Tel Aviv.

Vos, Ida. *Hide and Seek*. Translated by Terese Edelstein and Inez Smidt. Boston: Houghton Mifflin, 1991.
>   The Nazi occupation of the Netherlands forces Rachel and her family into hiding.

Watts, Irene. *Remember Me*. Toronto: Tundra Books, 2000.
>   Marianne is one of the first children to escape Nazi Germany on the Kindertransporte to a foster family in England, where she must learn English and adjust to living without her family.

Author-Related Sources

Berger, Laura Standley, ed. *Twentieth-Century Young Adult Writers*. Detroit, MI: St. James Press, 1994, 507–9.

Holtze, Sally Holmes, ed. *Seventh Book of Junior Authors and Illustrators*. New York: H. W. Wilson, 1996, 243–4.

" Uri Orlev." In vol. 30 of *Children's Literature Review*. Farmington Hills, MI: Gale Group, 1993, 162–7.

"Uri Orlev." In vol. 135 of *Something about the Author*. Farmington Hills, MI: Gale Group, 2000, 160–7.

Discussion Questions

For *Lydia, Queen of Palestine*

1. What kind of person is Lydia?

2. What does Lydia hope and wish for in life?

3. How does Lydia feel about leaving Romania?

4. How does Lydia feel about the communal living philosophy of a kibbutz? What does it teach her?

5. What does she do to try to keep her identity on the kibbutz while living within the rules?

6. Why does Lydia act out and misbehave so much?

7. How does Lydia's fairy-tale play help her?

8. Why are Lydia's dolls important, and what do they represent to her?

9. Where is Lydia happiest—Europe with her mother or in Palestine with her new sets of parents?

10. How has Lydia changed by the end of the story?

Matilda

By Roald Dahl, Illustrated by Quentin Blake

New York: Viking Kestrel, 1988

Reading Level: 4–6
Genre: . . . . Humorous fiction
Themes: . . . . Vengeance, gender stereotypes, bullies, self-reliance

Plot Summary

Matilda Wormwood, five years old, is a precocious, clever child with a brilliant mind who is thoroughly ignored and unappreciated by her uneducated, self-centered, grotesquely shallow-minded parents. Her father, a swindling used car dealer, views success through the stupidity and misfortune of others. Matilda's parents revere television and have no time for books, education, and reading, so Matilda discovers the public library on her own and learns about the world outside her limited home through the hundreds of books she begins to read, appreciate, and enjoy each week. Moving through every book in the children's section, she discovers, with the help of Mrs. Phelps, the librarian, the great classics of literature written by Dickens, Shakespeare, Kipling, and others. Her reading at home bewilders her mother and earns angry belittlement from her father, who in a series of successive rages, demeans her for her interest beyond the television set. As the mistreatment and verbal abuse grow intolerable, Matilda begins to devise ways to get back at her parents and succeeds in initiating several humorous episodes to make her father miserable. When she is finally enrolled in school, it is one where abuse and mistreatment are the norm. Headmistress Miss Trunchbull is the stereotypical oversized and overpowering bully who presents a new challenge to Matilda as she seeks justified revenge through her clever plots. Her ally, teacher Miss Honey, is another victim as the only living relative of Miss Trunchbull, who has been cheated out of her rightful inheritance following her parents' death. With Dahl's wonderful slapstick humor, Matilda is able to turn her anger and feelings of injustice into a powerful and magical conclusion scaring Miss Trunchbull away with some ghostly behavior and developing a lasting relationship with Miss Honey after her parents flee the country to avoid imprisonment for Mr. Wormwood's conniving business deals.

Main Characterization

Matilda is a sensitive, clever, brilliant girl with the intelligence level of a genius. She uses her abilities to protect herself from the paradoxically stupid adults she is forced to encounter each day, her parents and the school's headmistress, Miss Trunchbull.

Mr. and Mrs. Wormwood are presented as caricatures displaying stereotypical behaviors and attitudes. Mr. Wormwood is a cheat and thief; his wife is a dumb housewife who cares about physical appearance over intellectual stimulation. They both favor their son, Michael, because he is a male.

Miss Honey is a kind, intimidated young woman who immediately appreciates the unique abilities Matilda displays in her classroom and develops an affection and unusual friendship with her. In many ways, both Matilda and Miss Honey parallel each other in their childhood experience, but Miss Honey does not have the emotional strength of her young student to overcome her situation with her Aunt Agatha Trunchbull.

Miss Trunchbull is a classic bully who preys on the small, weak, and innocent but, when countered with some power and intelligence, is eager to flee.

Themes

Gender stereotyping that Mr. and Mrs. Wormwood display, blatantly limiting the ability, role, and potential of their daughter Matilda, is the dominant theme of this story, which leads into two subthemes of bullying behavior and the justified vengeance it can cause. Matilda also exhibits an extraordinary amount of self-reliance as she takes care of her emotional and intellectual needs through her creative pranks and planned mischief.

Books with Similar Issues or Themes

Creech, Sharon. *Ruby Holler*. New York: HarperCollins, 2001.
> Orphans and twins Dallas and Florida have spent most of their life in the Boxton Home for the Orphaned, run by the heartless Trepids. When they are sent to yet another foster home, that of an elderly, eccentric couple, they finally discover respect, caring, and love.

Elliott, David. *Evangeline Mudd and the Golden-Haired Apes of the Ikkinasti Jungle*. Illustrated by Andrea Wesson. Cambridge, MA: Candlewick Press, 2004.
> Evangeline must search for her missing primatologist parents who have left her with totally disinterested second cousins and gone to the Ikkinasti Jungle to research the golden-haired apes.

Horvath, Polly. *Everything on a Waffle*. New York: Farrar, Straus & Giroux, 2001.
> Losing her parents at sea in a typhoon and living with a series of less than competent guardians and foster parents, Primrose continues to believe that her parents are alive and will eventually be found.

Lindgren, Astrid. *Pippi Longstocking*. New York: Viking Press, 1985.
> The classic story of the nine-year-old Pippi who lives alone without parents in her funny house, Villa Villekula, with her monkey and horse.

Snicket, Lemony. *The Bad Beginning*. Illustrated by Brett Helquist. New York: HarperCollins, 1999.
> This is Book 1 in "A Series of Unfortunate Events" in which three orphaned children must outwit their appointed guardian to gain access to their rightful inheritance.

Author-Related Sources

Berger, Laura Standley, ed. *Twentieth-Century Young Adult Writers*. Detroit, MI: St. James Press, 1994, 167–9.

Dahl, Roald. *Boy: Tales of Childhood*. New York: Puffin Books, 1984.

Dahl, Roald. *Going Solo*. New York: Puffin Books, 1999.

"Roald Dahl." In vol. 41 of *Children's Literature Review*. Farmington Hills, MI: Gale Group, 1997, 1–50.

"Roald Dahl." In vol. 73 of *Something about the Author*. Farmington Hills, MI: Gale Group, 1993, 39–46.

Shields, Charles J. *Roald Dahl*. Philadelphia: Chelsea House, 2002.

Silvey, Anita, ed. *Children's Books and Their Creators*. Boston: Houghton Mifflin, 1995, 185–6.

Discussion Questions

For *Matilda*

1. What do Matilda's parents expect of their children, and of boys and girls in general?

2. What is Matilda's biggest problem or concern?

3. How does Matilda use her intelligence to make her life at home bearable?

4. When, if ever, is revenge justified?

5. Why do Miss Honey and Matilda develop such a strong relationship?

6. What is Matilda's greatest strength?

7. What does Matilda's hidden power represent? Why does she lose it after Miss Trunchbull leaves?

8. How does the author use his language style and slapstick humor to develop his characters?

9. Did you think this is a fantasy or a story that uses exaggeration? What is the author trying to say through his story?

10. What did you think of the way the story ended? How would you have written the ending?

My Louisiana Sky

By Kimberly Willis Holt

New York: Henry Holt, 1998

Reading Level: . . . . Grades 5–7
Genre: . . . . Historical fiction, realistic fiction
Themes: . . . . Family love, emotional strength, mental challenges
Awards: . . . . ALA Notable Book, YALSA Best Book of the Year

Plot Summary

Tiger Ann Parker is twelve years old but seems much more mature and advanced than her mentally deficient mother and father. Her Granny has always lived with them in the rural town of Saitter, Louisiana, taking charge, while her father, Lonnie Parker, has been able to work in a flower nursery to make a fair living, and her mother, Corinna, has tried to help with household chores under Granny's direction. Tiger Ann enjoys playing ball with the boys, has a special best-friend relationship with Jesse Wade, and tries hard to ignore the whispers and quiet teasing about her parents, wanting only to be popular with the girls in school and be invited to the parties and after-school get togethers. After Granny passes away suddenly, Tiger Ann's Aunt Dorrie Kay, her mama's sister, arrives to help out with funeral arrangements and household necessities to find that Corinna is completely devastated by the death and has not been able to even wash or change her clothes for several days. Dorrie Kay's city life in Baton Rouge has allowed her numerous opportunities and, wanting to give Tiger Ann a chance at leading a more normal life without taking charge of her parents, invites her to live and finish school in Baton Rouge. Tiger Ann is impressed with the sophisticated lifestyle her aunt leads and agrees to a brief trial period. She explores a bit, gets her hair cut in a new movie-star style, and is given a new wardrobe and name by her Aunt to help her adjust to a modern 1950s urban society. During this visit, she also learns of the childhood accident that caused her mother's brain damage and comes to the realization that she must stay with her family. Her return brings on a joyful and emotional reunion with her mother and the understanding that her father has his own talents and skills that are valued by the people who employ him.

Main Characterization

Tiger Ann Parker is a sensitive, caring twelve year old who aspires to be like her sophisticated city-dwelling aunt, yet is more comfortable with her country lifestyle. She is devoted to her family and takes on the responsibility of supporting them emotionally from a very young age.

Corinna Parker, Tiger Ann's mother, is fun-loving and childish with the mentality of a six year old and adores her daughter, serving more as a playmate than a parent.

Lonnie Parker, Tiger Ann's father, is also mentally challenged but has learned to do a job and is dedicated and devoted to his family and employer. Although his academic skills are low, his instincts for weather and animal behavior are quite high and serve him well in his position.

Jesse Wade is the son of Lonnie's employer and a good friend of Tiger Ann, having a better understanding of her family situation than most of the other kids in the community.

Aunt Dorrie Kay is Corinna's younger sister, who has broken away from the family's lifestyle, leading her own single life in the city. She maintains a connection through her financial assistance and long-distance monitoring, perhaps feeling responsible for her sister's accident and experiencing guilt or even resentment.

Themes

A strong love for family is a theme that is present in the actions and words of the major characters. Tiger Ann's decisive choice between the city and the home she has always known allows her the opportunity to see clearly what is important. She has the emotional strength to weather a life different from those of most children. With her Granny's passing, she is able and willing to take charge in ways that her parents cannot. In addition, the idea that mentally challenged adults can lead productive lives is also present in the portrayal of Lonnie.

Books with Similar Issues or Themes

Byars, Betsy. *Summer of the Swans*. New York: Viking, 1970.
> Feeling the pressures of a changing life, fourteen-year-old Sara Godfrey understands certain values when her mentally challenged brother, Charlie, is missing.

Lisle, Janet Taylor. *Afternoon of the Elves*. New York: Orchard Books, 1989.
> When Hillary accepts an invitation to Sara-Kate's neglected and overgrown yard to see her imaginative elf-filled village, Hillary learns about her friend's mother's illness and seclusion within the house and the reason for Sara-Kate's shabby and disheveled appearance.

Little, Jean. *Willow and Twig*. New York: Viking, 2000.
> Abandoned again by their drug-addicted mother, ten-year-old Willow and her emotionally disturbed younger brother must find a way to reach their grandmother's home in Toronto to begin a new life.

Slepian, Jan. *Risk N' Roses*. New York: Philomel Books, 1990.
> Wanting to make new friends in her new neighborhood, eleven-year-old Skip joins in a series of games and dares until the reality of cruel mischief affects her slow sister, forcing Skip to evaluate her loyalties and family bond.

Weeks, Sarah. *So B It*. New York: HarperCollins, 2004.
> Living a somewhat protected life with her severely mentally challenged mother and caring neighbor, Heidi's curiosity about an unintelligible word in her mother's vocabulary triggers an investigative trip across the country to her place of birth where the truth about her mother's former life is revealed.

Author-Related Sources

"Kimberly Willis Holt." In vol. 122 of *Something about the Author*. Farmington Hills, MI: Gale Group, 2001, 110–13.

Kimberly Willis Holt Web page: http://www.kimberlyholt.com/ (accessed 1 January 2005).

Discussion Questions

For *My Louisiana Sky*

1. What is Tiger Ann Parker's life like as a twelve-year-old girl in a small town?

2. What does family mean to Tiger Ann and to Aunt Dorrie Kay?

3. How do Lonnie's instincts serve him well in his life?

4. What does Granny provide to her family and how does it help Tiger Ann?

5. How does Tiger Ann feel about moving to the city?

6. Why does Tiger Ann choose to continue living with her parents?

7. Where does Tiger Ann gain her confidence and emotional strength to take charge after her grandmother's death?

8. How do you imagine Tiger Ann's life continued after she finished school?

9. What does the title *My Louisiana Sky* mean? What does this phrase mean to Tiger Ann?

The Ornament Tree

By Jean Thesman

Boston: Houghton Mifflin, 1996

Reading Level: . . . . Grades 6–8
Genre: . . . . Historical fiction
Themes: . . . . Feminism, education, class status
Awards: . . . . YALSA Best Books for Young Adults

Plot Summary

Bonnie Shaster, fourteen and recently orphaned, chooses to live with her mother's family, a group of educated and progressive women running a boarding house in Seattle, Washington. The women rally and work for several issues during this World War I period—women's suffrage, equal rights, birth control, and the education of the lower class. Although they have opened their home to a group of paying male boarders as a way to meet the mortgage, these women seem completely inept at running a household without hiring domestic help for the kitchen. Bonnie, accustomed to farm work and the organization of a well-run kitchen including basic cooking skills, is willing to help but is discouraged from doing so. Cousin Audra insists Bonnie maintain the higher-class behavior of a girl who will attend a preparatory academy and then continue with a university education. Bonnie's introduction to the progressive thinking of her new family members is both intriguing and amusing. She must also adjust to living and working with a variety of new personalities, male and female, and try to befriend her only peer in the household, twelve-year-old Clare, who seems resentful and ashamed of her grandmother and mother's involvement with the boarding house. Despite her cousin Audra's direction, Bonnie does help out, providing guidance and instruction when it becomes apparent that her new companions cannot operate a stove or cook at all after the hired woman quits. As the days continue, Bonnie begins to form relationships with both Clare and a new boarder, a young blind veteran, Carson Younger. Her fears and hopes for her future are expressed privately through letters to her close friend, Elena, living in California, and the paper notes she begins to hang on the family's backyard ornament tree. The year progresses, and Bonnie witnesses some difficult and frightening situations as Seattle struggles to achieve better conditions for the working class and Cousin Audra becomes personally involved in a boarder's abusive behavior with his institutionalized wife. Bonnie is able to appreciate her ability to better her opportunities in life with an education thanks to the encouragement from her supportive family.

Main Characterization

Bonnie, orphaned at the age of fourteen, is a sincere, bright girl who dares to break free from traditional expectations to better her future and position in life. Her strength of character is displayed several times as she leaves her nasty Aunt Suze, her father's stepsister, to make her new home in Seattle; challenges the depressed and sarcastic Mr. Younger; takes charge in the household when it becomes necessary; and makes the bold decision to attend college away from home.

Cousin Audra is the classic feminist of the day, providing encouragement and an unorthodox education for Bonnie.

Twelve-year-old Clare is Bonnie's youngest cousin, who is concerned about public appearances, interested in boys and the prospect of future marriage, and generally not quite convinced of all the progressive ideas circulating around her in her boarding house home.

Carson Younger, blinded in action during his tour in the Great War, is bitter, melancholy at times, and even sardonic about life in general. His one-sided romantic relationship with Bonnie is a positive influence on him, yet he retains the typical male attitude concerning women's traditional roles of the day.

Themes

Bonnie Shaster's farm and country upbringing is expanded as she moves in with her sophisticated, city-dwelling cousins, who introduce her to the feminist issues of the women's suffrage movement and the general idea that education is the key to women's independence. In addition, a distinct comparison is present between the working class and the upper- and middle-class segments of the population with the introduction of Melba, the preteen cook, and her illiterate and defiantly bawdy behavior.

Books with Similar Issues or Themes

Allan, Mabel Esther. *The Mills Down Below*. New York: Dodd, Mead, 1980.
> In England, fourteen-year-old Elinor Rillsden breaks away from her father's traditional Victorian upbringing when a classmate introduces her to the women's suffrage movement while the impending gunfire of World War I surrounds them.

Ingold, Jeanette. *Pictures, 1918*. New York: Harcourt, Brace, 1998.
> Coming of age in the World War I period, fifteen-year-old Asia uses her interest in photography to work through relationships and society's restrictions for young ladies and gains strength and confidence as she begins to understand Grandmama's mental decline.

Myers, Anna. *Fire in the Hills*. New York: Walker, 1996.
> Sixteen-year-old Hallie endeavors to take her dead mother's place raising her siblings as World War I brings change and fear to her small Oklahoma mountain town, harboring both German residents and a conscientious objector.

Rostkowski, Margaret I. *After the Dancing Days*. New York: Harper & Row, 1986.
> Visiting with wounded veterans in her father's hospital at the end of the Great War, thirteen-year-old Annie develops a friendship with a severely burned soldier and learns the truth about her Uncle Paul's death.

Author-Related Sources

Holtze, Sally Holmes, ed. *Seventh Book of Junior Authors and Illustrators*. New York: H. W. Wilson, 1996, 322–3.

"Jean Thesman." In vol. 124 of *Something about the Author*. Farmington Hills, MI: Gale Group, 2002, 205–10.

Jean Thesman Web site: http://www.jeanthesman.com/ (accessed 24 October 2004).

Discussion Questions

For *The Ornament Tree*

1. What impact does Bonnie's decision to live with her mother's family have on her life?

2. How does Bonnie feel about the feminist position her Cousin Audra holds?

3. How do Mr. Younger's attitude and predicament affect Bonnie?

4. What is the significance of the Ornament Tree?

5. What are Clare's concerns about living in the boarding house and why?

6. Why doesn't Melba appreciate or take advantage of the help Cousin Audra is willing to provide?

7. In the early nineteenth century, how did a woman's working status and education affect her position in society? How does this contrast with women's lives today?

Our Only May Amelia

By Jennifer L. Holm

New York: HarperCollins, 1999

Reading Level: . . . . Grades 5–7
Genre: . . . . Historical fiction
Themes: . . . . Gender roles, courage, defiance, death
Awards: . . . . Newbery Honor, ALA Notable Children's Book

Plot Summary

It takes quite a lot of spunk, courage, and fortitude and a bit of a miracle to be the only girl in a family of seven brothers living in a town full of boys. May Amelia Jackson endures the challenges, disappointments, and even heartbreak she faces during her twelfth year in the 1899 northwest Nasel River Settlement. In a first-person narrative, May Amelia recounts a series of circumstances, adventures, and happenings seen through her determined and inexperienced eyes. She boldly wears her overalls to keep up with the boys, eager to behave like them and be treated equally, resentful of the constant reminder that she is "just a girl." Her father is always worried she will get herself into trouble running around the logging camp and is continually yelling for her to stay home or be with one of her brothers. May Amelia cannot understand her father's concerns and confidently feels she can do anything her brothers do, even though she is expected to behave like "a proper young lady." At the same time, May Amelia longs for another miracle, a baby sister, so she can enjoy some female companionship. With her mother heavy with pregnancy, May Amelia is required to stay home more and help by doing the hard chores her mother cannot. This gives her the opportunity, however, to leave the settlement and go with the boys to the closest city, Astoria, a half-day's trip away, to shop for her mother. Seeing the city for the first time is an eye-opening wonder for May Amelia, having known only the immigrant Finnish lifestyle of her small town. Staying the night at her very Americanized Aunt Alice's home is another impressive treat that May Amelia cherishes. Returning home, May Amelia continues her tomboy behavior while helping out more and more with the women's chores. When her hateful Grandmother Patience arrives to live with the family, May's spirit and emotional health are threatened as the old woman openly and cruelly criticizes her behavior and actions without justification. Her brothers and parents are supportive yet powerless to prevent the old woman's abusive words. May Amelia's happy and optimistic attitude is tested when her grandmother first physically strikes and breaks a favorite doll, a gift from Aunt Alice, and then cruelly blames the untimely sudden infant death of the new baby on May Amelia's negligence. Despite the lack of truth in this accusation, May Amelia is hurt and grief stricken, and she runs away, eventually joined by her loving brother Wilbert, who takes her to their family in Astoria for a period of time. The love of all her family and the natural death of Grandmother Patience bring May Amelia home, grateful to be reunited and to move on.

Main Characterization

Twelve-year-old May Amelia is the youngest of eight children whose need for peer companionship is compounded by the lack of a girl playmate, friend, or sibling. Living, working, and playing alongside her brothers foster a rough-and-tumble lifestyle, much to the chagrin and worry of her family, who feel the need to protect her as their only girl. May is a daring, inquisitive girl, eager to take on anything her brothers can do. Her boldness sometimes overshadows her better judgment as she sets out to explore alone without understanding some possible consequences. She is brave and loyal, as is evident when Lonny, the neighbor's boy is nearly caught by a cougar and May Amelia risks her own life to run back and help him out of danger. On the other hand, May is also a fragile, sensitive, and sometimes vulnerable child who needs the protection of not just her brothers, but her parents as well. Her good intentions and desire to be included in the family as an important and useful member, are not always appreciated. Taking the responsibility of caring for her new infant sister while her mother recuperates from a difficult birth is an exciting and different role for May. Losing her sister in such an unfortunate and incomprehensible way is devastating enough, but having the guilt precipitated by the cruel words of her grandmother is more unbearable and brings May Amelia to an emotional low point in her life. Time, youth, and loving relatives allow May to heal from her emotional wounds, but a near-death episode on the Nasel River during a logging run allows May finally to see the beauty in her life with her loving brothers surrounding her.

Themes

Traditional roles for boys and girls are portrayed through May Amelia's father's expectations concerning his children. In addition, May Amelia's behavior is looked upon as unladylike by most of her family and friends. May Amelia displays a courageous outlook on her ability to achieve as her brothers do and a defiance to pursue her desires regardless of any disobedience she may exhibit. Accepting death as an inevitable and uncontrollable consequence of life is a difficult reality that May Amelia ultimately deals with.

Books with Similar Issues or Themes

Avi. *The True Confessions of Charlotte Doyle*. New York: Orchard Books, 1990.
> Thirteen-year-old Charlotte Doyle finds herself to be the only female passenger aboard the ship *Seahawk* and is thrust into an adventure of murder and mutiny making the 1832 transatlantic voyage from England to America one of daring survival.

Brink, Carol Ryrie. *Caddie Woodlawn*. Illustrated by Trina Schart Hyman. New York: Macmillan, 1973.
> Allowed to run "wild" with her brothers so she will be physically stronger, eleven-year-old Caddie Woodlawn refuses to behave like a lady as she begins to near the age when such comportment is required.

Cushman, Karen. *The Ballad of Lucy Whipple*. New York: Clarion Books, 1996.
> Transplanted to the Gold Rush state of California, Lucy tries to adjust to the Wild West ways that are so different than her previous East Coast city life.

Field, Rachel. *Calico Bush*. Engravings on wood by Allen Lewis. New York: Macmillan, 1931.
> Marguerite Ledoux, a young French orphan girl forced to work as an indentured servant for the Sargent family living off the coast of Maine, bravely endures all the hardships, skills, and emotions of the difficult colonial life of the 1700s.

Fleischman, Paul. *The Borning Room*. New York: HarperCollins, 1991.
> At the end of her life, Georgina Lott recounts her childhood and young womanhood on an Ohio farm where she encounters runaway slaves, social injustice, and the eternal life cycle of birth, courtship, marriage, and death.

Author-Related Sources

"Jennifer L. Holm." In vol. 120 of *Something about the Author*. Farmington Hills, MI: Gale Group, 2001, 123.

Jennifer Holm Web site: http://www.jenniferholm.com/ (accessed 22 October 2004).

Discussion Questions

For *Our Only May Amelia*

1. What is May Amelia's life like in her Finnish home and small settlement where her family lives?

2. How do her brothers feel about their only little sister?

3. Why is it important for May Amelia to be treated the same as her brothers?

4. What was acceptable and appropriate behavior for girls and young women in 1899?

5. Why can't her parents protect May Amelia from the hateful Grandmother Patience?

6. How does May Amelia work out her feelings and guilt about her sister's death?

7. What does May Amelia want most in her life and why?

8. How do you think May Amelia's adult life was affected by her young life as the only girl in her community?

Protecting Marie

By Kevin Henkes

New York: Greenwillow Books, 1995

Reading Level: . . . . Grades 5–7

Genre: . . . . Realistic fiction

Themes: . . . . Communication, trust, assertiveness, self-esteem, confidence

Awards: . . . . School Library Journal Best Books

Plot Summary

Fanny Swann, the only child of Henry and Ellen, has a difficult relationship with her artist father, who is worried about turning sixty, his creative block, and the small familial issues that trigger his angry outbursts. Fanny is very close to her mother and relies on her to provide emotional strength and understanding whenever things are tense with her father. Fanny's one dream is to own a dog, a pet that will not only provide a source of play and companionship but also bring a sense of happiness and fulfillment in her lonely home life. But as Fanny dreams, she cannot help but remember the hurtful and negative experience of several years ago when the family tried to keep a puppy, Nellie, whose overly destructive, untrained behavior was too much for her orderly and intense father. After Nellie got into her father's studio, it was decided, much to Fanny's grief and disappointment, that Nellie had to go to a new home, and the Swann's household would never include another dog. Paradoxically, after Henry skips out on his sixtieth birthday party, he returns the next day with a full-grown part German Shepard, part yellow Lab oddly named "Dinner," as a gift to the confused and skeptical Fanny. Dinner is well trained, loveable, and endearing, and once Henry explains and promises that this dog will stay, Fanny allows herself to fall in love. She is not completely trusting of her father's commitment, however, and arranges her life and schedule so that the care and well-being of the dog are carefully controlled and kept separate from her father's artistic work. Fanny's distrustful feelings go back not only to the time that Nellie was given away, but also to a clean-up game her father used to play with her called "Stupid Hunts" that resulted in his attempt to throw away meaningless junk in her room, without respecting her personal reasons for keeping each item. Thus arises Fanny's vigilant strategy to protect her homemade paper doll named Marie, which appears as nothing more than crumpled paper to her father but holds a very personal significance to Fanny. In the end, after much angst, misunderstanding, and reconciliation, Dinner succeeds in unifying this family of three and developing a feeling of satisfaction for both father and daughter.

Main Characterization

Fanny Swann is a twelve-year-old girl who is torn between her love and concern for her father and the fear and almost hate she feels when his actions and behavior appear cruel and inconsistent. She is reluctant to trust him—not just in his promise that Dinner will stay, but in his true feelings for her. She wants to believe that he loves her, yet she also feels he does not understand her. Her close relationship with her mother provides part of the support she craves, yet her insecurity is compounded without her ability to communicate clearly with her father.

Henry Swann is a man who loves his family but who is almost overpowered by his creative block. His adult issues are real but incongruous to a twelve-year-old girl, who only wants to feel loved and not responsible for his difficulty in his professional life.

Ellen Swann is a steady emotional base for Fanny, outlining an adult perspective while sympathizing with a young 'tween's feelings.

Mary Dibble is Fanny's best friend, who provides peer support and a voice of reason to her insecure feelings about her father and her concerns about maintaining a calm life with her new dog.

Timothy Hill is a minor character who provides an additional element of suspense and concern in Fanny's life, yet ends up representing a future of possibilities for her.

Dinner is everything Fanny has wished for in a dog, but, more importantly, acts as a surprisingly unifying force between her and her father.

Themes

Communication is the central theme in this book, depicted by the characters' varied abilities to express themselves in each relationship. Fanny and her father struggle throughout the book to tell each other their true feelings. Fanny's hurt about losing Nellie has prevented her from completely trusting her father, concealing her thoughts until the end when she tells him how she fears him. Her father, immersed in his work and professional problems, never quite understands his daughter and her emotional stress. Fanny must learn to become more assertive and confident, as does her father, not only in his relationship with her, but with his work as well.

Books with Similar Issues or Themes

DiCamillo, Kate. *Because of Winn-Dixie*. Cambridge, MA: Candlewick Press, 2000.
> India Opal Buloni adopts a stray dog that she calls Winn-Dixie and learns to accept life without a mother, but with a loving father and some endearingly eccentric friends.

Hall, Lynn. *Halsey's Pride*. New York: Charles Scriber's Sons, 1990.
> Moving in with her dog breeder father, thirteen-year-old March Halsey relies on Pride, the kennel's prize, to help her adjust to her new environment and her relationship with her father.

Hearne, Betsy. *Eliza's Dog*. New York: Margaret K. McElderry Books, 1996.
> On a trip to Ireland, Eliza falls in love with a sheepdog puppy and convinces her family to bring her home to Chicago.

Jennings, Patrick. *Faith and the Electric Dogs*. New York: Scholastic, 1996.
> Narrated by an "electric dog," a Mexican idiom meaning "mutt," Eddie tells the story of his mistress Faith and the new life she hates in San Cristobal de las Casas, Mexico. He also tells of the magical rocket ship trip they take while Faith longs to return to her real home in San Francisco.

Staples, Suzanne Fisher. *The Green Dog: A Mostly True Story*. New York: Farrar, Straus & Giroux, 2003.
> Finding a dog the summer before fifth grade fills Suzanne's heart with happiness and love but keeping the dog out of trouble proves to be quite a challenge.

Author-Related Sources

Holtze, Sally Holmes, ed. *Sixth Book of Junior Authors and Illustrators*. New York: H. W. Wilson, 1989, 123–4.

"Kevin Henkes." In vol. 23 of *Children's Literature Review*. Farmington Hills, MI: Gale Group, 1991, 124–31.

"Kevin Henkes." In vol. 108 of *Something about the Author*. Farmington Hills, MI: Gale Group, 2000, 105–10.

Kevin Henkes Web site: http://www.kevinhenkes.com/ (accessed 18 August 2004).

Silvey, Anita, ed. *Children's Books and Their Creators*. Boston: Houghton Mifflin, 1995, 303–4.

Discussion Questions

For *Protecting Marie*

1. The book is divided into three sections titled "Without," "With," and "Within." What do these three subdivisions in the story mean to you?

2. What does the title of the book tell you about Fanny?

3. This is a story of relationships. What kind of relationship does Fanny have with her father and her mother?

4. Why does Fanny feel so conflicted about her father, and what does she want most in life?

5. What is Henry's concern and conflict both with himself and with Fanny?

6. How does Dinner change the family, and mostly Henry and Fanny?

7. What does Henry learn from his daughter?

8. Why does Fanny destroy the original Marie and then create a new one?

9. The author, Kevin Henkes, uses a writing style that is filled with symbolism. Can you point out times in the book when what you are reading is very visual and can almost be imagined as a painting or a movie?

10. Why can we consider Henkes' writing to be as artistic as an artist's painting?

Ruby Electric

By Theresa Nelson

New York: Atheneum Books for Young Readers, 2003

Reading Level: . . . . Grades 5–7
Genre: . . . . Realistic fiction
Themes: . . . . Imagination, family relationships, friends, deception
Awards: . . . . ALA Notable Children's Book

Plot Summary

Twelve-year-old Ruby Miller and her seven-year-old brother Pete have moved to Los Angeles with their mother following the mysterious disappearance of their policeman father. Ruby uses her terrific imagination to write screenplays, anticipating a career in the movie industry. Her wishful thinking allows her to believe a variety of scenarios about her father's situation, including the possibility of his working on a secret case. After a couple of years, Frank Miller tries to meet with the family but never manages to show up at the appointed time and place. Ruby lives her life fluctuating between reality and fantasy as she longs for her father to return and escapes within her writing to create reasons and excuses for his absence. Spending much of her time alone, Ruby is bothered by two boys, the cut-ups in her grade, Matthew Mossbach (nicknamed Mouse) and Vincent Bogart (also known as Big Skinny). Both boys always seem to be hanging around, mostly because Big Skinny has a huge crush on Ruby and has tried to gain her attention and acceptance in a variety of clever ways. He embarrasses her by creating a large red graffiti sign on the concrete riverbank opposite her house stating his admiration. When Ruby attempts to cover the sign with more red paint, she is caught, arrested, and sentenced to community service with the two boys. Pete, interested in prehistoric woolly mammoths, receives a painting of such a scene from an anonymous artist, providing Ruby with the incentive to launch a community civic project to paint over the concrete riverbank dually hiding the graffiti and beautifying the neighborhood. An eventual reunion with their father proves disappointing but serves to anchor Ruby's future expectations more realistically.

Main Characterization

Ruby Miller, twelve years old, misses her father and wants to know the real story behind his disappearance. She invents reasons, excuses, and scenarios for his return to the family. Her imaginative mind works in screenplay format as her fictitious characters role-play life as she would like it to be. Her youthful aspirations to succeed in the movie world are ever present, as indicated by her written invitation to Steven Spielberg. Her strength lies in her determined persistence to find a positive solution to both her father's absence and her court-ordered community service.

Pete Miller, seven years old, barely remembers his father, has an interest in prehistoric life, and relies on his sister for basic familial support. His innocent, matter-of-fact attitude serves as a reality check for Ruby's dreams about finding their father and resuming their former life.

Mouse (Matthew Mossbach) and Big Skinny (Vincent Bogart) are the class clowns with very little interest in school; they are always in some sort of trouble, yet genuinely interested in providing emotional support to Ruby when Pete is in a serious accident. They have good hearts and a sincerity that shows through their comical approach to Ruby's problems and concerns.

Frank Miller is Ruby and Pete's father. He is a former policeman who has spent three years in jail for committing a white-collar crime.

Mama tries to protect Ruby and Pete by concealing the truth behind their father's disappearance. Her efforts to start a new life in a new town prove difficult for Ruby, who needs the truth to live her life happily.

Dr. Ed is both Mama's new boss and romantic interest, eventually serving as a positive father figure to both Ruby and Pete.

Themes

Ruby escapes her real-life problems through her imaginative thinking and creative writing. Her screenplay scenarios encompass more than her thoughts on her family's situation as she incorporates a certain melodrama into each vignette. Her relationship with both her brother and mother and her desire for contact with her father is an ongoing theme as well. The secondary theme of deception is important because it reflects Ruby's entire outlook on life. Without understanding or knowing the true reason for her father's disappearance, she is unable to accept the reality of her single-parent household. Friendship is also an important theme as the boys' presence in Ruby's life becomes psychologically beneficial despite her resistance.

Books with Similar Issues or Themes

Codell, Esme Raji. *Sahara Special*. New York: Hyperion Books for Children, 2003.
> Silently coping with her parents' divorce by refusing to participate or talk in school and by keeping a secret journal of her life behind a shelf at the public library, Sahara Jones is placed in special education. Her eccentric and unorthodox teacher later encourages her to write.

Crum, Shutta. *Spitting Image*. New York: Clarion Books, 2003.
> Seeking to do some good with a VISTA volunteer in her 1960s small Kentucky town, Jessie Bovey brings unexpected problems to her neighbors and learns the truth about her absent father.

DiCamillo, Kate. *Because of Winn-Dixie*. Cambridge, MA: Candlewick Press, 2000.
> Opal is frustrated about her mother's disappearance and must accept and adjust to her single-parent household with a loving father.

Naylor, Phyllis Reynolds. *Reluctantly Alice*. New York: Atheneum, 1991.
> Alice adjusts to seventh grade, deals with a new class enemy, and comically handles the romantic trials of her older brother and widowed father.

Snyder, Zilpha Keatley. *Libby on Wednesday*. New York: Delacorte Press, 1990.
> Accustomed to being home-schooled, smart and creative eleven-year-old Libby is enrolled in a regular school for "socialization" and must learn to interact with her peers and an intriguing group of kids in a writing workshop.

Author-Related Sources

Holtze, Sally Holmes, ed. *Seventh Book of Junior Authors and Illustrators*. New York: H. W. Wilson, 1996, 237–8.

"Theresa Nelson." In vol. 25 of *Authors and Artists for Young Adults*. Farmington Hills, MI: Gale Research, 1998. Reproduced on the Thomson Gale Biography Resource Center Web site: http://galenet.galegroup.com/servlet/BioRC (accessed 18 October 2005). Document no. K1603000331.

"Theresa Nelson." *St. James Guide to Young Adult Writers*, 2nd ed. St. James Press, 1999. Reproduced on the Thomson Gale Biography Resource Center Web site: http://galenet.galegroup.com/servlet/BioRC (accessed 18 October 2005). Document no. K1663000323.

Discussion Questions

For *Ruby Electric*

1. What is Ruby's main concern in her life?

2. How does Ruby express her feelings?

3. How does Ruby's screenplay writing affect her real-life situation?

4. Why does Ruby's mother keep the real reason for her father's absence a secret?

5. Why is Ruby's reunion with her father different than she imagined and so difficult for her?

6. How do Mouse and Big Skinny affect the lives of Ruby and the rest of her family?

7. How does Ruby creatively and effectively resolve her unwanted relationship with the two boys?

8. How do the lives of each character change in the story?

9. What did you think about the author using different formats and print to tell the story of *Ruby Electric*?

10. Why do you think the author chose the title *Ruby Electric*?

Rumpelstiltskin's Daughter

By Diane Stanley

New York: Morrow Junior Books, 1997

Reading Level: . . . . Grades 3–4

Genre: . . . . Fairytale

Themes: . . . . Greed versus social consciousness, empowerment

Plot Summary

In this altered version of the traditional fairytale, Meredith, the miller's daughter, decides she is better off marrying Rumpelstiltskin, who promises to be an excellent father to her firstborn child, rather than the greedy king. So, on the third night, Rumpelstiltskin spins a ladder of gold and helps Meredith escape her tower filled with straw to a happy life together far away from the palace. Their bright, clever daughter, named Hope, periodically visits the goldsmith with coils of gold spun by her father in exchange for the money the family needs to purchase necessities. Hearing of this girl's unusual gold trades from the goldsmith, the king orders his guards to kidnap her, thinking that, like her mother, he will be able to force her to spin gold from straw to add to his miserly wealth. Witnessing the country's poverty in sharp contrast to the king's greed, Hope realizes that allowing her father to spin gold for the king will only bring more despair to the poor citizens of the kingdom. She creatively devises a plan to fool the king into providing the means to a more prosperous livelihood for his subjects, which results in his overwhelming popularity. Ultimately pleased with all Hope has helped him achieve, the king offers to marry Hope, but she refuses and counters with a request to be made his prime minister. This gives her the powerful ability to influence the king's decisions to benefit the kingdom's good citizens.

Main Characterization

Meredith, the miller's daughter, is bold and willing to consider a different and better alternative to escape her situation in the tower filled with straw. Her boldness influences the life of her daughter Hope, who is a kind and clever girl with social consciousness. Hope's resourcefulness allows her the ability not only to improve the lives of the entire kingdom, but to help the king develop a fresh kind of cheerfulness through his newly inspired goodwill initiatives.

Themes

Greed at the expense of one's fellow citizens or neighbors countered by social consciousness to correct or improve a community's plight is the main theme. Hope's intuitive concerns for the ordinary folks and their basic needs for food and warm clothing are coupled with her bold attempt to carry out a plan and outsmart the king into thinking his wealth is enriched by his popularity. In addition, the ability to use a situation to a certain advantage empowers Hope to create a position of responsibility and authority for herself.

Books with Similar Issues or Themes

Andronik, Catherine, M. *Hatshepsut: His Majesty, Herself.* Illustrated by Joseph Daniel Fiedler. New York: Atheneum Books for Young Readers, 2001.
    A picture book biography of the female successor to ancient Egypt's throne after all the male successors had died, how she assumed more power over the years, eventually crowned herself pharaoh, and behaved and dressed as a man in a time when no word for a female ruler existed.

Mayer, Marianna. *Women Warriors: Myths and Legends of Heroic Women.* Illustrated by Julek Heller. New York: Morrow Junior Books, 1999.
    Twelve tales that explore the power of women warriors from mythical goddesses such as the East Indian Devi to the real warrior queen of Britain, Gwendolen.

San Souci, Robert D. *Cut from the Same Cloth: American Women of Myth, Legend, and Tall Tale.* Illustrated by Brian Pinkney. New York: Philomel Books, 1993.
    Twenty stories of legendary tall-tale women from American folklore.

Yolen, Jane. *Not One Damsel in Distress: World Folktales for Strong Girls.* Illustrated by Susan Guevara. New York: Silver Whistle/Harcourt, 2000.
    Thirteen tales of female characters who are fearless, strong, heroic, and resourceful.

Author-Related Sources

"Diane Stanley." In vol. 46 of *Children's Literature Review.* Farmington Hills, MI: Gale Group, 1998, 127–58.

"Diane Stanley." In vol. 115 of *Something about the Author.* Farmington Hills, MI: Gale Group, 2000, 191–8.

"Diane Stanley." In vol. 15 of *Something about the Author Autobiography Series.* Farmington Hills, MI: Gale Group, 1993, 277–91.

Diane Stanley Web site: http://www.dianestanley.com/ (accessed 8 November 2004).

Holtze, Sally Holmes, ed. *Sixth Book of Junior Authors and Illustrators.* New York: H. W. Wilson, 1989, 287–8.

Silvey, Anita, ed. *Children's Books and Their Creators.* Boston: Houghton Mifflin, 1995, 623–4.

Discussion Questions

For *Rumpelstiltskin's Daughter*

1. How is this version of "Rumpelstiltskin" different from the traditional one?

2. Why does Meredith make the choice to marry Rumpelstiltskin?

3. What kind of childhood do you think Hope had with her parents, Meredith and Rumpelstiltskin?

4. What concerns does Hope have after she is kidnapped?

5. What does Hope think of the greedy king, and how did her opinion help her to devise her plan?

6. Why does Hope ask to be prime minister instead of agreeing to be queen?

7. How would her life and influence with the king be different if she were queen instead of prime minister?

8. Why do you think the author chose the name "Hope" for Rumpelstiltskin's daughter?

9. Why do you think the author chose to wait until the end of the story to introduce Rumpelstiltskin's daughter's name?

10. Which version of "Rumpelstiltskin" do you like best? Why?

Seven Brave Women

By Betsy Hearne, Illustrated by Bethanne Andersen

New York: Greenwillow Books, 1997

Reading Level: . . . . Grades 3–4; discussion level: Grades 3–6
Genre: . . . . Picture book
Themes: . . . . Women's contribution, female strength, female courage, women's history

Plot Summary

Rather than marking history and time in the United States by the various wars that have been fought, the American story is recounted by the struggles, dreams, and accomplishments of one girl's seven maternal relatives going back to her great-great-great-grandmother during the Revolutionary War, continuing with six successive generations that cover the War of 1812, the Spanish-American War, World War I, World War II, and the Korean War, finally ending with her own mother who was raised during the Vietnam War. Each woman represents the bravery and steadfast endurance that was indelibly passed on to the next generation. Their brief stories mark the personal impact that women made to the family and their place in history during times of war.

Main Characterization

Elizabeth, a Mennonite, struggles to emigrate from Switzerland to the United States, arriving after a long, difficult sea journey to Revolutionary War Philadelphia, where she eventually bears nine children.

Eliza lives during the War of 1812 and the Civil War, works hard on an Ohio farm, and lives to the age of ninety-nine.

Nellie is an artist married to a preacher during the Spanish-American War, leaving painted dishware and pottery to her family.

Helen attends medical school in a male-dominated society during World War I and works as a missionary in India, saving lives by starting a hospital for women.

Betty becomes an architect—an all-male field during the World War II era—teaches, and writes a book about buildings at age eighty-nine.

Margaret lives through the Korean War, is widowed early, and supports her children, parents, and siblings working as a secretary.

Betsy lives through the Vietnam War period, grows up to be a librarian, tells stories to her young patrons, and passes on her family history by recalling the lives of these brave women across generations.

Themes

Each of these women, although not famous, represents a contribution to America's story, not through war service but through female strength, courage, and fortitude. Their struggles include both intellectual and emotional issues, as they tirelessly work to provide for their families and their communities.

Books with Similar Issues or Themes

Dietz, Heather. *Newbery Girls*. New York: Margaret K. McElderry Books, 2000.
Selections from fifteen Newbery Award–winning novels featuring strong female characters.

Hamilton, Virginia. *Her Stories*. Illustrated by Leo Dillon and Diane Dillon. New York: Blue Sky Press, 1995.
A collection of both true stories and folk tales of African American female characters and women portraying strength, shortcomings, accomplishments, and dreams.

McCully, Emily Arnold. *The Bobbin Girl*. New York: Dial Books for Young Readers, 1996.
Ten-year-old Rebecca, the bobbin girl in an 1830s Lowell, Massachusetts, textile factory, becomes part of a female workers' protest for better conditions.

Phelps, Ethel Johnston. *Tatterhood and Other Tales*. Illustrated by Pamela Baldwin Ford. New York: Feminist Press, 1978.
A collection of twenty-five traditional tales featuring witty, resourceful, heroic women characters from a variety of cultures.

Stamm, Claus. *Three Strong Women*. Pictures by Jean and Mou-Sien Tseng. New York: Viking Press, 1990.
When Forever-Mountain, the famously strong Japanese wrestler, meets Maru-me, he must learn a different kind of strength and power from three deceptively frail women.

Tchana, Katrin. *The Serpent Slayer and Other Stories of Strong Women*. Illustrated by Trina Schart Hyman. Boston: Little, Brown, 2000.
Eighteen folk and fairytales emphasizing feminine strength, courage, fortitude, and cleverness.

Author-Related Sources

"Betsy Hearne." In vol. 95 of *Something about the Author*. Farmington Hills, MI: Gale Group, 1998, 68–71.

Betsy Hearne homepage: http://www.lis.uiuc.edu/~hearne/ (accessed 18 July 2004).

Holtze, Sally Holmes, ed. *Sixth Book of Junior Authors and Illustrators*. New York: H. W. Wilson, 1989, 119–20.

Discussion Questions

For *Seven Brave Women*

1. Why are these women ordinary but extraordinary at the same time?

2. What are these women struggling or fighting for even though they never fight in a war?

3. How do these women symbolically change the course of U.S. history?

4. What do each of these women's experiences tell about their time in U.S. history?

5. Is it possible to tell the story of the United States without referring to the wars the nation has fought?

6. What do the themes of women's courage, strength, and bravery mean to you?

7. What does the author mean by telling "her story" as part of history?

Shadow Spinner

By Susan Fletcher

New York: Atheneum Books for Young Readers, 1998

Reading Level: . . . . Grades 5–7
Genre: . . . . Historical fiction
Themes: . . . . Survival, courage, ambition, loyalty, ingenuity

Plot Summary

In this tale of storytellers, Marjan weaves her own tale of courage, ambition, loyalty, and cunning ingenuity. Marjan is an orphan Persian girl employed as a servant in the home of a Jewish couple in the ancient Persian kingdom. Her idol is the famous Shahrazad, the queen who has been living with the sultan for the last three years, escaping his cruel death sentence each night by telling him a new story with a cliff-hanger ending. The sultan's revenge for having a former unfaithful wife is to marry a new one each night after killing the previous one until all young girls are at risk. Marjan's own mother, before taking her own life, is desperate to save her daughter and, unable to think of another plan, purposely breaks Marjan's foot so she will be maimed, unattractive, and suitable for a life of servitude rather than fated to the harem's certain death. Marjan has the utmost respect for the queen's clever ability to know and tell thousands of stories to save her own and the lives of all the young, available women in the kingdom. She models her own ambition to be a great storyteller on Shahrazad's talent. But, after three years, Shahrazad is out of stories to tell, and when she hears of Marjan's storytelling ability, she brings her to the palace and involves her in a daring plot to find the mysterious storyteller from the bazaar where Marjan has overheard a different tale, one that the sultan is expecting to hear. Along the way, Marjan must outwit the villainous mother of the sultan (the khatun) and her spies and create allies with other palace inhabitants—namely, the Shahrazad's sister Dunyazad and the messenger pigeon keeper, Zaynab. It is not until Marjan is imprisoned and brought before the sultan, however, that she courageously tells a story of truth to reveal the secret behind Shahrazad's talent. A combination of luck and bravery work to bring Marjan's plight to a satisfying conclusion, leaving the grateful Shahrazad with a reformed king and creating a new position for Marjan in a neighboring wealthy household.

Main Characterization

Shahrazad's character is based on the legendary Persian queen who was able to keep the sultan entertained with her 1,001 nights of stories and thus kept herself and the other women of the harem alive. She is portrayed here as someone with brave determination and resolve never to concede to the sultan's insanity. On the contrary, she is in love with him and views him as a wounded man who needs emotional healing through her understanding and affection.

Marjan is a thirteen-year-old girl whose ambition is to be a great storyteller. She is in awe of Shahrazad's talent and courageous schemes. She is also resentful of her mother's solution to the problem of girls losing their lives to the sultan's insane killings. Taking her emotional strength from her Auntie Chava's lessons and from the need to perform to save her queen, Marjan risks her life several times to bring the much needed information to Shahrazad and ultimately gambles, risking great danger, and wins by bringing the truth to the sultan.

Themes

Survival is at the core of everything both Marjan and Shahrazad do with their storytelling pursuits dovetailing with subthemes of courage, ambition, loyalty, and ingenuity. Both young women take chances with clever plans and schemes driven by their ambition. Each also displays a loyalty to each other and the unmarried women in the kingdom.

Books with Similar Issues or Themes

Alderson, Brian. *The Arabian Nights*. Illustrated by Michael Foreman. New York: HarperCollins, 1995.
> A classic collection of timeless stories from Arabia, India, and Persia.

Gorog, Judith. *Winning Scheherazade*. New York: Atheneum, 1991.
> A retelling in which Scheherazade is freed from her storytelling position at the palace and enters into a dangerous desert adventure with an unexpected visitor.

Lewis, Naomi. *Stories from the Arabian Nights*. Illustrated by Anton Pieck. New York: Holt, 1987.
> Thirty-one of the legendary tales used to amuse the sultan famous for killing one of his wives each day.

Napoli, Donna Jo. *Beast*. New York: Atheneum Books for Young Readers, 2000.
> An expansion of the traditional "Beauty and the Beast" fairytale told in an ancient Persian setting from the point of view of the Beast.

Author-Related Sources

"Susan Fletcher." In vol. 110 of *Something about the Author*. Farmington Hills, MI: Gale Group, 2000, 93–7.

Discussion Questions

For *Shadow Spinner*

1. Both Shahrazad and Marjan display great courage. Who do you think was braver?

2. Marjan's mother chose to end her life and maim her daughter. Why was Marjan so resentful, and what else could her mother have done?

3. How does love affect the choices that Shahrazad, Marjan, and Marjan's mother make?

4. What ambitions do both Marjan and Sharazad have in their lives?

5. Each chapter begins with a piece titled "Lessons for Life and Storytelling." How can some of these proverbs apply to our life today?

6. How do stories sometimes teach real themes in real life?

7. Why does Marjan risk everything to tell the sultan the truth through a story?

8. At the end of the story, Marjan talks about how real life differs from life in stories. What does she mean when she says, "What seems like an ending is really a beginning in disguise"?

Squashed

By Joan Bauer

New York: Delacorte Press, 1992

Reading Level: . . . . Grades 6–8

Genre: . . . . Realistic fiction

Themes: . . . . Competition, confidence, self-esteem, dedication, self-contentment

Plot Summary

Sixteen-year-old Ellie Morgan's passion in life is agriculture, and a major goal is to place first in the adult Rock River Pumpkin Weigh-In at the annual Harvest Fair. Growing a giant pumpkin to beat the nasty incumbent Cyril Pool is a twenty-four-hour commitment, leaving Ellie with little time for a teen's typical school and social life. Ellie nurtures her pumpkin beyond the basics of plant food, sunshine, and water, with the care and concern of a mother hen, giving her vegetable a name, Max, and treating it as if it has a human soul. Max is the largest pumpkin in Ellie's short farming history, measuring 107 inches in diameter with an estimated weight of more than 300 pounds. With five weeks left to the Harvest Fair, Ellie is determined to battle weather, insects, and human theft to help Max continue to grow and thrive. She is also battling another weight issue under pressure from her father, a professional motivational speaker, to lose some pounds herself and become more interested in her school work and social life, and less interested in farming—something he feels has a limited future. Without the emotional support and strength of her mother, who was killed in a car accident, Ellie draws her fortitude from her advocates, Nana, who tells her she has a grower's soul; Richard, her baseball-playing cousin; and a new friend and potential suitor, Wes, past president of the high school agricultural club. The passing weeks bring anxiety, doubt, continued determination, and resolve as Ellie perseveres recounting all her hopes and fears through a humorous, almost sarcastic voice. The final day brings a well-anticipated victory to Ellie amid the support and cheers of her neighbors, classmates, and friends, as the cheating Cyril tries to enter a rotting gigantic pumpkin but is rightly disqualified, leaving Ellie's Max the winner and champion.

Main Characterization

Ellie Morgan's love for farming and gardening gives her a sense of responsibility and dedication. She is a typical teen, concerned with appearance, popularity, and boys but keeps her uncertainty to herself while relating her needs and ambitions to the success of her pumpkin growing and her very competent cooking skills. Somewhat an underdog, she struggles to ignore her self-doubt, maintaining an outward confidence through her hard work and the emotional support of her allies.

At first, Dad has difficulty supporting Ellie's interest in farming, viewing it from a personal and selfish perspective. He is a concerned father who tries to motivate his daughter in the direction he thinks will lead to success, but eventually he is able to translate his perspective to Ellie's approach to and interest in life.

Richard is a self-confident boy who sees life as a baseball game, providing emotional support for his cousin Ellie.

157

Wes is the most agriculturally knowledgeable character, motivating Ellie to believe in her squash by communicating verbal encouragement to Max on a daily basis.

Cyril Pool is the arrogant, overly confident incumbent who disrespects Ellie for her youth, inexperience, and female status and depends on his bullying behavior to help him steal a win.

Themes

Hard work and dedication that bring a sense of satisfaction are portrayed through Ellie's voice, but more important, the idea of healthy competition that does not necessarily bring success in the form of a win, but through the triumph of self-esteem, contentment, and confidence are the basic concepts in this story.

Books with Similar Issues or Themes

Horvath, Polly. *The Canning Season*. New York: Farrar, Straus & Giroux, 2003.

> Two girls, Ratchet and Harper, are brought together under different circumstances to live with eccentric and very old twin sisters, Tilly and Penpen, in rural Maine. The girls begin to experience parental love and concern and eventually realize the happiness they harbor within themselves.

Naylor, Phyllis Reynolds. *The Grooming of Alice*. New York: Atheneum, 2000.

> The summer before high school, Alice and her friends Pamela and Elizabeth decide to embark on an exercise campaign to be in shape for their new school experience and work through some difficult situations concerning eating disorders, physical changes, and sexual feelings.

Peck, Richard. *A Year Down Yonder*. New York: Dial Books for Young Readers, 2000.

> During the Depression, fifteen-year-old Mary Alice spends a year in rural Illinois where she adjusts to and learns from the feisty and bold ways of her grandmother. Sequel to *A Long Way from Chicago* (1998).

Tolan, Stephanie S. *The Great Skinner Homestead*. New York: Four Winds Press, 1988.

> Stranded in the Adirondack Mountains after their motor home breaks down, sixteen-year-old Jenny is resigned to living with her family in this country setting without the comforts of city life until a good-looking college boy appears and is willing to share his rattlesnake research with her.

Wright, Betty Ren. *The Summer of Mrs. MacGregor*. New York: Holiday House, 1986.

> Twelve-year-old Caroline, jealous of her beautiful sister despite her heart illness, begins to gain confidence in herself the summer she meets the mysterious seventeen-year-old Mrs. MacGregor, soon to be a model in New York City.

Author-Related Sources

Hipple, Ted, ed. Vol. 1 of *Writers for Young Adults*. New York: Charles S. Scribner's Sons, 1997, 73–80.

"Joan Bauer." In vol. 117 of *Something about the Author*. Farmington Hills, MI: Gale Group, 2000, 10–14.

Joan Bauer Web site: http://www.joanbauer.com/jb.html (accessed 19 October 2004).

Discussion Questions

For *Squashed*

1. How does Ellie feel about herself and her ability to win?

2. Would Ellie have been a winner even if she didn't win the weigh-in?

3. What is Nana's advice to Ellie about farming and life in general?

4. How does the author use baseball as a way to help Ellie with her attitude on winning?

5. How does Wes help Ellie in a way that her father tried but could not?

6. What did Ellie gain from the last competition, in addition to the grand prize?

7. How does Ellie's relationship with her father change after the contest?

8. What do Ellie and her father learn from each other?

9. Why is competing more important than winning?

10. Do you think winning changes Ellie's life or makes no difference in the end?

Sweetgrass

By Jan Hudson

New York: Philomel Books, 1989

Reading Level: . . . . Grades 6–8
Genre: . . . . Historical fiction
Themes: . . . . Survival, maturity, gender roles
Awards: . . . . Canadian Library Association Book of the Year for
Children, Canada Council Children's Literature Prize

Plot Summary

Sweetgrass is a fifteen-year-old Blackfoot Indian girl being raised by her aunt and mother's sister, Almost-Mother, after her own mother passed away in childbirth. Life revolves around the seasonal work of the women in her tribe, preparing and storing food for the long, cold Canadian prairie winter. As is the custom, many girls her age, and even younger, are promised in marriage agreements by their families. Sweetgrass, however, is still the oldest unmarried girl of her tribe. Secretly in love with Eagle-Sun, she longs to be his wife. Her father, who favors her among all his children, is not convinced that she is ready to take on the responsibility of a first wife. Amid the everyday struggles of rival warrior attacks, wild bear threats, and tedious back-breaking work, Sweetgrass is encouraged by her vital, sharp grandmother to be brave, bold, alert, and vigilant in her life. Seeking the experienced knowledge of her newly wed friend Pretty-Girl, Sweetgrass longs to understand the nuances of married life. With the men away from the camp, the harsh winter brings death and disease to the tribe. Sweetgrass, with her courage and wits, is left to provide medical help to her dying baby brothers nurse Almost-Mother and her older brother Otter back to health from the smallpox infestation and starvation that eventually kill the majority of her tribe. With great resolve and determination, Sweetgrass ignores the traditional taboo of eating fish to provide the only sustenance available, thus bringing her aunt and brother back to life and clearly proving to her father, on his return, that she is ready and mature enough for marriage to Eagle-Sun.

Main Characterization

Sweetgrass, her father's favored child, is good yet impatient to be treated equally, longing to risk the idea of choosing her own mate. Raised with the traditional Blackfoot tribe customs, she is bold enough to think outside the rules to develop her own prospective marriage relationship and to save her family from starvation during the smallpox infestation. Her grandmother is a strong female role model for Sweetgrass, recounting the old ways of the tribe when women were respected more as equals and encouraging a sense of independence and fortitude.

Themes

This story of a girl's desires for future happiness and love quickly turns into one of survival as Sweetgrass is thrust into a struggle to keep her family well and alive. The difficult realities of disease, death, and destruction resulting from enemy warfare bring Sweetgrass to a level of maturity beyond even her father's expectations as she uses her emotional strength to provide for her family outside the Blackfoot expectations of a typical girl.

Books with Similar Issues or Themes

Burks, Brian. *Walks Alone*. New York: Harcourt, Brace & Company, 1998.
Wounded and having lost the rest of her family following a fierce attack from the White Eyes, Walks Alone and her young brother are determined to continue the journey to join their fellow Apaches in Mexico.

Koller, Jackie French. *The Primrose Way*. New York: Harcourt, Brace & Company, 1992.
Joining her missionary father in the New England colony in 1633, sixteen-year-old Rebekah questions the need for the salvation of the Pawtucket tribe once she is introduced to their way of life and culture.

Matcheck, Diane. *The Sacrifice*. New York: Farrar, Straus & Giroux, 1998.
Ignored at birth as the female half of fraternal twins, an eighteenth-century Apsalooka girl name Weak-One overcomes numerous obstacles including hunger, injury, and betrayal as she sets out to prove she is destined to be the Great One.

O'Dell, Scott. *Streams to the River, River to the Sea: A Novel of Sacagawea*. Boston: Houghton Mifflin, 1986.
A novelization of the Shoshone girl's heroic role and relationship with Lewis and Clark, the two men she guided, on their famous discovery expedition through the Southwest.

Osborne, Mary Pope. *Adaline Falling Star*. New York: Scholastic Press, 2000.
Left to live with her father's people in St. Louis, Adaline, daughter of the legendary Kit Carson and an Arapaho woman, runs away to learn more about her Native American family while making her own way in the wilderness of the west.

Author-Related Sources

Holtze, Sally Holmes, ed. *Seventh Book of Junior Authors and Illustrators*. New York: H. W. Wilson, 1996, 146–7.

"Jan Hudson." In vol. 40 of *Children's Literature Review*. Farmington Hills, MI: Gale Group, 1996, 92–8.

"Jan Hudson." In vol. 77 of *Something about the Author*. Farmington Hills, MI: Gale Group, 1994, 88–91.

Discussion Questions

For *Sweetgrass*

1. How does Sweetgrass feel about being the oldest unmarried girl in the tribe?

2. How does she feel about her status as a girl in the tribe?

3. Why does Sweetgrass's father feel she is not ready for marriage, and why does he postpone an arrangement?

4. What does Sweetgrass learn from her grandmother?

5. What choices or decisions does Sweetgrass have to make to save her aunt and brother?

6. How do religion and custom play a role in Sweetgrass's life?

7. How does Sweetgrass become a woman in her father's eyes?

8. What is the significance of the heroine's name, Sweetgrass?

Yolonda's Genius

By Carol Fenner

New York: Margaret K. McElderry Books, 1995

Reading Level: . . . . Grades 4–6

Genre: . . . . Realistic fiction

Themes: . . . . Individuality, belonging, gifted attributes, interracial relationships

Awards: . . . . Newbery Honor

Plot Summary

Yolonda's life in Chicago is less than her widowed mother would like it to be, exposed to drug pushers and precarious street crime that inner-city life can impart. On the other hand, Yolonda is a confident, strong fifth grader, physically large for her age, streetwise, and ready to protect her first-grade brother, Andrew. She loves the city for all its busyness, shopping opportunities, street fairs, museums, and concerts in the park. But when a gun incident at her school results in a death, Mother moves the family to a small, safer town in western Michigan. Yolonda's disdain for boring, small-town life is immediately apparent, but her need to belong and simultaneously maintain her individuality is typical of any child moving to a new school and neighborhood. At the same time, she is very concerned about her quiet brother, who spends a lot of his time playing a Marine Band harmonica he received from his policeman father before his death. The harmonica is more than a musical instrument for Andrew, it's a way of communication that only Yolonda seems to recognize. Andrew's school problems include his inability to read and understand text, and although he is assigned to a slow learner's resource room and a speech therapist, Yolonda feels that his abilities with music are not being acknowledged; she believes he may be a musical genius. Her research at the library confirms her feelings about her brother when she reads John Hersey's statement describing a genius as one who "rearranges old material in a way never seen before." Making new friends is difficult for Yolonda, who has found herself in a racially mixed environment and the target of much teasing for her size. Responsible for Andrew both before and after school while Mother works, she neglects him one day at the skateboard playground where they usually meet to have a cake-baking session at home with a new friend, Shirley, another unconventional girl in the class. Realizing too late that Andrew is not home, Yolonda arrives at the playground to find Andrew attacked by the local junior high bullies, who have crushed his harmonica beyond repair. Yolonda's fury and guilt drive her to seek both vengeance against the boys and to find a way to replace Andrew's harmonica. Yolonda knows that the loss of his instrument has psychologically affected Andrew, like the death of a dear friend. Andrew is completely withdrawn and uncommunicative without it. Yolonda's strong, brave response to the bullies gains her much respect from her classmates, and her vision to give her brother some exposure in a professional musical venue is realized when a vacation back to Chicago to visit Aunt Tiny during the Blues Festival in Grant Park inspires her to create an opportunity to meet B. B. King backstage.

Main Characterization

Yolonda is a determined girl who carries a sense of responsibility both for the way she lives her life and the way she protects her brother. Her streetwise experience allows her certain maturity beyond her age that seems to match her large physical size. Her single mother, who works full time, has forced her to be a surrogate parent to her brother, sometimes overshadowing Yolanda's own need to socialize and belong. She views herself as her father's daughter, sporting both his physical attributes and ambition to follow him in the police force.

Andrew is a withdrawn child, viewed as a slow learner by adults, yet capable of expressing his thoughts through his unique ability with the harmonica. His personal psychological struggle is virtually ignored by his mother, leaving Yolonda resolute to help him find his "voice" and spirit again.

Shirley is the opposite of Yolonda, white and small, yet she shares Yolonda's feelings of nonconformity and gravitates toward her as a fellow outcast of the class.

Themes

Yolonda's move to a small town from a large city places her in a situation in which she both appears and feels different than her newest classmates. She is comfortable with her individuality and staunchly defends herself, yet she needs to belong in some way and feel accepted. Her brave, forceful response to the school bullies gains her the respect she is looking for to balance both feelings. Andrew's abilities, whether they are truly of a gifted nature or not, represent another form of individuality. In addition, a loose subtheme of interracial relationships is present with Yolonda and Shirley's friendship and with the inclusion of a multiracial population in both her new town and at school.

Books with Similar Issues or Themes

Hamilton, Virginia. *Plain City*. New York: The Blue Sky Press/Scholastic, 1993.
> Buhlaire Sims is uncomfortable in her town, feels out of place, and begins to question the information or lack of it that her mother has about her past and her father.

Konigsburg, E. L. *The Outcasts of 19 Schuyler Place*. New York: Atheneum Books for Young Readers, 2004.
> Margaret Rose, miserably unhappy at summer camp, prefers not to compromise her identity. She is taken home by her summer guardian uncle and becomes involved in saving an unusually large, artistic tower structure in his front yard, created by both her uncles, from being torn down at a neighbor's request.

Spinelli, Jerry. *Stargirl*. New York: Alfred A. Knopf, 2000.
> At first intrigued by her uniqueness, other kids welcome new student Stargirl, but then begin to shun her for her differences.

Tolan, Stephanie S. *Surviving the Applewhites*. New York: HarperCollins, 2002.
> Thrown out of every conventional school, Jake Semple is forced into a home-schooling situation run by a very eccentric family. He must adjust to cooperative education and eventually realize his potential and talents.

Voight, Cynthia. *It's Not Easy Being Bad*. New York: Atheneum Books for Young Readers, 2000.
> Best friends and outcasts of their former school, Mikey and Margalo, try to break into the ever-popular clique environment of middle school.

Author-Related Sources

"Carol Fenner." In vol. 89 of *Something about the Author*. Farmington Hills, MI: Gale Group, 1997, 64–7.

"Carol Fenner" [obituary]. In vol. 132 of *Something about the Author*. Farmington Hills, MI: Gale Group, 2002, 76.

Discussion Questions

For *Yolonda's Genius*

1. How does Yolonda's life change when she moves to a small town?

2. How does Yolonda's experience in the city help her in her new small-town life?

3. How do Yolonda, Shirley, and Andrew keep their individuality?

4. How do Yolonda's feelings about her physical appearance help or hurt her relationship with other kids?

5. Why does Yolonda feel so responsible for Andrew?

6. How do the adults in Yolonda's life—her mother, Aunt Tiny, and her father—influence her thoughts and ideas?

7. What is most important to Yolonda?

8. What is most important to Andrew?

9. What has Yolonda learned from living in two different places and adjusting to her new school and town?

10. How do you think Andrew's life changes after the concert in Grant Park?

11. How do you think Yolonda's life continues the next year at school and in town?

Zel

By Donna Jo Napoli

New York: Dutton Children's Books, 1996

Reading Level: . . . . Grades 6–8
Genre: . . . . Fantasy
Themes: . . . . Possessive love, freedom of choice, coming of age
Awards: . . . . School Library Journal Best Books

Plot Summary

In this novelization of the traditional fairytale "Rapunzel," Zel has lived the past thirteen years with her mother in a happy, secure, warm home. She has been sheltered from the outside world because her mother has kept her close to home, avoiding other friendships. Zel is unaware that Mother is really a witch woman who, barren and desperate for a child, bargains away her soul for a magical power with plants and then bullies a neighbor woman into giving up her girl baby. When Zel meets a young man, Konrad, at the market and the possibility of a relationship seems imminent, Mother uses her overprotective powers of love and deceit to place Zel in the tower that will keep her isolated from any other human contact. Zel spends the next two years completely alone, except for the daily hour-long visits with Mother. The extreme loneliness drives her to rebel and long for freedom, despite Mother's coercive behavior to choose a secluded life together. Smitten with love, Konrad searches for Zel daily for the next two years. When he succeeds, Mother uses her destructive powers with plant life both to keep Zel imprisoned and ultimately to create a chaotic and violent conclusion to Zel's incarceration. The witch woman eventually succumbs to death after which the two lovers reunite two years later. Told from the perspective of the three individual characters in alternating chapters, we see the emotional and psychological thinking of each.

Main Characterization

Zel, raised in a protective environment and sheltered for her thirteen years, is still an independent and curious thinker. She longs to have a husband and family, expecting that at the right time her goals will be met. While only knowing the love of her mother, she nevertheless feels betrayal and revulsion when her imprisonment in the tower appears to serve a disturbed, possessive need of her mother.

Mother, a witch, is possessed by the need to have a child for herself. Her overprotection in the name of love stems more from a selfish desire that is ultimately harmful to the child. Ironically, imprisoning Zel in the tower causes Mother an unforeseen sense of loss and unhappiness.

Konrad comes from a wealthy household and appears to be arrogant and a bit pompous until he sees Zel and becomes enchanted with her ability to work sensitively with animals, in particular, his horse. His love for Zel and his obsessive search for her changes his outlook on life.

Themes

The possessive love of a parent dominates in this coming-of-age novel that places a young woman in the position of choosing her own direction in life. More than a story, Napoli presents a psychological drama in which the needs and will of three people play for and against each other.

Books with Similar Issues or Themes

McKinley, Robin. *Spindle's End*. New York: G. P. Putnam's Sons, 2000.
    Determined to save Briar Rose from Pernicias's curse of the spindle, a young fairy raises her in hiding to avoid any future contact with either the witch or any needles.

Napoli, Donna Jo. *Bound*. New York: Atheneum, 2004.
    The Cinderella story written in the context of the Chinese Yeh-Shen but set in the historical period of the Ming dynasty.

Roberts, Lynn. *Rapunzel: A Groovy Fairy Tale*. Illustrated by David Roberts. New York: Harry N. Abrams, 2003.
    A modern-day version in which Rapunzel has red hair, and is stuck in her aunt's tenement apartment with a broken elevator.

Stanley, Diane. *Petrosinella: A Neapolitan Rapunzel*. New York: Dial Books for Young Readers, 1995.
    An Italian version in which the heroine's mother steals parsley from the ogre, causing the inevitable entrapment that leads the young girl to find a way to break the vicious spell using a series of three acorns.

Author-Related Sources

"Donna Jo Napoli." In vol. 51 of *Children's Literature Review*. Farmington Hills, MI: Gale Group, 1999, 152–8.

"Donna Jo Napoli." In vol. 137 of *Something about the Author*. Farmington Hills, MI: Gale Group, 2003, 154–60.

Donna Jo Napoli Web site: http://www.donnajonapoli.com/ (accessed 30 May 2004).

Hipple, Ted, ed. *Writers for Young Adults*. New York: Scribner's, 2000, 217–26.

Silvey, Anita, ed. *Essential Guide to Children's Books and Their Creators*. Boston: Houghton Mifflin, 2002, 320.

Discussion Questions

For *Zel*

1. We read this story from the three separate views of each character. What wishes or expectations do Zel, Mother, and Konrad each have for themselves?

2. The views of Zel and Konrad are told with a narrator's voice, but Mother tells her own story in her own voice. Why do you think the author wrote the novel in this way?

3. What is Mother's motivation for wanting to keep Zel away from any other relationship?

4. What is the power of a mother's love, and can it ever be harmful to a child?

5. The prospect of communicating with animals is something Mother promises to Zel as a gift for making the right choice. What kind of choice did Zel really have to make all along?

6. Why can't the witch succeed in keeping Zel and Konrad apart and instead loses her own life?

7. Why are Konrad and Zel able to find each other and be reunited in the end?

8. How does the author keep aspects of the traditional fairy tale while creating a story of psychological need and desire?

Chapter 4

Father-Son Book Club

Starting a Father-Son discussion group in your library or community can be a positive, innovative way to attract the male component of your community to a literature experience despite the concept that book discussion has acquired a feminine association. Fathers generally bond with their sons through "guy" activities—sports, technology, adventure entertainment. Why not books? If positive male role models are formed through these other activities, why not use reading and discussion as another venue?

Women have comprised the overwhelming majority of participants in book discussion groups both historically and in today's literary world. Historically, many book groups were formed by women who did not work outside the home yet had a need for intellectual stimulation in a communal venue. In his essay "Reading Groups: Where Are All the Men?" columnist Bob Lamm (1995) states, "men don't join reading groups because it would violate the Guy Code." Because of the powerful conditioning that men receive in our sexist society, most men look at book clubs as "one more form of 'women's work' that should be avoided at all costs." He continues to explain that while that may have once been true, today's men avoid book groups for fear that they are too feminist. So although probably welcome in a female-dominated group, joining a male-only group is rarely considered (p. 205).

When it comes to boys, librarians and teachers have become increasingly concerned about their lack of interest in reading and their lower literacy achievement compared with girls. For years we have complained that there is never enough fiction with strong boy protagonists to entice and encourage reading. Society is also at fault here, because recreational sports and athletics are valued on a higher plane for boys than is recreational reading.

Kathy Odean notes in her introduction to her book *Great Books for Boys,* "as boys move toward adolescence, all too many quit reading for pleasure because it's not cool and a reader risks being labeled a 'sissy' or 'nerd' " (1998, p. 1) This is not unique to the United States. In a study done by the Programme for International Student Assessment and reported in the *Organization for Economic Cooperation and Development Observer,* "girls have overtaken boys in the literacy stakes when it comes to reading, both in their ability to understand what they read and in their tendency to read for pleasure. When it comes to reading, males in all OECD countries are more likely than females to be among the lowest-performing students" ("Girls Read More Than Boys," p. 53). Jon Scieszka, popular author of numerous children's books and a former elementary school teacher, has expressed the same concerns and started a campaign and Web site called "Guys Read." Much of what he advises for parents, teachers, and librarians revolves around using men as reading role models for boys. And what better way than to have dads participate in their own book group?

What Features in a Book Are Attractive to the Male Reader?

In their book *What Stories Does My Son Need?* (2000, pp. 8–10), Michael Gurian, family therapist, educator, and author of *The Wonder of Boys* and *The Good Son,* and Terry Trueman, educator and author of the young adult novel *Stuck in Neutral,* talk about "primal stories" and their appeal to male readers. They define primal stories as myths and legends, biblical parables, spiritual epics, and many fairy tales that help teach the lessons of life and are "stories that boys need in order to become good men." Gurian and Trueman further define these primal stories by whether they teach ten moral competencies: "Decency, fairness, empathy, self-sacrifice, responsibility, loyalty, duty, service, honesty, and honor." These ten competencies stimulate moral dialogue and interaction between adult and child about "what is compassionate, human, joy-advancing, and success-building."

It is no secret that boys and girls are different, and studies have shown that they learn and behave differently in school. In the study titled "Reading Don't Fix No Chevys," teachers Michael Smith and Jeffrey Wilhelm (2002, p. 11) researched gender and literacy over a year by evaluating how young adolescent boys deal with literacy in their lives. Here is what they found concerning choice of reading:

- Boys and girls express interest in reading different things, and they do read different things.
- Boys are more inclined to read informational texts.
- Boys are more inclined to read magazine articles and newspaper articles.
- Boys are more inclined to read graphic novels and comic books.
- Boys tend to resist reading stories about girls, whereas girls do not tend to resist reading stories about boys.
- Boys are more enthusiastic about reading electronic texts than girls are.
- Boys like to read about hobbies, sports, and things they might do or be interested in doing.
- Boys like to collect things and tend to like to collect series of books.
- Poetry is less popular with boys than with girls.
- Girls read more fiction.
- Boys tend to enjoy escapism and humor; some groups of boys are passionate about science fiction or fantasy.

These findings shouldn't surprise any of us. In fact, if you read further into their study, the qualities that seemed to engage boys in reading certain books are the key to having a successful father-son book group.

Qualities in books boys enjoy (pp. 149–57):

- **Texts with action**—often the primary feature of a story such as Philbrick's *The Young Man and the Sea*

- **Texts that are visual**—where the reader can visualize the action as it is written such as Dahl's *James and the Giant Peach* or Levine's *Dave at Night*

- **Texts that are exportable**—that could easily be brought into conversation because of what is said by characters or what happens in action such as Clements' *Frindle*

- **Texts that sustain engagement**—where they want to get to know a character better or see what happens such as Curtis' *Bud Not Buddy*

- **Texts that provide multiple perspectives**—such as Donahue's *An Island Far From Home* or Cormier's *The Chocolate War*

- **Texts that are novel**—that provide a new, different, or surprising feature or viewpoint such as Spinelli's *Wringer*

- **Texts that are edgy or subversive**—such as Paulsen's *Harris & Me* or DeFelice's *Weasel*

- **Texts that have powerful or positive ideas**—such as Hiaasen's *Hoot* or Gutman's *The Million Dollar Shot*

- **Texts that are funny**—such as Peck's *Soup*

Smith and Wilhelm also point out one other important aspect in their study, that of sociability and its significance to literary practices. The boys in this study placed a clear value on home connections and how literacy grew out of relationships they established through literature circles in school, reading buddies, book groups, and cooperative learning groups. Thus, the father-son book discussion group can be fostered with reasonable success.

Should You Handle Father-Son Discussion Groups Differently From Other Groups You Might Lead?

Yes and no. The basic format of using icebreakers, interpretive questioning, and snacks always worked for my group, regardless of gender. The difference came in the choice of titles and in respecting both the boys and fathers for their male viewpoints. As the only female in the group, which was, by the way, their choice, I was careful to step back and free discussion among them, only gently leading when the group went astray. The same would certainly apply with a male leader.

References

Brooks, Bruce. "Will Boys Be Boys?" *VOYA* (June 2000): 88–92.

"Girls Read More Than Boys." *OECD Observer* (January 2002): 53.

Gurian, Michael. *The Wonder of Boys.* New York: Putnam, 1996.

Gurian, Michael, and Patricia Henley with Terry Trueman. *Boys and Girls Learn Differently! A Guide for Teachers and Parents.* San Francisco: Jossey-Bass, 2001.

Gurian, Michael, and Terry Trueman. *What Stories Does My Son Need?* New York: Penguin Putnam, 2000, 8–10.

Lamm, Bob. "Where Are All the Men?" In *The Book Group Book: A Thoughtful Guide to Forming and Enjoying a Stimulating Book Discussion Group.* Edited by Ellen Slezak. Chicago: Chicago Review Press, 1995, 204–10.

Maughan, Shannon. "You Go, Guys" *Publisher's Weekly* (May 7, 2001): 41.

Odean, Kathleen. *Great Books for Boys.* New York: Ballantine Books, 1998.

Smith, Michael W., and Jeffrey D. Wilhelm. *Reading Don't Fix No Chevys: Literacy in the Lives of Young Men.* Portsmouth, NH: Heinemann, 2002.

Sullivan, Michael. "Why Johnny Won't Read." *School Library Journal* (August 1, 2004): 36–9.

Wilhelm, Jeff. "Getting Boys to Read: It's the Context!" *Instructor* (October 2002): 16–19.

Web Sites

A Literacy Initiative for Boys from Jon Scieszka: http://guysread.com/ (accessed 25 October 2004).

Bud, Not Buddy

By Christopher Paul Curtis

New York: Delacorte Press, 1999

Reading Level: . . . . Grades 4–6

Genre: . . . . Historical fiction

Themes: . . . . Family relationships, homelessness/survival, hope, racism

Awards: . . . . Newbery Medal, Coretta Scott King Award, Michigan Mitten Award

Plot Summary

The third abusive foster home in Flint, Michigan, for ten-year-old Bud Caldwell is the last straw. Determined to use the few questionable hints his mother left behind four years before her death in the form of worn-out jazz concert flyers for a band called "Herman E. Calloway and the Dusky Devastators of the Depression!!!!!!" Bud packs his suitcase with basic belongings—clothes, a blanket, and a collection of five specially marked rocks. Unsure where to go, now that he is "living on the lam," he decides to walk to Grand Rapids where he reasons this bandleader named Herman C. Calloway with a name so close to his must be the father he never knew. A black boy outside the city limits of Flint in the year 1936 can raise eyebrows, a situation that may prove to be dangerous for him. So when Lefty Lewis notices Bud at the early hour of 2:30 A.M. alone on the road, he stops to investigate. Bud's sense of self-protection keeps him alert, and rather than claiming he is from Flint, he lies about his situation, stating he has run away from Grand Rapids and his father, Herman C. Calloway. Good Samaritan Lefty Lewis brings Bud back "home" to the well-known, surprised, and cantankerously belligerent bandleader. Bud's unwavering purpose and conviction that he is related to Mr. Calloway together with the kind, enveloping care of singer Miss Thomas help him unravel the mystery behind his father's identity, his mother's childhood life in Grand Rapids, and the connection he really has with his grandfather, Herman E. Calloway.

Main Characterization

Bud Caldwell is a ten-year-old boy with a well-developed, tough perspective on life. His "rules and things for having a funner life and making a better liar out of yourself" are both insightful and hilarious. Minor characters of Lefty Lewis and Miss Thomas serve as helpful role models he fortuitously encounters to help him solve his quest. Grandfather Herman C. Calloway remains bitter about losing his only daughter, yet hopeful as he continually collects the rocks in each city he tours.

Themes

Curtis combines issues around family relationships, racism, hope, and survival as the story is told from the first-person narrative of an orphan boy unwilling to remain in a difficult situation and willing to take risks to create a better life for himself. The racist reality of the time period is blended in the experiences Bud encounters outside his Flint neighborhood, in the Hooverville shantytowns,

Lefty Lewis's urgent warnings about the road, and in his grandfather's need to have one white band member to bend the rules.

Books with Similar Issues or Themes

Kehret, Peg. *Searching for Candlestick Park*. New York: Dutton, 1997.
> Twelve-year-old Spencer decides to search for his estranged father after his parent's divorce when his mother insists they can no longer afford to keep his cat Foxey.

Levine, Gail Carson. *Dave at Night*. New York: HarperCollins, 1999.
> Dave runs away at night from his abusive orphanage to meet up with his new friends, Solly, a fortuneteller, and Irma Lee, the little girl of a wealthy beauty products manufacturer in the 1920s Harlem Renaissance neighborhood of late night jazz.

Townsend, John Rowe. *Dan Alone*. New York: J.B. Lippincott, 1983.
> Rather than live in an orphanage, Dan Lunn runs away and joins a band of thieves who "beg and sing" for their living and eventually finds the family he has always wanted.

Wynne-Jones, Tim. *The Maestro*. New York: Puffin Books, 1998.
> Fleeing an abusive father, fourteen-year-old Burl runs away to the Canadian wilderness where he comes upon a well-known pianist, "the maestro," trying to finish a composition.

Author-Related Sources

Christopher Paul Curtis Web site: http://christopherpaulcurtis.smartwriters.com/ (accessed 30 January 2005).

"Christopher Paul Curtis." In vol. 140 of *Something about the Author*. Farmington Hills, MI: Gale Group, 2003, 45–50.

Murray, Barbara. *Black Authors and Illustrators of Books for Children and Young Adults,* 3rd edition. New York: Garland Publishing, 1999, 95.

Discussion Questions

For *Bud, Not Buddy*

1. How does Bud protect himself from circumstances and situations in life?

2. Which of Bud's "rules" make sense to you, and which do you think are just plain humorous?

3. What kind of relationship did Bud have with his mother? How was it different from the relationship she might have had with her father?

4. How is the band a symbol of a family?

5. What makes Bud feel he was really at home with a family?

6. Throughout Bud's quest, what situations or ideas give him reason for hope in his future?

7. What did Bud's mother mean when she talked about "one door closing and another door opening"?

8. How can we tell that Herman E. Calloway has never given up on his daughter?

9. How does the author let us understand the racist environment of the time period?

10. How does racism affect the band and Herman E. Calloway?

11. How are things different today from the era when this story takes place?

The Chicken Doesn't Skate

By Gordon Korman

New York: Scholastic, 1996

Reading Level: . . . . Grades 3–5

Genre: . . . . Contemporary fiction

Themes: . . . . Competition, animal rights, animal/science experimentation, superstition

Plot Summary

This school setting combining science and sports employs a variety of characters, each with his or her individual concern or agenda to weave together a story of amusement, suspense, and controversy. When Milo Neal, son of a Noble Prize–winning scientist, seriously announces his topic for the school's science fair competition as "The Complete Life Cycle of a Link in the Food Chain" with a chicken as its subject, his classmates initially have different responses. Milo brings in a baby chick, which he continually calls his "specimen" and Kelly Marie, the resident animal activist, immediately adopts the bird, naming it Henrietta. Preparations to keep the chick in the classroom are made with the approval and help of the teacher, Mrs. Baggio. Adam Lurie, hockey star on his middle school team, is unimpressed, as are most of the boys, including the class's budding screenwriter, Zachary Gustafson. Taking control of the chicken's well-being over the ignored protests of Milo, who refuses to develop any emotional attachment to his specimen, Kelly Marie insists on caring for Henrietta on weekends and agrees to a rotation schedule among the other willing students. As the weeks progress, Henrietta, so well cared for, is gaining and growing at a greater than normal rate. She ends up at a hockey game where the team's bad luck streak is somehow reversed, and she is heralded by the whole school as a lucky charm—all to the dismay of Milo. When it becomes obvious that Henrietta will be slaughtered and eaten to complete the experiment, an outcry of inhumanity and outrage occurs throughout the school and town. Milo completes his experiment in a way he could not foresee, and Henrietta manages to take the team all the way to winning the championship trophy.

Main Characterization

Korman uses first-person accounts for each of his characters in alternating chapters. Adam Lurie is the hockey star, superstitious and only interested in Henrietta as a lucky charm. Kelly Marie is an animal activist who succeeds in developing Henrietta's status as a loveable, defenseless pet. Milo Neal is a studious, serious, budding scientist who analyzes everything from a clinical viewpoint and only shows an emotional side with his distress over his parents' divorce and the absence of his father. Zachary Gustafson is the class "dweeb," continually picked on by the cooler boys and only interested in his screenwriting aspirations.

Themes

In a playful and sarcastic tone, themes of animal rights and science experimentation are introduced from a variety of viewpoints as represented by all the characters. In addition, the concept of chicken humor with a middle school sensibility brings in the amusing idea of superstitious beliefs or the concepts of luck and confidence. Competition is a subtheme shown in both the science fair and hockey school settings.

Books with Similar Issues or Themes

Grunwell, Jeanne Marie. *Mind Games*. Boston: Houghton Mifflin, 2003.
> Six students recount their experience and perceptions with a joint science fair project relating the possibilities of extrasensory perception.

Hurwitz, Johanna. *Much Ado About Aldo*. New York: Morrow, 1978.
> When Aldo's class creates a food chain experiment with a tank full of crickets and introduces a chameleon, Aldo decides to become a vegetarian rather than participate in the real food ecosystem.

Mills, Claudia. *Standing Up to Mr. O*. New York: Farrar, Straus & Giroux, 1998.
> Animal rights supporter Maggie Macintosh is willing to risk an F in science rather than dissect a living animal for the purpose of looking inside.

Todd, Pamela. *Pig and the Shrink*. New York: Delacorte Press, 1999.
> When a seventh grader named Tucker convinces his friend Angelo Pighetti, aka "Pig," to be the subject of his science experiment on obesity and nutrition, he learns more about the value of friendship than about the scientific concepts of weight loss.

Author-Related Sources

Berger, Laura Standley, ed. *Twentieth-Century Children's Writers*. Detroit, MI: St. James Press, 1995, 534–5.

Gordon Korman. In vol. 119 of *Something about the Author*. Farmington Hills, MI: Gale Group, 2001, 95–101.

Gordon Korman's official Web site: http://gordonkorman.com/ (accessed 2 February 2005).

Hipple, Ted, ed. In vol. 2 of *Writers for Young Adults*. New York: Charles S. Scribner's Sons, 1997, 199–206.

Holtze, Sally Holmes, ed. *Seventh Book of Junior Authors and Illustrators*. New York: H. W. Wilson, 1996, 180–1.

Discussion Questions

For *The Chicken Doesn't Skate*

1. How does Milo view his science experiment, and why does he view Henrietta as just a chicken or "specimen"?

2. What effect does Henrietta have on each character in the story?

3. Why is it important for Milo to complete his experiment by slaughtering his specimen and then cooking and eating it?

4. How does Henrietta's status in the school and town make Milo's experiment more difficult?

5. What does Milo's experiment bring out concerning animal rights and science?

6. What does Henrietta do for the good of the hockey team?

7. How do you think the team would have played without Henrietta's presence?

8. Was this story a comedy or a serious drama?

9. How does the author write and describe the events in the story to make you feel as though you were part of the class?

10. If you were in this class, what kind of character would you portray?

The Chocolate War

By Robert Cormier

New York: Pantheon Books, 1974

Reading Level: . . . . Grades 6–8

Genre: . . . . Realistic fiction

Themes: . . . . Bullying, independence, conformity, intimidation

Awards: . . . . ALA Best Book for Young Adults, School Library Journal Best Book of the Year, New York Times Outstanding Book of the Year

Plot Summary

At Trinity, a Catholic high school for boys, freshman Jerry Renault must balance the tensions of academics, football, and teachers' demands against peer pressure and the expectations of an underground society called the Vigils. The school's annual fundraising chocolate sale is raised to a new level when Brother Leon, acting principal, commands the student body to sell double the normal quota of twenty-five boxes per boy for double the normal price of $1 per box. The Vigils, and in particular their leader Archie Costello, create a variety of school pranks that are "assigned" to students as a powerful form of intimidation from the influential Vigils. Selling the chocolates is voluntary, as acknowledged by the tyrannical Brother Leon, but everyone is nonetheless expected to take part. Jerry's "assignment" is to refuse to take his share of the selling for ten straight days as the boxes are handed out and the sales are recorded each morning at the general school assembly. At first, this has the shocking effect that Archie anticipated, but after ten days, when Jerry decides he will continue to refuse to sell the chocolates, a different and precarious environment develops as both Archie and Brother Leon feel they have lost their respective control over the student body. Jerry's continued defiance increases both his level of respect among his peers and his vulnerability for violence and retaliation from Archie and Brother Leon. The brutal yet realistic ending, involving the severe beating of Jerry Renault in a publicly arranged boxing match, explores humanity's struggle with vengeance and pride.

Main Characterization

Jerry Renault is adjusting to life after his mother's recent death from cancer. His strength of character is seen in his ability to go against expectations and stand his ground, regardless of the consequences. His individuality proves to be both his strength and weakness. He is able to tolerate the cruel psychological harassment of his classmates, but when he finally seeks the satisfaction of revenge, resorting to the violence of a boxing match with Emile Janza, his integrity and dignity are compromised along with his physical safety.

Archie Costello is a bully who prefers to use psychological rather than physical torment. He is a calculating and brilliant boy, constantly thinking ahead to keep himself in a position of authority and leadership with the Vigils, the student population, and Brother Leon.

Brother Leon uses his administrative position in the school to intimidate both students and faculty to conform to a set of standards. The chocolate sale represents not only a charitable fundraising event, but a way for him to gain financially and figuratively through the efforts of the boys.

Roland Goubert, "The Goober," is a loyal friend to Jerry. A nervous boy, he is actually terrified of Archie, never quite recovering from the traumatic experience of his own assignment, the disassembling of room nineteen. He is highly disturbed by the disquieting evil perpetrated both by the Vigils and the coercive administration.

Themes

This psychological drama includes themes of bullying and intimidation as the boys are expected to conform to the unofficial rules of both a dominating secret society and a powerful administrator. Jerry's defiance represents both independence and isolation as his behavior simultaneously makes him a hero and an ostracized victim.

Books with Similar Issues or Themes

Avi. *Nothing but the Truth: A Documentary Novel.* New York: Scholastic, 1991.
> A boy's mindless prank of humming the "Star Spangled Banner" develops into a series of escalating reactions by the administrators, media, and town residents, resulting in the unfortunate disruption and disparagement of a dedicated teacher's professional career.

Spinelli, Jerry. *Wringer.* New York: HarperCollins, 1997.
> A boy refuses to follow his town's tradition and convention, requiring him to perform the duties of a wringer at the annual park fundraising pigeon shoot.

Author-Related Sources

Berger, Laura Standley, ed. *Twentieth-Century Young Adult Writers.* Detroit, MI: St. James Press, 1994, 152–5.

Hipple, Ted, ed. In vol. 1 of *Writers for Young Adults.* New York: Charles S. Scribner's Sons, 1997, 291–302.

"Robert Cormier." In vol. 55 of *Children's Literature Review.* Farmington Hills, MI: Gale Group, 1999, 1–42.

"Robert Cormier." In vol. 83 of *Something about the Author.* Farmington Hills, MI: Gale Research, 1996, 35–40.

Silvey, Anita, ed. *Children's Books and Their Creators.* Boston: Houghton Mifflin, 1995, 170–2.

Thomson, Sarah L. *Robert Cormier.* New York: Rosen Central, 2003.

Discussion Questions

For *The Chocolate War*

1. What kind of boy is Jerry Renault?

2. Why do you think Jerry continued to refuse to sell the chocolates?

3. Why does Jerry choose to stand alone in his conviction to make his own decisions?

4. What do Archie and Brother Leon have in common that allowed them to work together?

5. How do Archie, Brother Leon, and Jerry each use their power in the story?

6. What does this novel say about individual choice?

7. How does the boxing match change Jerry emotionally and psychologically?

8. What does the author mean when he included the line "Do I Dare Disturb the Universe" in this novel?

9. The novel has both good guys and bad guys who are continually competing against each other in what Jerry calls "fun and games." In the end, who do you think are the winners?

10. What do you think is the most significant message in this story?

Dave at Night

By Gail Carson Levine

New York: HarperCollins 1999

Reading Level: . . . . Grades 4–6

Genre: . . . . Historical adventure

Themes: . . . . Friendship, loyalty, survival, race relations

Awards: . . . . ALA Notable Book, School Library Journal Best Books, ALA Best Book for Young Adults

Plot Summary

Dave Caros, a streetwise and dare-devilish eleven-year-old boy living in the Jewish quarter of New York City's lower East Side in the 1920s, is taken to the Hebrew Home for Boys (HHB) in Harlem after his stepmother refuses to care for him following his father's unexpected death. Resentful that his older, more studious and serious brother Gideon has been invited to live with Uncle Jack in Chicago and that his other relatives feel they cannot financially support him, Dave vows to take care of himself and run away to a better life. The HHB and its cavernously large, poorly heated building, meager food portions, and abusively powerful superintendent Mr. Bloom, is a rough place even for a smart, tough-acting boy like Dave. Forced to wear the uniform of the orphanage while his few precious possessions are confiscated, Dave thinks only of escaping and manages to find a way out during the first night by climbing a tree close to the surrounding fence. Once out, he begins to roam the late-night streets of Harlem, finds a dollar bill, then meets Solly Gruber, an older, grandfatherly Jewish man who makes a living telling fortunes at the "rent parties," fundraisers to help pay the rent that were popular during the Harlem Renaissance period. Solly lets him "work" the crowds with him and eventually takes him to the home of Odelia Packer, modeled after the famous beauty products business woman, Madame C. J. Walker, where he meets Irma Lee Packer, the most intriguing little girl he has ever known. Getting back to the orphanage just in time to sneak in behind the milkman, Dave's new buddies are curious and impressed with his late-night escapade. Time in the orphanage continues with Dave developing close ties with his new friends, both the boys in his grade and with Solly and Irma Lee at night. Orphanage life includes dodging the older bullies, learning to appreciate teacher Mr. Hillinger's art lessons, and scheming to retrieve his father's carving, the only thing left of his papa, before escaping for good to Irma Lee's basement. But the plan is foiled when Dave is caught by Mr. Bloom, who takes back the precious carving; Dave is forced to flee into the cold winter city. He eventually finds his way back to his old neighborhood and to Solly, the only adult with a positive solution to his situation. With the influential assistance of his powerfully wealthy friends in Harlem, Solly joins Mrs. Packer in a visit to the orphanage to straighten out Mr. Bloom. Dave, on the other hand, is torn between his loyalty and care for his buddies and his feelings of gratitude for Irma Lee and her mother. Dave continues to live at the orphanage with a new superintendent while maintaining his ties with Solly (his adopted grandfather) and Irma Lee, feeling part of a family once more.

Main Characterization

Dave Caros is a bright, clever, eleven-year-old who feels alone and abandoned yet is able to transfer his feelings of loyalty to his new family of buddies. His daring sense of bravado gets him in trouble but also helps him survive in the tough environment of the orphanage. He is resentful that his real family of aunts and uncles was unwilling to care for him, as they were able to for his brother, and is confused by but grateful for Solly's interest and help.

Themes

Survival both in an abusive environment and in a world without family dominates this story, but it is friendship and loyalty that are stressed in Dave's newfound relationships with his buddies, Irma Lee and Solly. The power of money and the intoxicating pleasure of jazz erase any color barrier as whites and blacks interact in the scenes of Dave's nighttime escapades set in the Harlem Renaissance period of New York City.

Books with Similar Issues or Themes

Collier, James Lincoln. *The Jazz Kid*. New York: Henry Holt, 1994.
> Wanting to play the cornet more than anything, thirteen-year-old Paulie Horvath runs away with a jazz group and becomes involved in the 1920s Chicago gangster life.

Curtis, Christopher Paul. *Bud, Not Buddy*. New York: Delacorte Press, 1999.
> A young boy runs away from his orphanage and foster home to follow clues that will lead to the father he has never met.

Snyder, Zilpha Keatley. *Gib Rides Home*. New York: Delacorte Press, 1998.
> Orphan Gibson Whittaker is sent from the cruel and difficult environment of the Lovell House Home for Orphaned and Abandoned Boys to work on the ranch of the wealthy Mr. Thornton and discovers the history behind his own circumstances.

Wallace, Barbara. *Sparrows in the Scullery*. New York: Atheneum, 1997.
> Ten-year-old Colley ends up in the Dickensian-style orphanage of the nineteenth century, the Broggin Home for Boys, run by the evil Mr. and Mrs. Crawler, who place boys in child labor factories.

Lasky, Kathryn. *Vision of Beauty: The Story of Sarah Breedlove Walker*. Illustrated by Nneka Bennett. Cambridge, MA: Candlewick Press, 2000.
> An illustrated biography of life from poverty to wealth for the pioneering businesswoman known as Madam C. J. Walker, who serves as a model for Levine's character of Mrs. Odelia Packer.

Author-Related Sources

"Gail Carson Levine." In vol. 85 of *Children's Literature Review*. Farmington Hills, MI: Gale Group, 2003, 111–15.

"Gail Carson Levine." In vol. 98 of *Something about the Author*. Farmington Hills, MI: Gale Group, 1998, 97–8.

Gail Carson Levine Home Page: http://www.harperchildrens.com/authorintro/index.asp?authorid=12385 (accessed 18 August 2004).

Discussion Questions

For *Dave at Night*

1. How does Dave ultimately survive losing a father and living in the tough world of the HHB?

2. What does Dave learn from his buddies about life and how to live in an orphanage?

3. How does Dave really feel about leaving the HHB and living in Irma Lee's basement?

4. Why does Solly help Dave and continue to visit him at the orphanage, even though he is not a real relative?

5. Why are art and art lessons so important to Dave?

6. What does Dave enjoy most about his nighttime outings? How does he like the music he hears?

7. How does writing letters help Dave, even though he never mails them?

8. Why do Dave and Irma Lee become such good friends even though they come from different backgrounds and lifestyles?

9. What does Dave feel is most important in his life?

10. What does Irma Lee feel is most important in her life?

11. What do you think was Dave's fortune?

Frindle

By Andrew Clements, Illustrated by Brian Selznick

New York: Simon & Schuster Books for Young Readers, 1996

Reading Level: . . . . Grades 3–5
Genre: . . . . Realistic fiction
Themes: . . . . Free speech, conformity, inventiveness
Awards: . . . . Christopher Award

Plot Summary

Nick, a fairly good student, is always clever in creating a diversion in class. Just when a new assignment is about to be introduced, Nick can redirect the teacher with a distracting question. Fifth grade, the year before middle school, brings a new seriousness to all the students with more challenging work and with language arts teacher Mrs. Granger, known for long vocabulary assignments and for her no-nonsense classroom. On the first day of school, as the first vocabulary assignment is about to be given, Nick raises his hand and throws out what he considers to be "a perfect thought-grenade" to distract and delay just before the final bell is about to ring. Nick innocently questions how all the words in the dictionary got there, and with a bit of a smile and a less than amused look in her eye, Mrs. Granger responds by giving Nick an extra assignment. He is to research the answer to his question and present an oral report the following day. Outmaneuvered by his experienced teacher, Nick is at first angry and annoyed but then rises to the challenge by presenting quite a long and factual report using up most of the English period. "The Lone Granger" still manages to fit her lesson and new assignment in the remaining eight minutes, but not before Nick launches another question on how word meanings are decided. When Mrs. Granger responds that meanings are created by how people speak and communicate, Nick develops another idea in his head, creating a new challenge for himself and the entire school and community. Experimenting with the term for "pen," Nick renames the item a "frindle" and begins to use it continually everywhere he goes. Soon other students and even adults begin to catch on, as the fad develops. Mrs. Granger, unable to accept this behavior as innocent experimentation, refuses to allow the term frindle in her classroom and at first forbids use of it in any context, assigning detention and writing punishments. But the power in numbers prevails as everyone begins to use the term freely and the press and adults become involved in a debate over free speech. In the end, a new word is created, proving Mrs. Granger's theory that word meanings develop as people use them.

Main Characterization

Nick Allen is a bright fifth grader willing to take some harmless risks to prove a point. His teacher, Mrs. Granger, is at first perceived as a typically strict and rigid woman but is ultimately responsible for inadvertently allowing Nick the freedom to pursue his experiment, leading to a positive outcome for many in the town.

Themes

Through the concept of words and word meanings, the issue of free speech is raised here as Nick is asked to stop his experiment by the school authorities. Nick's inventive ideas and his pursuit of his experiment also encourage a kind of conformity throughout the school and town as everyone eventually realizes the use of a new word is harmless and fun.

Books with Similar Issues or Themes

Avi. *Nothing but the Truth: A Documentary Novel*. New York: Orchard Books, 1991.
> Humming quietly and refusing to adhere to the silent rule during the school's daily national anthem recording, Philip Malloy triggers a national free speech issue and exaggerated political drama to the detriment of his teacher and parents.

Byars, Betsy. *The Burning Questions of Bingo Brown*. New York: Viking, 1988.
> Sixth grader Bingo Brown begins to write some of life's questions in his school journal, wondering how he will find the answers and whether his teacher Mr. Markham has answers to his own questioning thoughts.

Gilson, Jamie. *Thirteen Ways to Sink a Sub*. Illustrated by Linda Strauss Edwards. New York: Lothrop, Lee & Shepard, 1982.
> When their very healthy teacher succumbs to illness, Hobie Hanson and his classmates are confident that their surefire way to sink their new substitute teacher, Miss Ivanovitch, will work, only to find that she may have her own plan in place.

Kaye, Marilyn. *Real Heroes*. New York: Harcourt Children's Books, 1993.
> When Kevin decides to support the rights of his HIV-positive teacher, he clashes with his police officer father, who supports the community and school board's wishes to fire the well-loved instructor.

Peck, Richard. *The Teacher's Funeral: A Comedy in Three Parts*. New York: Dial, 2004.
> When the teacher of a one-room 1904 rural Indiana schoolhouse dies, Russell hopes that the school board and his father will see reason to close it down, but he is completely taken by surprise when the new teacher happens to be his bossy, yet highly capable, older sister, who is quite a match for his shenanigans.

Author-Related Sources

"Andrew Clements." In vol. 104 of *Something about the Author*. Farmington Hills, MI: Gale Group, 1999, 21–6.

Official Web site for *Frindle:* http://www.frindle.com/ (accessed 1 January 2005).

Discussion Questions

For *Frindle*

1. Why is it important for Nick to create a new word and prove Mrs. Granger's original theory?

2. Why does Nick's experiment work so easily?

3. Is there any justification for the school authorities to try and stop Nick? Why?

4. How does Nick's little experiment turn into an issue of free speech for the entire town?

5. What is so surprising about the secret letter that Mrs. Granger kept for Nick?

6. Why do you think Mrs. Granger writes what she does in the letter, and how does she realize that Nick would succeed?

7. Why does Mrs. Granger secretly support Nick?

8. What new words or fads can you think of that have been started in the last two years?

Grape Thief

By Kristine L. Franklin

Cambridge, MA: Candlewick Press, 2003

Reading Level: . . . . Grades 5–7

Genre: . . . . Historical fiction—Depression era

Themes: . . . . Poverty, family responsibilities, education, multicultural relationships, religious faith, self-sufficiency

Plot Summary

Twelve-year-old Slava Petrovich, also known as "Cuss" for his unique talent of cursing in a variety of languages, is one of five children in an immigrant Croatian family living and trying to eek out a living during the Depression in the mining town of Roslyn, Washington. Fatherless, his mother earns money through her modest dairy cow business. Destined to become a miner like his two older brothers, Cuss loves to study and read books—he is determined to stay in school as long as possible. His other pleasures in life are fooling and playing with best friends, Perks, a boy from the black part of town, and Skinny, an Italian boy. The three work on a scheme to come away with the biggest grape heist from the annual grape train that passes through town from the vineyards of California for the bootleg wine-making business. When Slava's brothers are threatened by prohibition gangsters and must leave town to start new lives in California, Cuss assumes the oldest son's responsibility to make a living and realizes that his dream of getting an education is threatened. Facing the reality that work is also scarce in a town that is laying off miners, Cuss hatches a plan with Perks to stowaway on the returning grape train to California, where work is plentiful. His plan is complicated by several situations including younger brother Philip's life-threatening illness along with the stunning revelation that he will need $26 to bribe the train conductor and the railroad bull, Big Swede. Feeling desperate to help out his mother financially, who is about to lose the house to the mortgage bank, Cuss "borrows" the money from the church collection plate and gets on the train with Perks, but as they reach the outskirts of the town, Cuss changes his mind about his strategy and jumps off. Adult male role models Father Duval and Dr. Moody provide new direction through faith, encouragement, and a scholarship to attend a boarding school, and Mother and Philip find a way to continue to earn money even though they will live as boarders elsewhere. Slava's dream of finishing his education rather than working his life away in the mines is achieved.

Main Characterization

Slava Petrovich, known as Cuss, loves his family and feels his mother's burden of having to earn enough to support her family. He worries over his brothers' safety and situation and is willing to do the right thing to help the family by quitting school and going to work, even though his dream is to get an education. He is a good boy in every sense of the word, knowing right from wrong, and is unable to deal with his guilt after stealing money to leave town for a better chance at a job. He tells his story honestly and with the humor of a boy about to enter the responsible adult world.

Themes

Poverty is the central theme in this story, and it affects just about everyone's life in the town of Roslyn. Slava's voice offers a look into family relationships and subtly exposes the unique multicultural friendship he has with his buddies, Perks and Skinny, in contrast to the sometimes prejudicial attitude his mother has concerning marriage out of their Croatian ethnic group. Mother's deep religious faith helps her cope with hard times, and her pride fosters self-sufficiency in all her hardworking children.

Books with Similar Issues or Themes

Ayres, Katherine. *Macaroni Boy.* New York: Delacorte Press for Young Readers, 2003.
> In the 1933 Pittsburgh factory district, Mike Costa makes a connection between the dead rats he keeps finding on the street and an illness that is killing the hoboes and has affected his grandfather. He works with the neighborhood bully to prove his suspicion.

Collier, James Lincoln. *The Jazz Kid.* New York: Henry Holt, 1994.
> The jazz world of 1920s Chicago lures music lover and aspiring horn player Paulie Horvath into a world of gangsters and late-night jazz club life.

Levine, Gail Carson. *Dave at Night.* New York: HarperCollins, 1999.
> Living in the Hebrew Home for Boys, set in the Harlem Renaissance era of the 1920s, "Dave the Daredevil" finds a way to sneak out at night to enjoy the music and society life of the neighborhood.

Author-Related Sources

Kristine L. Franklin. In vol. 124 of *Something about the Author.* Farmington Hills, MI: Gale Group, 2002, 70–4.

Discussion Questions

For *Grape Thief*

1. Why do you think the three boys—Cuss, Perks, and Skinny—are such good friends despite their different cultural backgrounds?

2. How is Cuss different from his two friends and most of the boys in the town?

3. How do the three boys keep their lives interesting and upbeat despite the poverty and difficult situations of their families?

4. Why is Mary's gift of a poetry book so important to Cuss?

5. What is Cuss's big dilemma? What does his Latin essay tell you about what he thinks he should do?

6. What has Mrs. Petrovich taught all her children despite the hard times they face?

7. Why does Cuss jump off the train and give up his chance to reach California?

8. Why does Father Duval justify Cuss's stealing from the collection plate?

9. Why do both Father Duval and Dr. Moody encourage and help Cuss to continue his education? Why does his mother agree?

10. What does this story tell you about what is important in life, even in difficult times?

Harris and Me:
A Summer Remembered

By Gary Paulsen

San Diego: Harcourt, Brace, 1993

Reading Level: . . . . Grades 5–7

Genre: . . . . Humorous fiction

Themes: . . . . Friendship, rural versus city life, taking risks

Awards: . . . . ALA Notable Book, YALSA Best Books for Young Adults

Plot Summary

In this novel of characters, two cousins, boys aged nine and eleven, are brought together one summer when Harris, a rough and crude farm boy, must help his city cousin acclimate to a very different lifestyle. The nameless narrator is introduced to everything from milking cows, to catching mud-slippery pigs, to jumping from a hayloft, to the hard work of running a farm all intermixed with the crazy and almost always dangerous and hilarious exploits of his scheming younger cousin, Harris. The unsuspecting narrator learns quickly to follow along—with trepidation—as his boisterous, sometimes swearing, cousin involves him in much imaginative play. The result is some pretty funny, if precarious, real-life consequences. In the end, both boys are glad to have spent the summer together, each gaining insight and respect for each other. From the narrator's perspective, coming from his alcoholic home life, Harris's crazy family and lifestyle represent the real home that love and hard work can create.

Main Characterization

Harris is a daring, young, energetic boy who represents the culturally acceptable ideas of masculinity. He takes risks, is impulsive, and is unafraid of the dire consequences he may be creating through his actions. He is truly happy to have a playmate participate in all of his wild escapades.

The narrator ("Me") is a city boy, on a respite from his alcoholic home and totally inexperienced with rural farm life. Although older than his cousin Harris, he continues to follow his younger playmate's more "experienced" lead, despite previous negative outcomes. His humorous retelling brings to light his feelings of inadequacy marked by his intellectual sensibilities.

Themes

The contrast between a city and a country boy is evident in this novel of friendship. The need for mutual acceptance is evident as Harris continually convinces his cousin, the narrator, to join him, and the narrator always hesitantly follows, despite his misgivings. In addition, the idea of taking risks and not realizing consequences is explored through the humorous and almost always realistic, harmless results.

Books with Similar Issues or Themes

Fitzgerald, John Dennis. *The Great Brain*. Illustrated by Mercer Mayer. New York: Dial Books for Young Readers, 1967.
> Ten-year-old Tom, the "Great Brain," creates one adventure after another all the while scheming to make some money and sometimes getting his younger brother in a mess.

Gantos, Jack. *Heads or Tails: Stories from the Sixth Grade*. New York: HarperCollins, 1994.
> Jack relates many of his humorous and eye-opening experiences of his sixth-grade year.

Soto, Gary. *Summer on Wheels*. New York: Scholastic, 1995.
> Hector and his friend (*amigo*) Mando set out on an adventurous week-long bike trip from their neighborhood in East Los Angeles to the Santa Monica beach, with some unexpected results.

Peck, Robert Newton. *Soup*. Illustrated by Charles C. Gehm. New York: Alfred A Knopf, 1974.
> In an earlier and simpler time period, two boys use their imagination and surroundings to play and get into some humorous mischief.

Author-Related Sources

Berger, Laura Standley, ed. *Twentieth-Century Children's Writers*. Detroit, MI: St. James Press, 1995, 745–7.

"Gary Paulsen." In vol. 82 of *Children's Literature Review*. Farmington Hills, MI: Gale Group, 2003, 54–160.

"Gary Paulsen." In vol. 111 of *Something about the Author*. Farmington Hills, MI: Gale Group, 2000) 136–45.

Gary Paulsen's official Web site: http://www.randomhouse.com/features/garypaulsen/ (accessed 2 February 2005).

Hipple, Ted, ed. In vol. 2 of *Writers for Young Adults*. New York: Charles S. Scribner's Sons, 1997, 455–63.

Holtze, Sally Holmes, ed. *Sixth Book of Junior Authors and Illustrators*. New York: H. W. Wilson, 1989, 219.

Marcus, Leonard S., ed. *Author Talk: Conversations with Judy Blume et al.* New York: Simon & Schuster, 2000, 76–82.

Paulsen, Gary. *My Life in Dog Years*. With drawings by Ruth Wright Paulsen. New York: Delacorte Press, 1998.

Silvey, Anita, ed. *Children's Books and Their Creators*. Boston: Houghton Mifflin, 1995, 510–11.

Thomson, Sarah L. *Gary Paulsen*. New York: Rosen Central, 2003.

Discussion Questions

For *Harris and Me: A Summer Remembered*

1. What kind of person is the narrator?

2. How does he feel about farm life?

3. What kind of person is Harris?

4. Why does Harris do the things he does? Why is it important for his city cousin to join him?

5. What contrasts can you make between the two boys and their knowledge of the world?

6. Harris's language and use of swear words are pretty colorful. Why do you think the author felt it necessary to tell this story with that kind of dialogue?

7. What is the Larson family like?

8. Why do you think the narrator feels at home with the Larsons at the end of the summer?

9. What do both boys learn from each other?

10. What makes the boys' relationship so special?

Hoot

By Carl Hiaasen

New York: Alfred A. Knopf, 2002

Reading Level: . . . . Grades 5–7
Genre: . . . . Realistic fiction
Themes: . . . . Environmental protection, activism, bullying
Awards: . . . . Newbery Honor, ALA Notable Book, YALSA Best Books for Young Adults

Plot Summary

Roy Eberhardt's new city of Coconut Cove in south Florida, along with his new middle school, are as different from his Montana home as he can imagine. In addition to a lack of four seasons, Roy is unimpressed by the flat, expansively ugly terrain of the area. Avoiding Dana Matherson's unpleasant bullying tactics on the school bus has taken priority over making new friends. Riding the bus one morning with his head plastered against the window, thanks to Dana's surprise ambush from behind, Roy sees a boy running barefoot, without a book bag, and is intrigued by his speed and destination. Roy's curiosity is strong, and he begins to do some investigating to find out who this boy is and what he's up to. At the same time, the construction site of a proposed restaurant is being continually vandalized in strange ways. As Roy follows the boy, he learns this runaway is on a mission to save a group of burrowing owls from losing their natural home to the proposed site of the new restaurant. Roy has two major issues concerning his life. First is to take care of the seriously dangerous Dana in a way, without violence, that will get him out of his life. Second is to help the boy, known as Mullet Fingers, to expose the illegal actions of the restaurant company's construction in violation of the protection of the miniature owls. Heeding advice from his supportive parents about deciding right from wrong and settling the argument between his heart and brain, Roy decides to make the owls' fate public by bringing it out in his current events class. With the media's attention at the restaurant's groundbreaking photo opportunity, Roy and his classmates demonstrate and expose the corporation's wrongdoings.

Main Characterization

Roy Eberhardt is a smart, reasonable boy, who abhors violence and enjoys nature and the beauty of the environment. Through his relationship with Mullet Fingers and the hidden creek he brings him to, Roy learns to appreciate Florida's tropical scenery. He is able to take a proactive role both in his situation concerning Dana's threatening behavior and in helping to save the burrowing owls' existence with clever solutions.

Mullet Fingers is a boy neglected and abused by his mother who has managed to live his life on the run, hiding and taking care of himself. He appears as a somewhat legendary character, able to pull off certain feats of vandalism that are quite impressive and troublesome to both the police and the construction company.

Beatrice Leep is a large, strong, tough girl who fiercely protects her stepbrother, Mullet Fingers, and develops a loyalty to Roy.

Dana Matherson is a classic bully, with a violent attitude and behavior that becomes seriously dangerous when he attacks Roy at school.

Themes

Two simultaneous plots are woven together to bring out themes of environmental protection, activism, and bullying. Roy's involvement with the protection of the burrowing owls and his activist's role in helping to take on a powerful corporation and corrupt city government is balanced against the bullying tactics of both the company's management and the more serious and physical bullying of Dana Matherson.

Books with Similar Issues or Themes

Cooper, Susan. *Green Boy*. New York: Margaret K. McElderry Books, 2002.
> Twelve-year-old Trey and seven-year-old mute Lou work to save the natural environment of both an alien world and a Bahamian island.

DeFelice, Cynthia. *Lostman's River*. New York: Macmillan, 1994.
> Thirteen-year-old Ty must decide whether helping to earn a living to ease his family's poverty is worth a job that will destroy the ecosystem of the Florida Everglades.

George, Jean Craighead. *The Missing 'Gator of Gumbo Limbo*. New York: HarperCollins, 1992.
> Liza Poole is determined to protect a ten-foot alligator named Dajun, living in one of the last balanced ecosystems in the nation, from being shot by the state official hired by the neighboring threatened residents.

George, Jean Craighead. *Who Really Killed Cock Robin?* New York: HarperCollins, 1971, 1991.
> Eighth-grader Tony unravels an ecological mystery that has caused the death of a well-known town bird and left the town park overrun with ants and no singing frogs.

Sharpe, Susan. *Waterman's Boy*. New York: Bradbury Press, 1990.
> Eleven-year-old Ben helps a government scientist clean up the Chesapeake Bay oil spill at the risk of hurting the livelihood that his waterman father depends on.

Author-Related Sources

Carl Hiaasen's official Web site: http://www.carlhiaasen.com/ (accessed 29 January 2005).

Discussion Questions

For *Hoot*

1. What was important in Roy's life before he met Mullet Fingers?

2. What sparks Roy's curiosity about what Mullet Fingers is doing?

3. What is right or wrong about how Roy handled Dana's bullying?

4. What is Roy's dilemma in telling everyone about the burrowing owls?

5. In deciding right from wrong, how does Roy settle the argument between his heart and his brain?

6. What is important to Mullet Fingers?

7. How does Roy find a way to use the media to his advantage to help save the owls?

8. What lets you know that Roy has finally adjusted to his new Florida life?

An Island Far from Home

By John Donahue

Minneapolis, MN: Carolrhoda Books, 1995

Reading Level: . . . . Grades 4–6
Genre: . . . . Historical fiction
Themes: . . . . Friendship, prejudice

Plot Summary

The Civil War is nearly over, but thirteen-year-old Joshua Loring hopes it will continue until he reaches the age to enlist and avenge the death of his physician father who was killed at the Battle of Fredericksburg. His Uncle Robert is the commanding officer at the prisoner-of-war camp on George's Island off the coast of Boston and a frequent visitor to Joshua's home in Tilton, Massachusetts. On one such visit, Uncle Robert makes an unusual request of Joshua. A new confederate prisoner named John Meadows, a boy the same age as Joshua, has arrived at the camp. Uncle Robert suggests that Joshua write him a letter to help allay his loneliness and isolation in a prisoner-of-war camp full of men. Joshua is outraged and resentful that such a request be made of him when he feels such hatred and disdain for the "Rebs" that killed his father. He also worries that others would view him as a traitor. But Uncle Robert explains that John is just a boy in a rough situation and urges Joshua to think about writing. Similarly, in his classroom, Joshua's teacher, Mr. Rawson, introduces a letter-writing campaign for the Yankee soldiers who are currently fighting in the war. As the class works on this project from week to week, Joshua thinks about his uncle's request, becomes curious about the boy prisoner and cautiously drafts a brief introductory letter. With John Meadows's response, a pen-pal relationship develops along with mutual respect, as Joshua realizes the many similarities they share and begins to understand the Southern perspective on the war. When it is Joshua's turn to offer the name of a soldier to whom the class should send letters, his choice is John Meadows, a Rebel prisoner. This results in an immediate reaction of anger and resentment throughout the classroom. Feeling the isolation of lost friendships, including that of his best friend Hogan, Joshua is determined to meet John before the war ends and all the prisoners are sent home. Disobeying his uncle's statement that George's Island is for army personnel only, Joshua finds a way to sneak onto a barge headed for the island, only to get caught and thrown into the prison as a possible spy. Luck plus the goodwill of another prisoner bring Joshua in contact with John for some brief, harrowing moments as they try unsuccessfully to implement an escape plan, only to be rescued by Uncle Robert as he enters the perilous scene.

Main Characterization

Joshua Loring is thirteen with a romantic view of war and a negative, preconceived idea of Confederate soldiers. Eager to join the army, he dreams of a heroic battle in which he emerges a famous victor. His curiosity sparked by the respect he holds for his Uncle Robert lets him write the first letter to John Meadows. It is that same curiosity that leads him to the daring visit on George's Island.

John Meadows, from his letters, appears to be a thoughtful, quiet, and sad boy, years beyond his age in experience. When confronted with Joshua's situation in the prison, he is willing to help him escape regardless of the added danger it might bring him.

197

Themes

Friendship is an overall theme here, shown through the two relationships that Joshua maintains, first with his best school friend Hogan, and second with the correspondence relationship he develops with John. Both boys are willing to risk their own well-being to help a friend. In addition, we see how preconceived thinking can prejudice a person's outlook as John opens Joshua's eyes to reality with reasons for his fighting that seem reasonable—protection of family, property, and one's rights. Their pen-pal relationship indicates that, as two American boys, the two have more similarities than differences.

Books with Similar Issues or Themes

Avi. *The Fighting Ground*. New York: J. B. Lippincott, 1984.
> Thirteen-year-old Jonathan disobeys his father and joins a small group of Revolutionary War fighters only to learn that his enemy may be very much like himself.

Collier, James Lincoln. *With Every Drop of Blood*. New York: Delacorte Press, 1994.
> Feeling the need to earn money to help his family after his father is killed in the Civil War, Johnny agrees to transport food to the Confederate troops and is caught by a black Union soldier, who provides a unique friendship.

Perez, Norah. *The Slopes of War*. Boston: Houghton Mifflin, 1984.
> Cousins are forced to fight on opposite sides in the Battle of Gettysburg.

Polacco, Patricia. *Pink and Say*. New York: Philomel Books, 1994.
> An African American soldier and a white boy are brought together under dire and brutal circumstances during the Civil War.

Wisler, G. Clifton. *Red Cap*. New York: Lodestar Books, 1991.
> During the Civil War, Ransom, thirteen years old, runs away to become a drummer boy for the Union Army and is taken prisoner to Libby and Andersonville prisons in the South.

Discussion Questions

For *An Island Far from Home*

1. How does Joshua Loring feel about the war?

2. How does John Meadows feel about the war?

3. What are some of the problems or conflicts that Joshua and John face?

4. How do they resolve the conflicts they have?

5. Why does Joshua decide to send the first letter to John?

6. Why do both boys continue writing to each other?

7. How do the war and the pen-pal relationship change Joshua and John's life?

8. How is Joshua and Hogan's relationship affected by Joshua's experience? Why does Hogan help him out in the end?

9. What does the author tell us about friendship in this story?

10. Can you compare Joshua's conflict and situation with a similar one in our world today?

James and the Giant Peach: A Children's Story

By Roald Dahl, Illustrated by Nancy Ekholm Burkert

New York: Alfred A. Knopf, 1961

Reading Level: . . . . Grades 4–6

Genre: . . . . Fantasy/adventure

Themes: . . . . Good versus evil, imagination/ingenuity, friendship, differences

Plot Summary

James Henry Trotter's happy childhood takes a turn for the worse when his parents are eaten by a London zoo runaway rhinoceros and he is forced to live with his only relatives, the evil Aunt Sponge and wicked Aunt Spiker. In the midst of his misery, James encounters a strange little man in the garden who presents him with a small bag full of magical things that look like tiny green crystals. The crystals have the power to make everything enormous, and when they are accidentally dropped on the ground, they infiltrate nature. In a matter of minutes, the peach tree has developed one gigantic peach. Rather than cutting it and eating it, the enterprising Aunt Spiker sees the opportunity to sell tickets to view the peach, but before her fortune can be made, the downtrodden and neglected James, fending for himself in the dark, is mysteriously drawn to the peach, crawls through a tunnel, and finds himself within the colossal fruit pit, welcomed by six overgrown insects and creatures. Old-Green-Grasshopper, Miss Spider, Ladybug, Centipede, Earthworm, Glow-worm, and Silkworm all behave differently and tell James about their unique talents. Making James at home, they all settle down for the night only to awake in the morning to the sounds and sensation of movement. The peach has broken off its branch and is rapidly rolling down the hill squashing everything in sight including James's two Aunts. Thus begins an adventurous journey across the Atlantic Ocean for James and his new friends, who must escape numerous threats from sharks, nasty cloud men, hail and rainstorms before reaching a new life in New York City.

Main Characterization

James, beleaguered, neglected, and abused by his aunts, possesses resourcefulness, curiosity, and ingenuity that help him flee his dire circumstances and embark on a remarkably new and different life. He is a well-mannered boy, courageous and clever in his unique ability to create workable, albeit inventive solutions to the perilous predicaments that arise on his wondrous journey. His new friends represent a variety of personalities and talents as diverse as any group of people. Old-Green-Grasshopper is cheerful, reasonable, and quite musical. Miss Spider is encouraging and helpful with her spinning. Ladybug is dainty and sweet. The cantankerous and grumpy Centipede clashes with the pessimistic and unhappy Earthworm, while the quiet Glow-worm is barely heard like her sleepy counterpart, Silkworm.

Themes

The powerful force of good over evil is evident in how the good child James is provided with an opportunity to leave the wickedness of his environment. The adventurous trip is not without its own evil occurrences that are also overpowered by the cooperative efforts of the travelers, working together toward a successful conclusion.

Books with Similar Issues or Themes

Bellairs, John. *The House with a Clock in its Walls*. Illustrated by Edward Gorey. New York: Dial Books, 1973.
> Lewis knows he must find the hidden clock in the walls of his Uncle Jonathan's house, placed there by the former owner and evil wizard Isaac Izard with a plan to bring about the end of the world.

Fleischman, Paul. *Half-a-Moon Inn*. Illustrated by Kathy Jacobi. New York: Harper & Row, 1980.
> Searching for his lost mother in a blizzard, a mute boy stumbles upon an inn where the scheming Miss Grackle holds him captive.

Pinkwater, Daniel. *Borgel*. New York: Macmillan, 1990.
> Melvin takes an extraordinary trip across time and space with his supposed 111-year-old Uncle Borgel in his 1937 hot-wired Dorbzeldge Sedan.

Scieszka, Jon. *Time Warp Trio*. Illustrated by Lane Smith. New York: Viking, 1991.
> In this series, three boys find their way across many time periods through the magic of "the book."

Author-Related Sources

Berger, Laura Standley, ed. *Twentieth-Century Young Adult Writers*. Detroit, MI: St. James Press, 1994, 167–9.

Dahl, Roald. *Boy: Tales of Childhood*. New York: Puffin Books, 1984.

Dahl, Roald. *Going Solo*. New York: Puffin Books, 1999.

"Roald Dahl." In vol. 41 of *Children's Literature Review*. Farmington Hills, MI: Gale Group, 1997, 1–50.

"Roald Dahl." In vol. 73 of *Something about the Author*. Farmington Hills, MI: Gale Group, 1993, 39–46.

Shields, Charles J. *Roald Dahl*. Philadelphia: Chelsea House, 2002.

Silvey, Anita, ed. *Children's Books and Their Creators*. Boston: Houghton Mifflin, 1995, 185–6.

Discussion Questions

For *James and the Giant Peach: A Children's Story*

1. What kind of boy is James?

2. How does James view his new friends at first? How does he view them by the end of their journey?

3. What talents and personalities do the insects and other creatures bring to the adventure?

4. What kind of talent does James have?

5. Why are the characters successful in meeting all the challenges on their adventurous trip?

6. Would you consider James to be a hero in this story?

7. What does James gain from the little man's gift?

8. How does James's adventure change his outlook on life?

9. How does author Roald Dahl depict good and evil in his story?

10. What message does Roald Dahl give in this fantasy?

11. Compare the original illustrations done by Nancy Ekholm Burkert in the 1961 Knopf edition to the illustrations done by Lane Smith in the 1996 Knopf edition. Which do you like better? What are the differences that give the story a different view?

Jim Ugly

By Sid Fleischman, Illustrated by Jos. A. Smith

New York: Greenwillow Books, 1992

Reading Level: . . . . Grades 4–5

Genre: . . . . Adventure/mystery

Themes: . . . . Trust, suspicion, honesty

Plot Summary

Jake Bannock has a mystery to solve involving the "deadly" disappearance of his father, Sam, and the appearance of a series of strange people who think his father is involved in a diamond theft scheme. After the funeral staged by his Uncle Axie, Jake refuses to believe his father is really dead and is left with Jim Ugly, Sam's mongrel wolf-dog, as the only way to search out the truth. Using the dog's keen sense of smell, Jake embarks on a wild chase in pursuit of his vaudeville actor father's whereabouts, followed keenly by the villainous D. D. Skeats, alleged bounty hunter for the diamond thieves. Along the way, from the mountains of Blowfly, Nevada, to the city of San Francisco, Jake meets actors Wilhelmina and Cornelius, who also play roles in the mysterious diamond entanglement. The magical world of the theatre brings Jake to a reunion with his father and to an understanding about a false report of a diamond mine, a swindler's deal Cornelius made with D. D. Skeats, and Wilhelmina's engagement and upcoming marriage to Sam. Jake gains a respect for Jim Ugly's indispensable sniffing talents, and in the end, the two come to their own understanding as Jake begins to call the dog by the name his father originally gave him: Amigo, Spanish for "friend."

Main Characterization

The characters in this story are drawn in a somewhat exaggerated style of a "Wild West" scenario. Jake Bannock is a curious, determined, and courageous boy, distrustful of his immediate circumstances and eager to find out the truth behind his father's mysterious disappearance. D. D. Skeats, Wilhelmina, and Cornelius are all caricatures of nineteenth-century western figures representing the gun-slinging bounty hunters and vaudeville traveling actors that bring a comedic atmosphere to the story.

The character of the dog, Jim Ugly, is developed as a loyal yet independent animal who holds the key to the mystery's solution.

Themes

Themes of trust and honesty are employed in this story—somewhat of a tall tale—of a western mystery, as Jake is distrustful of most of the adults he has encountered trying to understand his father's disappearance. Suspicion is woven throughout the story as each character's personality and motives are continually muddled until the last revealing scene.

Books with Similar Issues or Themes

Clifford, Eth. *The Dastardly Murder of Dirty Pete*. Illustrated by George Hughes. Boston: Houghton Mifflin, 1981.
    On a road trip to the west coast, a family stumbles on a ghost town and a mysterious adventure.

Glass, Andrew. *Sweetwater Run*. New York: Doubleday, 1996.
    Thirteen-year-old Cody is given a chance at riding the Pony Express when two riders are injured and a mailbag with some top-secret important information must be delivered.

Hahn, Mary Downing. *The Gentleman Outlaw and Me—Eli: A Story of the Old West*. New York: Clarion Books, 1996.
    Twelve-year-old Eliza Yates, dresses as a boy, changes her name to Elijah Bates, sets out to look for her missing father, and teams up with Calvin Featherbone, a naïve eighteen-year-old con artist whose schemes result in more trouble.

Sachar, Louis. *Holes*. New York: Farrar, Straus & Giroux, 1998.
    When Stanley Yelnats finds himself in a boys' detention camp for a theft he did not commit, he becomes involved in uncovering a mysterious crime of greater proportions.

Author-Related Sources

Berger, Laura Standley, ed. *Twentieth-Century Children's Writers*. Detroit, MI: St. James Press, 1995, 357–8.

"Sid Fleischman." In vol. 148 of *Something about the Author*. Farmington Hills, MI: Gale Group, 2004, 71–9.

"Sid Fleischman." In vol. 15 of *Children's Literature Review*. Farmington Hills, MI: Gale Research, 1988, 101–13.

Sid Fleischman Web site: http://www.sidfleischman.com/ (accessed 3 January 2005).

Silvey, Anita, ed. *Children's Books and Their Creators*. Boston: Houghton Mifflin, 1995, 245–7.

Discussion Questions

For *Jim Ugly*

1. Who do you think is the main character of this story, Jake or Jim Ugly?

2. Why does Jake put so much trust in Jim Ugly's sniffing talents?

3. How does Jake and Jim Ugly's relationship differ from the beginning to the end of the story?

4. How does the author make trust an important issue in this story?

5. How does the author make this story seem like a cartoon in some scenes?

6. How do Jake's descriptions using similes and metaphors let you visually see the scenes without the use of illustrations?

7. How important are the pen-and-ink illustrations in the book?

8. What makes this story believable and yet somewhat like a tall tale?

The Kite Rider

By Geraldine McCaughrean

New York: HarperCollins, 2001

Reading Level: . . . . Grades 6–8
Genre: . . . . Historical fiction/thirteenth-century China
Themes: . . . . Family responsibility, bravery, betrayal, obedience

Plot Summary

The chance to work as a kite-rider in the Jade Circus offers twelve-year-old Haoyou a way out of the poverty and despair he and his mother suffer after the tragic death of his father. His father, Pei, a sailor, died in the sky tied to a kite testing the direction of the winds for the cruel and villainous first mate, Di Chou. Haoyou is a talented kite maker and is motivated to fly with the circus to protect his beautiful mother from being married off to Di Chou, whom Haoyou views as his father's murderer, to seal a financial arrangement his Great Uncle Bo has made as head of the family. So Haoyou follows the Great Miao, the circus master, and begins to perform for audiences throughout Cathay (thirteenth-century China), eventually appearing before the court of Kublai Khan. He takes with him a distant cousin, Mipeng, who has fooled many with her clairvoyant abilities, acting as a medium between the dead and living. Haoyou's relationship with his father continues almost every time he flies, for he believes he sees his spirit helping him stay safe and make decisions. But the danger from Di Chou and even his greedy Uncle Bo is always present; both men try to have their way with the money Haoyou earns and with the unfulfilled promise of marriage. Haoyou's greatest ally is his trusted employer, Miao, who tries to protect him from both the physical and emotional abuse of his family's leader. Haoyou's biggest problem is his obligation to obey his uncle, behavior he reasons is one his father would have expected, thus creating conflict and renewed despair as he turns over his earnings to a man who will simply gamble it away. Finding his mother and baby sister living in squalor on a return trip from the circus, Haoyou comes to the realization that his uncle along with Di Chou will selfishly use his family for their pleasure and gain. Haoyou rescues his family and leaves with the help of Miao and Mipeng to live a proud life with the circus, earning an honest living.

Main Characterization

Haoyou is a family boy, devoted to his mother, eager to behave obediently as he believes his father would have wanted. He is blinded by this virtue, at first unable to admit that obedience to an elder should not be maintained if it means sacrificing his family's well-being. His adventurous and harrowing escapes from the evil Di Chou eventually turn his thinking around, bringing a new understanding of the need for self-protection and independence.

Mipeng is a wise young woman who lives her life beyond and outside the traditional role of a woman in thirteenth-century China. She makes her own choices and speaks out against her uncle, trying to instill a sense of independence to her less experienced younger cousin Haoyou.

Miao Jie, or the Great Miao, is the circus owner and master, a kind-hearted gentleman who is disgusted by the behavior of the two villains, the greedy and thieving Great Uncle Bo and the evil-minded Di Chou. He serves as a fatherly role model to the young Haoyou.

Themes

Following his father's death, Haoyou feels the weight and burden of his family's well-being and takes responsibility for their support. He is continually betrayed by both his great uncle and the evil Di Chou but must bravely decide to disobey rather than risk the dangerous life his mother and sister will have to endure. Haoyou is torn between respecting his elders at any cost and making the right choice for his family.

Books with Similar Issues or Themes

Park, Linda Sue. *The Kite Fighters*. New York: Clarion, 2000.
    In fifteenth-century Korea, two brothers overcome their sibling rivalry to work together as creator and skilled flyer to compete in a New Year's kite-fighting contest.

Paterson, Katherine. *Rebels of the Heavenly Kingdom*. New York: Lodestar Books, 1983.
    Fifteen-year-old Wang Lee is encouraged to join the followers of the Taiping Rebellion as he is rescued from kidnapping slave-trade bandits.

Author-Related Sources

Berger, Laura Standley, ed. *Twentieth-Century Young Adult Writers*. Detroit, MI: St. James Press, 1994, 434–6.

"Geraldine McCaughrean." In vol. 38 of *Children's Literature Review*. Farmington Hills, MI: Gale Research, 1996, 131–52.

"Geraldine McCaughrean." In vol. 139 of *Something about the Author*. Farmington Hills, MI: Gale Group, 2003, 157–62.

Discussion Questions

For *The Kite Rider*

1. At first, Haoyou is reluctant to fly the kites he has made. Once he has made his first flight, how does he feel about kite-riding and why?

2. What gives Haoyou the courage and fortitude to become a kite-rider?

3. In what ways do Miao, Uncle Bo, and Mipeng play significant roles in Haoyou's life?

4. What does Haoyou believe about obedience and respecting his elders? How does this create a conflict for him?

5. Why is Mipeng an unusual character for this story's setting and time period?

6. Would you consider Haoyou to be a hero?

7. How does superstition affect the way Haoyou and Mipeng lead their lives?

8. Why is the circus a good place for Haoyou and Mipeng to earn a living?

9. What does Haoyou learn about life and family by the end of the story?

The Master Puppeteer

By Katherine Paterson, Illustrated by Haru Wells

New York: Thomas Y. Crowell, 1975

Reading Level: . . . . Grades 5–7
Genre: . . . . Historical fiction eighteenth-century Japan
Themes: . . . . Responsibility, values, honor
Awards: . . . . National Book Award

Plot Summary

The famine in eighteenth-century Osaka, Japan, forces many to search for food and rise up in angry desperation. Twelve-year-old Jiro is fortunate to apprentice at Hanaza, the puppet theater company where his father sells handcrafted dolls and where food for the staff is plentiful. At the theater, Jiro is mentored by Kinshi, who is older, more experienced, and the son of the master puppeteer, Yoshida. There is also the kindly, old blind chanter, Okada, who narrates the stories during the performances. The starvation in the city has spawned mass riots encouraged by the legendary Saburo, a Robin Hood–type character who steals from the wealthy to give to the poor. When night rovers infiltrate the theatrical life, Jiro is disturbed to make a connection between the elder figures in the theater and the mysterious Saburo. He also learns that his father is part of the riotous throng and has been secretly working with Saburo, abandoning his mother, Isako, and leaving her with no means to buy food. Saburo is really Okada, who, as the genuine master puppeteer, manipulates and gives his orders through the stern Yoshida. Jiro and Kinshi work together to rescue Jiro's mother and are caught in the dangerous chaos of the streets. They must come to terms with the knowledge that both their fathers are involved with the uprising as their own values of right and wrong are questioned. In the end, the boys come to an understanding with both men and the elder, Okada, that their silence concerning the deception will protect Isako until the uprisings have proven effective in the struggle for the oppressed.

Main Characterization

Jiro loves both his parents very much and is eager to help their financial situation by working as an apprentice. His naïveté about his father's involvement with Saburo's thievery places him in a precarious situation with the elder puppeteers at the theater. He is torn between his own sense of values and his attempt to understand his father's reasons for maintaining a secret allegiance with Saburo at the expense of abandoning his wife and son. Simultaneously, Kinshi is also different from his stern, rigid father, emotionally sensitive and willing to risk his life to help Jiro find his mother. He routinely helps his work mates by "stealing" the scripts so that they will learn their roles and cues more easily.

Themes

Jiro displays a sense of responsibility for his mother and for his behavior. Both he and his friend Kinshi struggle to justify and understand their fathers' behavior beyond the basic concept of theft and destruction within the larger concept of working against a government of an oppressed society.

Moral values play alongside honor and respect as Jiro vows to maintain Okada's secret as the identity of Saburo to shelter his mother at the theater away from the chaotic and famished outside world.

Books with Similar Issues or Themes

Haugaard, Erik Christian. *The Samurai's Tale*. Boston: Houghton Mifflin, 1984.
    The orphaned son of a samurai is brought to the general Takeda Shingen, where he learns the skill of a samurai and vows to fight the enemies of his murdered family.

McCaughrean, Geraldine. *The Kite Rider*. New York: HarperCollins, 2001.
    Trying to save his widowed mother from a brutal second marriage, twelve-year-old Haoyou joins the thirteenth-century Chinese Jade Circus and performs by soaring through the sky attached to a beautiful scarlet and gold kite.

Namioka, Lensey. *Den of the White Fox*. San Diego, Harcourt, Brace, 1997.
    In sixteenth-century Japan, two samurai warriors, Konishi Zenta and Ishihara Matsuzo, become involved in the mystery of the White Fox—is he a rebellious political leader or a man with more sinister motives?

Park, Linda Sue. *A Single Shard*. New York: Clarion Books, 2001.
    Thirteen-year-old Tree-ear becomes the apprentice to a potter in medieval Korea and aspires to create the unique and honored celadon ceramics.

Author-Related Sources

Berger, Laura Standley, ed. *Twentieth-Century Children's Writers*. Detroit, MI: St. James Press, 1995, 740–2.

Cary, Alice. *Katherine Paterson*. Santa Barbara, CA: Learning Works, 1997.

Hipple, Ted, ed. In vol. 2 of *Writers for Young Adults*. New York: Charles S. Scribner's Sons, 1997, 443–54.

"Katherine Paterson." In vol. 50 of *Children's Literature Review*. Farmington Hills, MI: Gale Group, 1999, 165–207.

"Katherine Paterson." In vol. 133 of *Something about the Author*. Farmington Hills, MI: Gale Group, 2002, 134–44.

Katherine Paterson's Official Web site: http://www.terabithia.com/ (accessed 30 May 2004).

Paterson, Katherine. *Gates of Excellence: On Reading and Writing Books for Children*. New York: Dutton/Lodester, 1981.

Paterson, Katherine. *A Sense of Wonder: On Reading and Writing Books for Children*. New York: Plume, 1995.

Schmidt, Gary D. *Katherine Paterson*. New York: Twayne, 1984.

Discussion Questions

For *The Master Puppeteer*

1. Why do you think Jiro's father, Hanji, does not want his son to join the Hanaza puppet theater company?

2. What do you think Okada or Saburo are trying to achieve by leading the night roving riots?

3. Why do Jiro and Kinshi become such good friends?

4. How do Jiro and Kinshi feel about their fathers' actions and involvement with Saburo?

5. Why does Jiro agree to keep Okada's identity secret from the police despite the reward money he would receive to help his mother?

6. What does Yoshida mean when he tells Jiro, "Sometimes a man must pay a heavy price to maintain his oath"?

7. Why does Jiro feel he has offended Okada's honor? How does he maintain his own honor?

8. Which important values do both boys, Jiro and Kinshi, believe in?

9. How does the author symbolically use the make-believe world of puppets to tell this story of Jiro's world?

10. What is the role of the master puppeteer in both worlds?

The Million Dollar Shot

By Dan Gutman

New York: Hyperion Books, 1997

Reading Level: . . . . Grades 3–4

Genre: . . . . Realistic fiction

Themes: . . . . Ethical behavior, honesty

Plot Summary

Eddie Ball likes to play basketball as a diversion from his humble trailer-park life. His Mom, along with others in the community, have recently been laid off from the Finkle Foods company that produces candy bars as its main product. When factory owner George Finkle offers an advertising promotional poetry contest with a chance at winning a million dollars by sinking one ball into the net at the NBA finals, Eddie leaps at the opportunity as a way to solve his home financial problems. His rap version of an advertising jingle is totally rejected by his new friend Annie Stokely, a pretty good basketball player herself with her own two-line lyrical version. Annie refuses to enter the contest, resentful of her father's lost job and unwilling to help Finkle with his own financial business woes. Eddie, however, takes her poem, sends it to the contest, and actually wins the chance to throw the million dollar shot at the finals game in New York City's Madison Square Garden. Offering to share the winnings with Annie, Eddie begins to practice with her father, a former college basketball star who teaches him the secret to the basketball throw. Eddie's practice and concentration start to work and when George Finkle realizes he might actually have to come through with his million dollar prize, he makes Eddie another clandestine offer—a college scholarship and the promise to rehire his mother. All Eddie needs to do is purposely miss the shot. Finkle's factory is in financial jeopardy and the million dollar winnings will contribute to the company's demise. Faced with the dilemma of a sure chance at some financial relief versus the fortuitous chance at a successful basketball shot, Eddie must also come to terms with an ethical decision and whether he wants to participate in George Finkle's fraudulent ways.

Main Characterization

Eddie Ball is confronted with an unusual choice. Eager to help his unemployed mother and provide some financial relief, he must weigh his options between a sense of job security (albeit through a low-wage factory position) against the somewhat improbable, one-time throw of a lifetime. Ultimately, doing the right thing rather than making the wrong choice, coupled with his pride and encouragement from those who care about him, become the issues that help him make an honest decision regardless of whether he will win the prize.

Annie Stokely is a strong-minded, independent girl unafraid to express her thoughts honestly.

George Finkle is a stereotypical villain and bully with the somewhat humorous attributes of a desperate man eager to take advantage of every opportunity for his own gain.

Themes

Themes of ethics and making choices with a sense of good values and morals are evident in Eddie's dilemma as he is pressured to do the right thing while worrying about the ultimate financial outcome for his family. Honesty is another theme seen through George Finkle's behavior and reflecting on Eddie's decision.

Books with Similar Issues or Themes

French, Michael. *The Throwing Season*. New York: Delacorte Press, 1980.
> Rather than lose his chance for a scholarship, Henry Chevrolet, known as Indian, is determined to compete fairly in the state high school shot-put competition despite an angry, corrupt businessman's bribe to coerce Henry to purposely lose the shot.

Konigsburg, E. L. *The View from Saturday*. New York: Atheneum for Young Readers, 1996.
> Four sixth graders are teamed to compete for the championship academic quiz bowl and learn about each other in the process.

Korman, Gordon. *Maxx Comedy*. New York: Hyperion, 2003.
> Eleven-year-old Max Carmody dreams of being a stand-up comic and enters a contest to find the funniest kid in America.

Peck, Robert Newton. *Soup Ahoy*. Illustrated by Charles Robinson. New York: Knopf, 1994.
> The humorous series continues when Soup and his best friend Rob enter a radio contest and win the prize—a visit from the radio personality Sinker O. Sailor to their Vermont town.

Author-Related Sources

"Dan Gutman." In vol. 139 of *Something about the Author*. Farmington Hills, MI: Gale Group, 2003, 111–14.

Dan Gutman's Web site: http://www.dangutman.com/ (accessed 30 January 2005).

Discussion Questions

For *The Million Dollar Shot*

1. What is Eddie's dilemma?

2. How does Mr. Stokely help Eddie, beyond teaching him the techniques of shooting baskets?

3. What helped Eddie make a decision that he felt was the right one?

4. What rules does Eddie try to follow as he thinks about the choice he has to make between Mr. Finkle's offer and the contest?

5. What does Eddie gain beside the money from his experience with the contest?

6. Would Eddie and his mother have been winners if he had missed the shot honestly?

7. What would Eddie and his mother have gained if he had taken Mr. Finkle's offer?

8. How does fame affect Eddie and his mother?

9. What do you think of Dan Gutman's writing style at the end of the book?

10. What ending did you expect the story to have? What ending would you have written if you were the author?

Run, Boy, Run

By Uri Orlev, Translated by Hillel Halkin

Boston: Houghton Mifflin, 2003

Reading Level: . . . . Grades 6–8

Genre: . . . . Historical fiction

Themes: . . . . Survival, the Holocaust

Awards: . . . . ALA Batchelder Award

Plot Summary

Eight-year-old Srulik Frydman finds himself alone losing his Jewish family to the death and destruction of Nazi rule in his Polish village. Remembering the last words his father told him, Srulik changes his name to Jurik Staniak and learns to live as a Christian, wandering for the next two years from village to village, hiding out in the neighboring forest, foraging for anything edible, and accepting offers of food and temporary shelter in exchange for work from the Polish farmers he continually encounters. But the danger of his Jewish identity being discovered is always foremost and present as many of the Polish farmers are eager to turn in Jews for a reward. Jurik must always keep his clothes on to hide his circumcision and learn the Christian way of praying. Over the course of the two years, Jurik is captured, turned in to Gestapo headquarters, and made to work on the farm of a German officer's girlfriend. Well fed and taken care of, Jurik nevertheless has a tragic accident when his arm is caught in a threshing machine. Taken to the hospital, the German doctor refuses to operate on a Jew, and Jurik eventually loses his arm to gangrene. Remembering his father's words and instruction to live at all cost, Jurik manages to teach himself many skills, using one arm and hand. But he is marked now as the one-armed Jewish boy and is continually being chased or captured. Finally during one of his clever and bold escapes, Jurik passes into Russian-held territory and is befriended by one of the soldiers. His two-year ordeal finally ends with the liberation of Poland. Thinking he can lead his life now as a Christian within a family that is willing to keep him, Jurik is nevertheless taken by a Jewish refugee agency and then given a new life, with education and a future, in Israel. This story is all the more amazing and poignant because it is based on the true experiences of one such Polish boy.

Main Characterization

Srulik/Jurik is a boy forced to keep himself alive and hidden through any means. From some older Jewish boys, he quickly learns the arts of stealing, looting, and, most important, self-preservation. He learns hard lessons for an eight-year-old, yet ones necessary for his only mission—survival. Jurik is clever, bold, daring, and also vulnerable in his dependence on the Christian Polish community. He also manages to keep a certain boyish mentality, willing to play with others when the opportunity arises.

Themes

Survival at all costs in a brutally cruel wartime environment is portrayed in a realistically descriptive story of a daily endurance requiring both mental and physical fortitude.

Books with Similar Issues or Themes

Matas, Carol. *Daniel's Story*. New York: Scholastic, 1993.
> Daniel secretly records with a hidden camera the brutal and devastatingly cruel life he lives and witnesses during his deportation to Auschwitz and Buchenwald.

Napoli, Donna Jo. *Stones in Water*. New York: Dutton Children's Books, 1997.
> Roberto, an Italian boy, is taken with his Jewish friend Samuele by German soldiers to work in a labor camp. Following Samuele's death from a cruel beating, Roberto escapes and must survive a hellish river trip, navigating his way back to his own country.

Orlev, Uri. *The Island on Bird Street*. Translated from the Hebrew by Hillel Halkin. Boston: Houghton Mifflin, 1984.
> A young boy is left to forage and survive on his own in the Warsaw Ghetto.

Spinelli, Jerry. *Milkweed: A Novel*. New York: Alfred A. Knopf, 2003.
> Told from an orphaned five year old's perspective filled with awe and amazement, this Warsaw ghetto story describes the atrocities of murder, starvation, and public beatings in an almost clinical context.

Author-Related Sources

Berger, Laura Standley, ed. *Twentieth-Century Young Adult Writers*. Detroit, MI: St. James Press, 1994, 507–9.

Holtze, Sally Holmes, ed. *Seventh Book of Junior Authors and Illustrators*. New York: H. W. Wilson, 1996, 243–4.

"Uri Orlev." In vol. 30 of *Children's Literature Review*. Farmington Hills, MI: Gale Research, 1993, 162–7.

"Uri Orlev." In vol. 135 of *Something about the Author*. Farmington Hills, MI: Gale Group, 2003, 160–5.

Discussion Questions

For *Run, Boy, Run*

1. How would you describe Jurik's character and personality?

2. Why is it so important for Jurik to stay alive through any means, as his father expressed?

3. How does losing his arm affect Jurik in his ability to survive?

4. Why do you think Jurik fights the rescue plans of the Jewish agency after the war is over?

5. How do you think his life would have been different had Jurik stayed with his adoptive Christian family?

6. Why isn't Jurik allowed to make a free choice on his future?

7. What impressed you most about Jurik's story?

Singularity

By William Sleator

New York: E. P. Dutton, 1985

Reading Level: . . . . Grades 5–7
Genre: . . . . Science fiction
Themes: . . . . Sibling rivalry, time travel

Plot Summary

What if a black hole or "singularity" existed here on earth as a portal to another universe? While their parents are on a business trip, sixteen-year-old twins Barry and Harry Krasner undertake the responsibility of house watching an old Illinois farmhouse bequeathed to their mother from a distant eccentric uncle. Arriving from their Boston home, the boys begin to explore the creepy contents of the house, finding skeletons of strange creatures, books on science and physics, and keys to a small locked structure made of steel called "the playhouse," which rests at the outskirts of the property. Barry is eager to discover what the mysterious structure holds, while Harry is reluctant and nervous. The twins' relationship is strained because they each have different personalities and views on life. While Barry is impulsive, eager to show his bravado, and unhappy about always being viewed as part of a twin rather than as an individual, he resents any advice or heeding that his brother offers. Harry, somewhat intimidated by his brother's teasing and bullying, tends to go along with Barry's ideas, to keep the peace and lessen the conflict between them. What they discover is that time moves faster within the enclosed walls of the playhouse to the equation of one minute of real time equaling one hour of playhouse time. Daring to take more and more risks with this discovery, Barry ignores Harry's more scientific reasoning and explanations based on his researching the books in the house. He charges ahead with plans of his own, threatening to stay in the structure long enough to age and change their twin status. But it is Harry's thoughtful reasoning and need to become more assertive with his brother that allow him to develop a plan of action to stay secretly in the structure for several hours one night to age one year. By changing the dynamics between himself and his brother, his "year in hiding" brings emotional growth and maturity.

Main Characterization

Barry Krasner is a sixteen-year-old twin resentful of having to live his life as a "second half" and eager to break away through his arrogant, impulsive, somewhat daring behavior of a maturing teen boy. Although physically identical in appearance, his twin Harry is both emotionally and intellectually his opposite. Barry's goading, teasing, and challenging ideas continually overpower Harry's kind, reasonable, gentle behavior. Harry's lack of assertiveness gives Barry free reign to control the boys' choices and decisions. However, it is Harry's ability to comprehend some of the scientific principles and the ramifications of misusing the black hole's power that sparks a change in his meek behavior and inspires his bold, life-changing decision to use their discovery to his advantage.

Themes

The sibling rivalry of the twin brothers is the overwhelming theme interwoven in this science fiction novel of time travel and its ability to change future events.

Books with Similar Issues or Themes

Garfield, Leon. *The Empty Sleeve*. New York: Delacorte Press, 1988.
> Fourteen-year-old twin Peter is eager to break away from his "saintly" twin brother, Paul, apprenticed to a locksmith but finds himself in mortal danger when the ghostly appearance of a former apprentice appears and he must rely on his twin to save him.

L'Engle, Madeleine. *Many Waters*. New York: Farrar, Straus & Giroux, 1986.
> Fooling with their scientist parents' computer, the Murray twins are taken to an alternate time and desert that is about to be flooded with "many waters."

Lubar, David. *Flip*. New York: Tom Toherty Associates, 2003.
> Twins Taylor and Ryan have an opportunity to become anyone other than themselves when they discover the magical, mysterious disks that were dropped from an alien space ship.

Stolz, Mary. *A Ballad of the Civil War*. Illustrated by Sergio Martinez. New York: HarperCollins, 1997.
> Twin brothers Tom and Jack separate with different ideals to fight on opposite sides of the Civil War.

Yolen, Jane. *The Bagpiper's Ghost*. New York: Harcourt, 2002.
> Twins Jennifer and Peter become involved in a dangerous supernatural struggle as they hunt for ghosts in a Scottish cemetery.

Author-Related Sources

Berger, Laura Standley, ed. *Twentieth-Century Young Adult Writers*. Detroit, MI: St. James Press, 1994, 593–4.

Hipple, Ted, ed. In vol. 3 of *Writers for Young Adults*. New York: Charles S. Scribner's Sons, 1997, 157–82.

Silvey, Anita, ed. *Children's Books and Their Creators*. Boston: Houghton Mifflin, 1995, 605–6.

"William Sleator." In vol. 29 of *Children's Literature Review*. Farmington Hills, MI: Gale Research, 1993, 196–208.

"William Sleator." In vol. 118 of *Something about the Author*. Farmington Hills, MI: Gale Group, 2001, 201–6.

Discussion Questions

For *Singularity*

1. What kind of relationship do the twin brothers, Barry and Harry, have?

2. What are Barry's reasons for exploring the playhouse?

3. How are Barry and Harry different? How did their view of the playhouse affect their reasoning and decisions?

4. Why is Harry able to accomplish his goal of living a year in isolation even though it is so difficult?

5. How does his year in isolation change Harry?

6. What does Harry hope to achieve by aging one year, and why do you think he succeeded?

7. If Barry had decided to lock himself in the playhouse as Harry had done, what do you think might have happened?

8. How does Barry's life change after he realizes that Harry is now a year older?

9. What kind of relationship do you think the twins might develop after they return to their life in Boston?

10. If you had the opportunity to alter your age, would you do it? Why?

Soup

By Robert Newton Peck, Illustrated by Charles C. Gehm

New York: Alfred A Knopf, 1974

Reading Level: . . . . Grades 4–5
Genre: . . . . Historical/realistic fiction
Themes: . . . . Friendship

Plot Summary

Seven episodic chapters introduce the character of Soup (Luther Wesley Vinson) and Rob (Robert Peck) in this humorous, semi-autobiographical novel about two best friends and the troubles and predicaments that dominate their boyhood lives. Set in an earlier time period when play consisted of outdoor sport and shenanigans and when movies cost a dime, these stories range from innocent misbehavior at school, to taking a first smoke, to cheating an honest businessman, to taking a daring barrel ride down Dugan's Hill, to using a bit too much hair oil, to sharing a new pair of shoes with a best friend who isn't as fortunate.

Main Characterization

Rob is author Robert Newton Peck, reminiscing about his childhood in the early 1930s with best friend Soup. Both boys are fun-loving, sincere individuals who are dedicated to their parents and to each other. They are imaginative and clever in their play, living in a time period without our modern-day technology and media that allows for simple outdoor fun.

Themes

Friendship is the overall theme of this episodic novel, but there are some serious issues that come forth in some of the stories, including honesty, vandalism, cheating, compassion, and sympathy.

Books with Similar Issues or Themes

Fitzgerald, John Dennis. *The Great Brain*. Illustrated by Mercer Mayer. New York: Dial Books for Young Readers, 1967.
> Ten-year-old Tom, the "Great Brain," creates one adventure after another all the while scheming to make some money and sometimes getting his younger brother in a mess.

Paulsen, Gary. *Harris and Me*. San Diego: Harcourt Brace, 1993.
> Two cousins—one from the city, the other from a rural farm—get to know each other one summer and become involved in numerous escapades, some perilous but most hilarious.

Peck, Robert Newton: other books in the Soup series

Soto, Gary. *Summer on Wheels*. New York: Scholastic, 1995.

    Hector and his friend (*amigo*) Mando set out on an adventurous week-long bike trip from their neighborhood in East Los Angeles to the Santa Monica beach, with some unexpected results.

Author-Related Sources

Berger, Laura Standley, ed. *Twentieth-Century Young Adult Writers*. Detroit, MI: St. James Press, 1994, 526–8.

Hipple, Ted, ed. In vol. 3 of *Writers for Young Adults*. New York: Charles S. Scribner's Sons, 1997, 15–26.

"Robert Newton Peck." In vol. 15 of *Children's Literature Review*. Farmington Hills, MI: Gale Research, 1988, 146–66.

"Robert Newton Peck." In vol. 111 of *Something about the Author*. Farmington Hills, MI: Gale Group, 2000, 145–51.

Robert Newton Peck's official Web site: http://my.athenet.net/~blahnik/rnpeck/> (accessed 2 February 2005).

Discussion Questions

For *Soup*

1. Which episode did you like best and why?

2. What kind of boys are Rob and Soup?

3. How is life different for these two best friends than it is for you and your best friend? How is it the same?

4. Did any of these stories seem true to you? Why?

5. How do Rob and Soup show loyalty and friendship to each other throughout the book?

6. Would you consider this book humorous?

7. There are some serious issues hidden in these episodes—honesty, cheating, vandalism, having compassion, and showing sympathy. How does the author bring out these issues in the stories?

Squids Will Be Squids: Fresh Morals, Beastly Fables

By Jon Scieszka, Illustrated by Lane Smith

New York: Viking, 1998

Reading Level: . . . . Grades 3–5
Genre: . . . . Fables
Themes: . . . . Family life, behavior, school life

Plot Summary

This contemporary, amusing collection of tongue-in-cheek fables with morals and some gross humor display concepts typical of modern school society and family lifestyles. They introduce situations such as parent-child homework interaction, calling home to check in, flatulence, sharing responsibilities, boasting, and truthful and polite behavior.

Main Characterization

A variety of insects, animals, sea creatures, and inanimate objects make up the plethora of characters that represent humanity ala Aesop and his classic fables.

Themes

Disguised in these comical and grotesquely amusing parodies, the author and illustrator bring out issues of human behavior that will be recognizable to most kids and will serve as a springboard for discussion of some serious school politics, behavior dos and don'ts, and family responsibilities such as homework, table manners, curfews, friendships, and advertising deception.

Books with Similar Issues or Themes

Demi. *A Chinese Zoo: Fables and Proverbs*. Adapted and illustrated by Demi. San Diego, CA: Harcourt Brace Jovanovich, 1987.
> Thirteen fables offering Chinese wisdom.

Kherdian, David. *Feathers and Tails: Animal Fables from around the World*. Retold by David Kherdian. Illustrated by Nonny Hogrogian. New York: Philomel Books, 1992.
> A collection of fables from diverse cultures, including Indian, Inuit, African, Armenian, European, and Native American.

Lester, Julius. *Ackamarackus: Julius Lester's Sumptuously Silly Fantastically Funny Fables*. Illustrated by Emilie Chollat. New York: Scholastic Press, 2001.
> Six original fables offering some preposterously absurd morals that stretch the truth.

Lobel, Arnold. *Fables*. New York: HarperCollins, 1980.
A collection of twenty tales illustrating the flaws of human behavior with a parade of humorous animals.

Rosenthal, Paul. *Yo, Aesop!: Get a Load of These Fables*. Illustrated by Marc Rosenthal. New York: Simon & Schuster Books for Young Readers, 1998.
Nine humorous fractured fables based on the Aesop originals.

Author-Related Sources

Berger, Laura Standley, ed. *Twentieth-Century Children's Writers*. Detroit, MI: St. James Press, 1995, 851–2.

Holtze, Sally Holmes, ed. *Seventh Book of Junior Authors and Illustrators*. New York: H. W. Wilson, 1996, 289–90.

"Jon Scieszka." In vol. 105 of *Something about the Author*. Farmington Hills, MI: Gale Group, 1999, 200–7.

Jon Scieszka's official Web site: http://www-personal.ksu.edu/~aec8484/biography.html (accessed 29 January 2005)

Marcus, Leonard S., ed. *Author Talk: Conversations with Judy Blume et al.* New York: Simon & Schuster, 2000, 83–9.

Silvey, Anita, ed. *Children's Books and Their Creators*. Boston: Houghton Mifflin, 1995, 581–2.

Discussion Questions

For *Squids Will Be Squids: Fresh Morals, Beastly Fables*

1. Which fable is the most logical or sensible?

2. Which fable is the funniest to you?

3. Which fable had the most serious truthful moral?

4. How does your life at school relate to some of these fables and morals?

5. What do you think the author tried to say in the fable called "Gee ... I Wonder"?

6. Why do the authors choose animals and creatures to illustrate human behavior?

7. What do the authors try to say about squids and slugs?

8. What animal or object would you use to tell a fable and moral of your own?

Sticks

By Joan Bauer

New York: Delacorte Press, 1996

Reading Level: . . . . Grades 5–7

Genre: . . . . Realistic fiction

Themes: . . . . Competition, perseverance, self-confidence

Plot Summary

Trying to live up to his father's championship billiards career, Mickey Vernon wants nothing more than to win the youth tournament held at his family-owned pool hall. Losing his father to cancer when he was a baby, Mickey is surrounded by relatives and friends who knew his dad, and he has inherited a talent that makes him a fantastic ten-year-old pool player. His serious competition is the thirteen-year-old tough bully Buck Pender, who is constantly threatening Mickey and his friends. Mickey's best friend, Arlen Pepper, is a math whiz and has figured out geometrical possibilities in billiards, the secret weapon, to help Mickey with possible strategies for a better game. Even with his best practice and coaching from Arlen, Mickey is still not confident that he can win until one day, when a strange man in a cowboy hat walks into the hall, takes an interest in Mickey's game, and begins to train with him every Saturday. The stranger is Joseph Alvarez, an old friend of Mickey's father, who has been gone for nine years and has come back with a new trucking business. He begins to give Mickey coaching advice and ways to develop skills for winning, while teaching him the importance of having *ganas,* or "desire." Mickey is still bothered by Buck's intimidation, loses his cool, gets into a physical fight with the older boy, and sprains his left hand badly—just four weeks before the tournament. Heartsick that he cannot practice and may even have to forfeit the competition, Mickey is quite down for the next couple of weeks. However, when Joseph returns from a trip and his hand is almost healed, Mickey manages to play in the tournament and wins a very difficult and painful championship that brings him a sense of justified pride and accomplishment.

Main Characterization

Mickey Vernon is living with his mother and grandmother above the pool hall that earns their living. Eager to do the best he can to live up to his father's reputation, he is encouraged by Joseph's psychological strength, continuing on even when the game is literally too physically painful to bear. But Mickey doesn't realize that he is a winner regardless of the competition, simply because he has persisted to attain his goal.

Arlen Pepper's brilliant interest in math has him connecting life with formulas and pool with geometry. He provides peer support when Mickey needs it most.

Joseph Alvarez appears in the story at convenient times to bring courage, advice, and emotional strength to a boy who needs confidence and assurance.

Themes

Fair competition and the concept of winning are stressed in this story of hard work, perseverance, and self-confidence.

Books with Similar Issues or Themes

Gutman, Dan. *The Million Dollar Shot*. New York: Hyperion Books, 1997.
> A boy uses all his skill and practice coached by a neighboring former basketball college star to win a candy company's promotional contest and a million dollars.

Hite, Sid. *An Even Break*. New York: Henry Holt, 1995.
> In a summer job at the local pool hall, Frisk Tilden learns the game, wins a tournament, and earns enough money to buy a new bicycle.

Weaver, Will. *Hard Ball*. New York: HarperCollins, 1998.
> The rivalry between two boys on the same baseball team is settled with compromise and effective coaching.

Author-Related Sources

Hipple, Ted, ed. In vol. 1 of *Writers for Young Adults*. New York: Charles S. Scribner's Sons, 1997, 73–80.

"Joan Bauer." In vol. 117 of *Something about the Author*. Farmington Hills, MI: Gale Group, 2000, 10–14.

Joan Bauer's Web site: http://www.joanbauer.com/jb.html (accessed 19 October 2004).

Discussion Questions

For *Sticks*

1. What allows Mickey to play so well and win with a sprained hand, even though he is one of the youngest players?

2. What is Mickey trying to prove to himself and his family by competing?

3. Why is winning the competition so important to Mickey?

4. In what ways is Mickey already a winner?

5. What does Joseph Alvarez teach Mickey besides the art of shooting pool?

6. Why is it so important to have *ganas* to be a winner?

7. What did Mickey's teacher imply when she said, "Courage rarely comes without fear"?

8. What do you think about how Arlen related math to the pool game?

9. What message does the author hope to convey in this story of a pool game and a boy?

Stuck in Neutral

By Terry Trueman

New York: HarperCollins, 2000

Reading Level: . . . . Grades 6–8

Genre: . . . . Realistic fiction

Themes: . . . . Physical disability, family relationships, euthanasia versus murder

Awards: . . . . Printz Honor

Plot Summary

Fourteen-year-old Shawn McDaniel is severely disabled with cerebral palsy, living his life with a fully capable mind in a broken body. Shawn describes his life in a way only he understands and enjoys through his mental and emotional abilities. Viewed as equally brain damaged and slow by all the experts, his family has become accustomed to assuming his lack of comprehension as well. But Shawn recounts, through his very intelligent narrative, his thoughts, feelings, and desires and describes how he has learned to read and understand through his everyday surroundings. Although his family loves him deeply, they are unaware of his mental abilities and treat him as an infant and hold discussions and arguments in his presence fully confident that he has no cognitive skills. Shawn tells us he is happy and optimistic, enjoying life his way, the best he can. But his overall concern of late is that of his award-winning father, who has been doing research on families with disabled children and is expressing a great interest in allowing the suffering of severely disabled children to end in death. Shawn is terrified that his father is planning to kill him out of extreme love and pity.

Main Characterization

Shawn McDaniel is a bright, inquisitive, imaginative boy who is incredibly optimistic and views life through a funny and sometimes sarcastic lens. Forced to place his trust in all who work and live with him, he develops a fear of his father yet ultimately is resigned to trust whatever decision and fate awaits him.

Themes

The serious and controversial issue of euthanasia to end suffering is explored within the context of a boy's perception of life based on his experience as a cerebral palsy victim living in a very caring and loving family situation.

Books with Similar Issues or Themes

Fleischman, Paul. *Mind's Eye*. New York: Henry Holt, 1999.
> Sixteen-year-old Courtney, paralyzed in an accident, learns to appreciate life through the imaginary trip to Italy that she takes with her blind, elderly roommate with the help of a 1910 travel guidebook.

Mikaelsen, Ben. *Petey*. New York: Hyperion Books, 1998.

  Misdiagnosed as retarded as a child in the 1920s, Petey, who has cerebral palsy, later in life befriends eighth-grader Trevor, who is having trouble adjusting to his family's move to a new town. Trevor grows emotionally through this unusual relationship with the elderly Petey.

Philbrick, W. Rodman. *Freak the Mighty*. New York: Scholastic Press, 1993.

  Two boys, one very large with learning disabilities, the other brilliant with a birth defect that has left him grossly small and deformed for his age, combine friendship and their unique abilities to "take on the world."

Voigt, Cynthia. *Izzy, Willy-Nilly*. New York: Atheneum, 1986.

  When fifteen-year-old Izzy loses her leg in a car accident, she must face a new life as an amputee.

Author-Related Sources

"Terry Trueman." In vol. 132 of *Something about the Author*. Farmington Hills, MI: Gale Group, 2002, 224–5.

Terry Trueman's Web site: http://www.terrytrueman.smartwriters.com/ (accessed 14 January 2005).

Discussion Questions

For *Stuck in Neutral*

1. What is Shawn's outlook on life?

2. What does Shawn want most out of life?

3. How does Shawn view his classmates in relation to what is "normal" when he says, "we retards are retards only because normal people call us that"?

4. What fears does Shawn have about his father's behavior?

5. What is Shawn's father feeling?

6. How is suffering portrayed and displayed in this story?

7. Who suffers the most in this story?

8. What do you think happens at the end of Shawn's story?

9. What do you think the author is trying to convey in this story?

Taking Sides

By Gary Soto

New York: Harcourt Brace Jovanovich, 1991

Reading Level: . . . . Grades 5–7
Genre: . . . . Realistic fiction
Themes: . . . . Friendship, loyalty, prejudice, racism

Plot Summary

When Lincoln Mendoza moves from his inner-city Latino neighborhood to a quiet, almost all-white suburban community, he still feels a loyalty to his old school, Franklin, despite playing basketball for Columbus Junior High. In addition, he maintains a connection with his best friend, Tony Contreras, through phone calls and visits to his old neighborhood. Linc is adjusting to his new surroundings. His basketball ability has earned him some respect, new friends, and even a new girl. But Linc feels a certain uneasiness being one of very few nonwhite students, especially when his coach displays resentment toward Linc at each practice and game. A league game between his former and present schools is approaching, and Linc's confusion grows. When he falls and hurts his knee in a silly accident during a basketball date with new girl, Monica, he cannot continue with practice and is benched for the game by the less than sympathetic coach. In the meantime, Lincoln learns about another game, played in the 1970s, that involved the coach and his mother's boyfriend as teammates playing opposite a mostly Mexican team. That game resulted in the coach's suspension for disrespectfully referring to an opposing team player with the disparaging word "Spic." Watching the game from the bench and chastised by the coach for talking to students from the other school, Lincoln realizes that he cannot deny who he is. But as Franklin is up 23 to 16 and the coach instructs Lincoln to enter the game in the last quarter, Linc decides that he will not allow Columbus to look like a losing team and will play his best, helping raise the score at the end with a respectable loss for Columbus. In the end, Lincoln enjoys a fair game victory dinner with his former teammates while earning the respect of his new ones.

Main Characterization

Lincoln Mendoza is a twelve-year-old boy caught between two communities and two worlds. His mother, unhappy with the dangers of street life in his older, Mexican community, has moved them to a suburban life, hoping to offer her son better opportunities. However, Linc learns firsthand that each neighborhood can have its positive and negative aspects and that he has to find a balance between his ethnicity and his new way of life.

Themes

Strong themes of friendship and loyalty play against undertones of racism and prejudice. Lincoln manages to develop binding ties with his former and present schoolmates through basketball.

Books with Similar Issues or Themes

Cooper, Ilene. *Choosing Sides*. New York: Morrow Junior Books, 1990.
Sixth-grader Jonathan Rossi feels the pressure and resentment of his expected participation on the basketball team from both his father and a demanding coach.

Deuker, Carl. *Night Hoops*. Boston: Houghton Mifflin, 2000.
Nick Abbott deals with a host of personal problems and the divorce of his parents by concentrating on his basketball game and the one-on-one nighttime practices with his difficult neighbor and angry teammate.

Klass, David. *Danger Zone*. New York: Scholastic, 1995.
Playing for an all-American basketball team in an international tournament in Rome, Jimmy Doyle must first face racism from his black teammates for being white and then face the entire team's abuse by a group of skinhead fans from Germany.

Myers, Walter Dean. *Slam!* New York: Scholastic, 1996.
Seventeen-year-old Greg, nicknamed "Slam," learns to approach life in the same way he approaches his basketball game in order to have some success.

Author-Related Sources

Berger, Laura Standley, ed. *Twentieth-Century Young Adult Writers*. Detroit, MI: St. James Press, 1994, 600–2.

Gary Soto's official Web site: http://www.garysoto.com/ (accessed 12 February 2005).

Hipple, Ted, ed. In vol. 3 of *Writers for Young Adults*. New York: Charles S. Scribner's Sons, 1997, 183–92.

Holtze, Sally Holmes, ed. *Seventh Book of Junior Authors and Illustrators*. New York: H. W. Wilson, 1996, 303–4.

Silvey, Anita, ed. *Children's Books and Their Creators*. Boston: Houghton Mifflin, 1995, 613–15.

Discussion Questions

For *Taking Sides*

1. What does Lincoln realize about his two schools and neighborhoods?

2. What helps Lincoln adjust to his new school and make new friends?

3. How does Lincoln feel about playing in the league game against his old school?

4. How does Lincoln show his loyalty to both schools in the end?

5. What is the author, Gary Soto, trying to say in this story? What does the title *Taking Sides* really mean?

Weasel

By Cynthia DeFelice

New York: Macmillan, 1990

Reading Level: . . . . Grades 6–8
Genre: . . . . Historical fiction
Themes: . . . . Revenge, racial prejudice

Plot Summary

In the unsettled state of Ohio in 1839, eleven-year-old Nathan and his younger sister, Molly, have been alone for the last several days. Their father remains missing from a hunting trip. Trying to stay positive and go about a normal routine, the children are visited by a strange, speechless white man dressed in the clothes of the Shawnee tribesman holding their deceased mother's locket, which their father always keeps with him. Nathan deduces that Pa must be hurt somewhere and that this wordless man can bring them to him. The man is Ezra, a former government Indian enforcement agent who chose to live among the Shawnees, married a Native American, and fathered a child. Nathan's Pa is hurt with an infected wound from an animal trap and is resting at Ezra's place. When they reunite with their father, the children learn that the area is being terrorized by another former government agent, dubbed "Weasel," who has gone on a rampage, killing indiscriminately and stealing food and ammunition whenever he can. He is responsible for killing Ezra's wife and baby and for cutting out Ezra's tongue in revenge for his adopting an Indian life. Weasel has come upon Nathan's Pa, and instead of aiding in his accident, has stolen his rifle and left him to die of his wound. Nathan must return to their farm to take care of the animals and boldly sets out on his own, promising to beware of the dangerous Weasel. But Weasel has already invaded the small settlement and taken or killed the family's animals. Nathan's sorrow quickly turns to rage and after burying the only animal left, their old sow, Nathan sets out into the dark night once again to return to Ezra's place only to be captured by Weasel and held prisoner in his cabin. With a combination of ingenuity, guts, and luck, Nathan manages to escape with his father's rifle, giving up his only chance for revenge—to kill Weasel in cold blood. After contemplating his lost opportunity for many days, Nathan finally sets out on his own again, against his father's judgment, determined to confront this crazed monster and boldly kill him, only to discover that Weasel has already died from wounds inflicted by his own hand.

Main Characterization

Nathan is a boy whose ideals are being shaped by the evil he has witnessed, countered with his desire for revenge. He is confused by his father's philosophy that killing Weasel would not change the past and would only bring Nathan closer to the evil that Weasel represents.

Themes

Nathan's boyhood outlook on life is stretched to understand the evil ways of people based on racial prejudice and the powerful urge to right a wrong through revenge.

Books with Similar Issues or Themes

Cooper, Susan. *Dawn of Fear*. Illustrated by Margery Gill. New York: Harcourt Brace Jovanovich, 1970.

> After a tough gang destroys their secret camp, Derek and his friends Peter and Geoff seek revenge and experience violent hatred and fear.

Cormier, Robert. *In the Middle of the Night*. New York: Delacorte Press, 1995.

> Twenty-five years after the exoneration of his father in the tragic death of many children in the movie theater where he was employed, sixteen-year-old Denny is lured by a mysterious and obsessive caller into a dangerous game of vengeance.

Author-Related Sources

"Cynthia DeFelice." In vol. 121 of *Something about the Author*. Farmington Hills, MI: Gale Group, 2001, 69–74.

Cynthia DeFelice's official Web site: http://www.cynthiadefelice.com/ (accessed 2 February 2005).

Holtze, Sally Holmes, ed. *Seventh Book of Junior Authors and Illustrators*. New York: H. W. Wilson, 1996, 78–9.

Discussion Questions

For *Weasel*

1. Why doesn't Nathan kill Weasel when he has the opportunity?

2. Why does Nathan later feel he must kill Weasel and that it is the right thing to do?

3. Why does Pa feel that killing Weasel is not important?

4. Why does Ezra choose to live with the Shawnees and change his white man's views?

5. How do Nathan and his family help Ezra go on with his life?

6. What does Ezra teach Nathan about racial prejudice?

7. What does Ezra mean when he writes to Molly and tells her "Weezl is small now"?

8. Why does Nathan feel that Weasel will never really be dead for him or for others who have known him?

The Winter People

By Joseph Bruchac

New York: Dial Books, 2002

Reading Level: . . . . Grades 4–6
Genre: . . . . Historical fiction
Themes: . . . . Family responsibility, heroism, coming of age, survival

Plot Summary

In this French and Indian War novel, Saxso, a fourteen-year-old Abenaki boy, is wounded in an attack on his village of St. Francis by the opposing British. He uses his uncle's wisdom and the foresight of the community's wiseman, known as "the Worrier," to rescue his mother and sisters from their captors with a cunning and daring plan. Losing his father several years earlier in another battle, Saxso remains the male figure in his family of females. Both his mother's brother and the Worrier act as mentors for him. When Saxso is warned of a new attack on the village, he brings the news to the French and Abenaki residents at a harvest celebration in the Council Hall. Remembering the massacre by the Bostoniaks that killed virtually everyone in the village of Turner Falls, Saxso's warning is heeded, and the women and children begin quietly to retreat to the woods. Saxso is torn between his responsibility to stay with his family and protect them and to join the other men in preparing a defense. Saxso stays to help recover a young girl who is left behind in her house, when the attack begins from three sides, and he is immediately shot in the shoulder. Bleeding and weak, he eventually passes out and wakes up in the care of the Worrier who instructs him in his mission to leave the fighting to the others and to follow his family and their kidnappers. Struggling with feelings of guilt and the need for vengeance, Saxso heeds the Worrier's advice and stealthily moves through the woods for several days until he finds his family at a campsite and puts together a strategy using secret communication techniques with his mother and the element of a surprise boulder avalanche to help them all escape to a neighboring village.

Main Characterization

Saxso is the sole male bearing the responsibility to provide and protect his family. He experiences a variety of emotions, including guilt and revenge, and also exhibits a certain bravado, but he is able to keep his head as his rescue attempt becomes increasingly possible.

The Worrier represents a man of wisdom and knowledge, giving Saxso an attitude of faith and confidence as he encourages him to follow the trail of his kidnapped family.

Themes

This coming-of-age novel includes themes of heroism as Saxso bravely creates a rescue plan, of survival as the livelihood of one group of people is virtually destroyed by another, and of family responsibility as a young man is burdened with the welfare of his mother and sisters when an attack places them in a defenseless position.

Books with Similar Issues or Themes

Cooper, James Fenimore. *The Last of the Mohicans*. New York: Dodd, Mead, 1979.

Cooper, James Fenimore. *The Deerslayer*. New York: Scribner's Sons, 1925.
> These two books from the classic Leatherstocking series focus on the French and Indian Wars and the clash between the various cultures of the British, French, and Native American tribes.

Dubois, Muriel L. *Abenaki Captive*. Minneapolis, MN: Carolrhoda Books, 1994.
> Recounts the capture of two New England settlers by the Abenaki Indians, focusing on a Native American boy named Ogistin and his desire to avenge his brother's death by the English.

Fleischman, Paul. *Saturnalia*. New York: Harper & Row, 1990.
> A fourteen-year-old Narraganset Indian boy working as a printer's apprentice in colonial Boston tries to maintain his culture through the legends secretly passed on to him by his uncle.

Houston, James. *River Runners*. New York: Atheneum, 1979.
> The story of two boys sent to the Canadian wilderness to set up a fur trade business and their developed friendship with the Naskapi Indians.

Author-Related Sources

Bruchac, Joseph. *Bowman's Store: A Journey to Myself*. New York: Dial Books, 1997. (The author's personal autobiography of his family and his Abenaki heritage.)

"Joseph Bruchac." In vol. 46 of *Children's Literature Review*. Farmington Hills, MI: Gale Group, 1998, 1–24.

"Joseph Bruchac." In vol. 131 of *Something about the Author*. Farmington Hills, MI: Gale Group, 2002, 31–8.

Joseph Bruchac's Web page: http://www.josephbruchac.com/ (23 December 2004).

Silvey, Anita, ed. *Children's Books and Their Creators*. Boston: Houghton Mifflin, 1995, 99.

Discussion Questions

For *The Winter People*

1. Why does Saxso let his family retreat without him after they receive warning of an attack?

2. Why is it important for Saxso to use his weapons only to hunt, allowing the other men to do the fighting?

3. What do Saxso's two mentors, the Worrier and his uncle, teach him? How does he use their advice?

4. Why does the Worrier call Saxso "White Man Talker"?

5. How can some of Uncle's lessons or sayings such as "wait, do nothing quickly" or "the best plan is often the simplest one" apply to your life today?

6. Why is this story of the French and Indian Wars from the point of view of the Abenaki people important?

7. Who are the winter people?

8. What does Saxso mean when he says that the English and the Bostoniaks have winter in their hearts?

Wringer

By Jerry Spinelli

New York: Joanna Cotler Books/HarperCollins, 1997

Reading Level: . . . . Grades 4–6

Genre: . . . . Realistic fiction

Themes: . . . . Courage, trust, responsibility, peer acceptance, defending one's values

Awards: . . . . Newbery Honor, ALA Notable Children's Book, School Library Journal Best Books of the Year

Plot Summary

Unlike most boys in his town, Palmer LaRue dreads the day he will turn ten. Reaching your tenth birthday in the town of Waymer marks a milestone and a right of passage that Palmer would rather avoid. The town has a history and reputation for running an annual pigeon shoot as a fundraiser for the recreational community park maintenance where five thousand pigeons are released and shot down. Those that don't die instantly are put out of their misery by the "wringer" boys who are initiated into this activity at age ten. Not conforming to the ritual is easier said than done as it would alienate Palmer from his peers, Beans, Henry, and Mutto, and even embarrass his father, a former champion pigeon shooter. This is a tough boys town with certain fraternal traditions that require stamina and courage. As boys reach a certain age, they are also expected to pass "the treatment" by the older boys, a kind of arm-bruising ceremony that indicates manhood. Wringing the necks of half-dead pigeons follows suit. As Palmer contemplates his dilemma with each day his birthday draws closer, something unbelievable happens. A pigeon lands on his windowsill and seems to want to stay. Chasing it away at first, Palmer begins to enjoy keeping the bird as a pet, names him Nipper, allows him in his room, creates a hide out, and feeds him regularly, always mindful that his friends might discover his secret. Palmer's anxiety grows with his love and concern for Nipper and he eventually confides his fears to neighbor and classmate, Dorothy. But it is when Nipper's life is truly threatened as he gets caught in the pigeon crates ready to be released for the shoot that Palmer courageously takes a stand and rescues the bird in a dramatic public expression of his true feelings about the town's annual event.

Main Characterization

Palmer LaRue is unhappy about the significance of his tenth birthday if it means he has to behave cruelly and against his values. Wanting peer acceptance and the respect of his father, however, he is nervous about making his own views clear. Erroneously thinking that he cannot turn even to his parents for support, he is eventually able to come to terms with his feelings and thereby take dramatic steps to save his pet Nipper, willing to stand alone with his views on the pigeon shoot.

Wise Dorothy Gruzik is the only ally Palmer has in his environmental and humane struggle. For the sake of his reputation, however, Palmer must keep their relationship a secret among their peers.

Beans, Henry, and Mutto are the tough-acting boys in Palmer's peer group, adhering to society's expectations and imitating their fathers and other older male role models. Henry, however, is closer to Palmer in his thinking and clandestinely supports him by providing mysterious clues to the boys' plans to expose Palmer's love for pigeons.

Themes

Palmer's dilemma tests his courage and resolve to withstand peer pressure to conform and join the crowd rather than risk his friendships. It becomes more important for Palmer not only to save Nipper's life, but also to stand up publicly for what he believes. Responsibility and trust are co-themes as Palmer accepts a greater role in taking care of Nipper and begins to trust his own values. In addition, his relationship with Dorothy indicates another form of trust as he is able to confide his true fears and emotions to her.

Books with Similar Issues or Themes

Avi. *Nothing but the Truth: A Documentary Novel*. New York: Scholastic, 1991.

A boy's mindless prank of humming the "Star Spangled Banner" develops into a series of escalated reactions from the administrators, media, and town residents, resulting in the unfortunate disruption and disparagement of a dedicated teacher's career.

Cormier, Robert. *The Chocolate War*. New York: Pantheon Books, 1974.

A freshman stands his ground and refuses to participate in the school's chocolate fundraising sale despite coercion, intimidation, and psychological harassment from both the school administrators and the secret student society called the Vigils.

Author-Related Sources

Hipple, Ted, ed. In vol. 3 of *Writers for Young Adults*. New York: Charles S. Scribner's Sons, 1997, 193–202.

Holtze, Sally Holmes, ed. *Sixth Book of Junior Authors and Illustrators*. New York: H. W. Wilson, 1989, 284–5.

Jerry Spinelli. In vol. 82 of *Children's Literature Review*. Farmington Hills, MI: Gale Group, 2002, 161–80.

Jerry Spinelli's Web site: http://www.jerryspinelli.com/newbery_001.htm (accessed 30 May 2004).

Silvey, Anita, ed. *Children's Books and Their Creators*. Boston: Houghton Mifflin, 1995, 619–21.

Spinelli, Jerry. *Knots in My Yo-Yo String: Autobiography of a Kid*. New York: Knopf, 1998.

Discussion Questions

For *Wringer*

1. What is Palmer's dilemma? Why does he have so much trouble dealing with it?

2. How do the other boys, Beans, Mutto, and Henry, like to express their manhood? Are they truly "men"?

3. Why could Palmer's values and way of thinking be considered just as bold and strong as the behavior of his peers?

4. Why did the men and boys of this town feel it was justified, even fun, to participate in the pigeon shoot?

5. Why is Palmer able to relate to Dorothy and develop a trusting bond with her but is unwilling to support her publicly when she is teased by the other boys? Why is Beans so disturbed by Dorothy's reaction to his teasing?

6. What does Palmer begin to see about himself as he becomes aware of Nipper's entrapment in the pigeon shoot crates?

7. What do you think of the way this town chooses to raise money for the park?

8. The story has an open ending with Palmer leaving the park and the newspaper article reporting Palmer's act as "an unexpected episode." How do you think the story ended?

9. What do you think Palmer might do next year?

10. What is the significance of the small child's question, "can I have one too, Daddy?" following Palmer's exit on the field with Nipper in his arms?

The Young Man and the Sea

By Rodman Philbrick

New York: The Blue Sky Press, 2004

Reading Level: . . . . Grades 4–6

Genre: . . . . Adventure/survival

Themes: . . . . Bullying, taking charge, perseverance, survival

Awards: . . . . School Library Journal Best Books

Plot Summary

Coping with the loss of his mother and his fisherman father's subsequent alcoholic depression, twelve-year-old Skiff Beaman is determined to bring some fishing money home and hopefully encourage his father to begin working again. Their neglected boat, the *Mary Rose,* has sunk to the bottom of the dock, and even though Skiff has been able to bring it back up with the advice of Mr. Woodwall, the engine has been damaged by the water and needs $5,000 worth of repair. Using the small wooden boat given to him for his ninth birthday, Skiff reasons he can trap lobsters by setting two hundred traps and earn money by the pound to repair the *Mary Rose.* Working diligently and carefully, Skiff begins to catch what he can but is soon sabotaged by rich kid and bully Tyler Croft. For no other reason than pure meanness, Tyler has been sneaking out at night and cutting loose the buoys so that the traps and the lobster will get away. Furious but unable to prove Tyler's crime, Skiff observes the sale of a giant blue fin tuna one day to the businessman Mr. Nagahachi, who pays anywhere from $8 to $18 per pound to ship the giant tunas to Japan for expensive sushi meals. Thinking of the opportunity to make a large sum of money in one fishing trip, Skiff makes the desperate and daring decision to take his little skiff out thirty miles to sea and harpoon his own blue fin tuna for profit. In a suspenseful, episodic, first-person narrative, Skiff recounts the harrowing struggle to stay alive as the 900-pound tuna he manages to harpoon pulls him out of the boat and into the depths of the sea and back up again. Alternately talking to himself and to his deceased mother, Skiff uses all the skill, knowledge, and wherewithal he can muster to save himself and keep hold of the giant fish until it finally succumbs to its wounds and is captured. Skiff's father ultimately rescues the boy just five miles from shore with the help of Tyler's dad. The frightening experience for both boy and dad sparks a new understanding between them.

Main Characterization

Through the course of his mother's unfortunate early death and his father's depressive neglect of himself, Skiff Beaman has learned that he must find a way to create an income. He is sincere, resourceful, courageous, and a bit impulsive, yet ready to follow his mother's advice about never giving up. He chooses his battles carefully, knowing that the bully Tyler Croft is not worth the effort of a real fight, finding another way to achieve his goal to earn a large sum of money.

Themes

Themes of survival and perseverance are apparent in Skiff's struggle to help his father return to making a living as a fisherman. Skiff displays a take-charge attitude, despite the overwhelming odds of his succeeding, his father's alcoholic depression, and his attempt to catch a goliath tuna for profit. Bullying, seen through Skiff and Tyler's negative relationship, is a subtheme.

Books with Similar Issues or Themes

Melville, Herman. *Moby Dick, or, The White Whale,* adapted by Geraldine McCaughrean. Illustrated by Victor G. Ambrus. New York: Oxford University Press, 1996.
>An excellent adaptation and lead-in to the classic sea-venturing novel.

Ransome, Arthur. *We Didn't Mean to Go to Sea.* Boston: Gregg Press, 1981 (first published in 1938).
>Four children embark on a dangerous adventure when their small sailboat is swept out to sea in a powerful tide.

Rosenbaum, Robert A., ed. *Best Book of True Sea Stories.* Illustrated by Kiyoaki Komoda. New York: Doubleday, 1966.
>An exciting collection of adventure and escape stories set on the unpredictable sea.

Salisbury, Graham. *Blue Skin of the Sea: A Novel in Stories.* New York: Delacorte, 1992.
>Sonny Mendoza, living in Hawaii and a descendant of Portuguese fishermen, overcomes his fear of the sea in these inviting and unpredictable stories.

Sperry, Armstrong. *Call It Courage.* New York: Simon & Schuster, 1940.
>The Newbery Medal classic featuring Mafatu, the Stout Heart, who conquers his fear of the sea in his canoe.

Author-Related Sources

Hipple, Ted, ed. *Writers for Young Adults.* New York: Charles S. Scribner's Sons, 2000, 227–36.

"Rodman Philbrick." In vol. 122 of *Something about the Author.* Farmington Hills, MI: Gale Group, 2001, 180–5.

Rodman Philbrick's Web site: http://www.rodmanphilbrick.com (accessed 25 December 2004).

Discussion Questions

For *The Young Man and the Sea*

1. What gives Skiff the encouragement and tenacity to find a way to earn money?

2. How do the three rules Skiff's mother taught him help him succeed?

3. Why are these rules important for everyone in general?

4. How does Skiff keep his will and spirit alive even when he is in mortal danger in the sea?

5. Do you think that Skiff's choices are heroic or risky?

6. Why does Skiff choose to go out to sea alone and attempt to catch the fish without help from others?

7. How do Skiff and his father feel about each other after the rescue?

8. Why is Skiff a hero in your mind?

9. What makes this story exciting and adventurous?

Chapter 5

Readers' Rap

Discussion groups led for and with children exclusively, what I call a Readers' Rap, fall into a more traditional programming category of storytimes, film hours, craft sessions, and summer reading clubs. School settings often provide opportunities either during informal lunch sessions or within formal classroom literature circles. Attracting and developing a strong, motivated, and interested core of boys and girls who like to talk about books with each other on a continual basis can be a somewhat greater challenge than the previously explored family-oriented series. Children looking for intrigue, excitement, and the feeling that they are doing something of *their* choosing will more readily attend and continue to read than those coaxed by an eager parent or teacher, ready to help that child become a better reader through your discussion program. One objective this program can fulfill over any other is to allow children free choice of participation and the impetus to develop lifelong recreational reading pleasure.

How can we accomplish this goal? Working within your community of readers, you can begin by selecting books that again have universally appealing themes and issues appropriate for both boys and girls. Protagonists of either gender should deal with conflicts and situations that are not gender sensitive such as the concept of eternal life explored in Natalie Babbitt's *Tuck Everlasting*. Stories favoring animal protagonists, such as Avi's *Ereth's Birthday* bring out a variety of personalities to analyze and generate basic critiquing. Books such as Konigsburg's *The View from Saturday* with a mixed gender of co-protagonists that offer individual and unified conflicts in the story, also work well.

Children who are already pressured with extra activities may not participate willingly or commit to the sessions if the choices prove to be too long or difficult every time. Providing easier-to-read choices that have meaty discussion concepts such as Leslea Newman's recent *Hachiko Waits,* might allow greater interest and commitment among a variety of reading abilities so that your group is encouraged to return and even grow. For older children, selecting themes with current global and political settings, such as Nye's *Habibi* or *Fish* by L. S. Matthews, places the reader in the context of a conflict that otherwise might only be seen through the detached view of the media. Finally, combining initial choices with recent film productions, such as *Because of Winn-Dixie*, might help initiate and invigorate the group, encouraging participants to continue with similar discussions. Encouraging input on book selection by providing a series of titles you introduce with energized booktalks will create a feeling of autonomy and allow for some independence within the group. If your group meets over a period of time and is able to bond, offering the ability to share your facilitator role with a rotating co-leader from the group might also instill a shared direction as your group develops over the program series.

The Cats in Krasinski Square

By Karen Hesse, Illustrated by Wendy Watson

New York: Scholastic Press, 2004

Reading Level: . . . . Grades 3–4; discussion level: Grade 3 and up
Genre: . . . . Holocaust picture book
Themes: . . . . The Holocaust, resistance, bravery

Plot Summary

A young girl and her sister work with the resistance movement amid the danger and terror brought on by the Gestapo to help smuggle food to those trapped in the Warsaw ghetto. Based on a true story told in a short article about the use of cats to outfox the Gestapo soldiers at a train station, this poetic verse recounts the little girl's relationship with all the homeless cats that have lost their families to the war. Needing diversion from the destruction around her, the girl bravely risks walking outside to play and cuddle with the cats knowing that they can feed themselves on mice as they let her see the cracks and holes in the wall separating her from the ghetto. When a plan to smuggle food in satchels at the train station to the other side is uncovered by the Germans, the girl, with her sister and friends, use the cats to create a chaotic distraction so that the plan is carried out successfully.

Main Characterization

The little girl in this story is brave and resilient beyond her years. She serves as the voice of the resistance to recount its courageous actions. The cats represent both friendship and a subversive weapon in a struggle that sometimes achieves glimmers of success.

Themes

This triumphant Holocaust story brings to light the incredible bravery of people who risked their lives in the face of brutality to work together in a resistance movement.

Books with Similar Issues or Themes

Innocenti, Roberto, and Christophe Gallaz. *Rose Blanche*. New York: Harcourt, Brace, 1985.
  A little German girl discovers a place in the woods where some hungry children with bright yellow stars sewn on their clothes are kept behind a barbed wired fence. She then brings them food daily, hiding it in her school bag.

McCann, Michelle P. *Luba the Angel of Bergen-Belsen*. Illustrated by Anne Marshall. Toronto: Tricycle Press, 2003.
  A concentration camp prisoner comes across a group of children left behind her barracks to starve and freeze to death. She secretly hides them with her fellow women prisoners, sharing or smuggling what food they are given or that she can find.

Polacco, Patricia. *The Butterfly*. New York: Philomel Books, 2000.

> During the Nazi occupation of France, a young Jewish girl is hidden by a family that is working with the French Resistance.

Rappaport, Doreen. *The Secret Seder*. Illustrated by Emily Arnold McCully. New York: Hyperion Books for Children, 2005.

> Pretending to be Catholics in Nazi-occupied France, Jacques and his father risk everything to attend a secret Seder in the mountains to observe the Passover holiday.

Author-Related Sources

Hipple, Ted, ed. *Writers for Young Adults*. New York: Charles S. Scribner's Sons, 2000, 93–102.

"Karen Hesse." In vol. 103 of *Something about the Author*. Farmington Hills, MI: Gale Group, 1999, 80–6.

"Karen Hesse." In vol. 113 of *Something about the Author*. Farmington Hills, MI: Gale Group, 2000, 67–82.

Discussion Questions

For *The Cats in Krasinski Square*

1. What do you notice about this city and its residents?

2. How do you think the little girl feels when she plays with the stray cats?

3. What does the little girl mean when she says, "I wear my Polish look, I walk my Polish walk"?

4. How does playing with the cats help the little girl cope with her war-torn life?

5. Why do you think the little girl and her friends did what they did with the cats even though it was so dangerous?

6. How do the illustrations tell you this is a city during wartime?

7. Why do you think the little girl wears red against the duller shades of grays and browns?

8. What does the merry-go-round symbolize for the little girl?

9. Do you think this is a sad or a happy story? Why?

10. There are countries in the world today where brave people are resisting and fighting a cruel government. How does this story relate?

Ereth's Birthday

By Avi, Illustrated by Brian Floca

New York: HarperCollins, 2000

Reading Level: . . . . Grades 4–6
Genre: . . . . Animal fantasy
Themes: . . . . Responsibility, survival, friendship

Plot Summary

Upset and annoyed that his birthday has been all but forgotten by his neighboring mouse family, a cantankerous, old, and nasty porcupine named Erethizon Dorsatum decides to travel out of Dimwood Forest in search of salt, a special tasty treat he is sure he deserves. The surest place to find salt is in the cabin of animal fur trappers, and this sets Ereth on a precarious and foolish pursuit. As snowfall makes his journey increasingly more difficult and dangerous, Ereth comes upon Leaper, a female fox caught in one of the trapper's mutilating metal spring traps, bleeding and near death. Begrudgingly and against his judgment, Ereth agrees to find Leaper's three baby kits and promises to take care of them. At the same time, Ereth is unaware that Marty the Fisher is watching and patiently waiting for Ereth to place himself in a dangerous position so that he can make his move. Finding the three fox kits, Tumble, Nimble, and Flip, Ereth behaves in his characteristically belligerent fashion, but nevertheless keeps his promise to care for and provide food until their father, Bounder, has returned. Continually feeling sorry for himself and eager to pursue his quest for salt, Ereth leaves the fox family, having warned and shown them how to watch out for other traps beneath the snow, only to be caught by Marty the Fisher in the fight for his life. Rescued by the three rambunctious and brave fox kits in a flurry of snapping and biting, Marty retreats and is caught by one of the trappers. Ereth decides to return home and bring the kits with him. His neighbors, Poppy and Rye, express their worry, not knowing their birthday friend's whereabouts for the last month and greet him with a gift of salt, much to Ereth's surprise.

Main Characterization

Ereth is an old, crotchety soul, always ready with a whip-lashing barrage of words to describe his thoughts and feelings of self-interest. However, his experience with Leaper and her kits brings out responsibility and altruism in Ereth, who takes on their care and feeding. Despite his outwardly harsh verbiage that attracts enemies such as Marty the Fisher and Bounder, Ereth has a kind, inner strength that is seen by those who truly care about him.

Themes

Friendship and responsibility are depicted through the surrogate parental role that Ereth adopts. Survival is a constant theme as the animals in the story deal with everything from the basic need for food to perilous hunters to other animals of prey.

Books with Similar Issues or Themes

Jarrell, Randall. *The Animal Family*. New York: HarperCollins, 1997.
A hunter living in the forest makes himself a family with a mermaid, a bear cub, a lynx, and a boy.

King-Smith, Dick. *Martin's Mice*. New York: Crown, 1989.
Martin, the cat, adopts a mouse family, keeps them in an old bathtub, and feeds and protects them despite their wish to be left free.

Lawson, Robert. *Rabbit Hill*. New York: Viking Press, 1944.
When a new family moves into the house on Rabbit Hill, the animals wonder if their meager subsistence will improve with the gardening and livelihood the humans may provide.

Selden, George. *The Old Meadow*. Illustrated by Garth Williams. New York: Farrar, Straus & Giroux, 1987.
The animals in the meadow join forces to save Mr. Budd and his dog from certain eviction after the town council of Hedley, Connecticut, has declared Old Meadow a landmark.

Van de Wetering, Janwillem. *Hugh Pine*. Illustrated by Lynn Munsinger. Boston: Houghton Mifflin, 1980.
The intelligent porcupine, Hugh Pine, searches for a solution to save his less fortunate brethren from the dangers of roadkill.

Author-Related Sources

"Avi." In vol. 68 of *Children's Literature Review*. Farmington Hills, MI: Gale Group, 2001, 1–46.

"Avi." In vol. 108 of *Something about the Author*. Farmington Hills, MI: Gale Group, 2000, 5–13.

Avi's official Web site: http://www.avi-writer.com/ (accessed 19 February 2005).

Berger, Laura Standley, ed. *Twentieth-Century Young Adult Writers*. Detroit, MI: St. James Press, 1994, 40–2.

Bloom, Susan P., and Cathryn M. Mercier. *Presenting Avi*. Woodbridge, CT: Twayne, 1997.

Hipple, Ted, ed. In vol. 1 of *Writers for Young Adults*. New York: Charles S. Scribner's Sons, 1997, 63–72.

Markham, Lois. *Avi*. Santa Barbara: Learning Works, 1996.

Silvey, Anita, ed. *Children's Books and Their Creators*. Boston: Houghton Mifflin, 1995, 38–9.

Discussion Questions

For *Ereth's Birthday*

1. How would you describe Ereth's feelings?

2. How does the author use words and language to express Ereth's feelings?

3. Why does Ereth keep his promise to Leaper to take care of her kits?

4. What does Ereth gain from his experience in the forest with the fox family?

5. Why do the three fox kits risk their lives for Ereth?

6. What does Ereth realize when he returns home?

7. Why is this the best and worst birthday of Ereth's life?

8. What does this story say about friendship and responsibility?

9. What makes the life of any animal in the forest a challenge?

Fish

by L. S. Matthews

New York: Delacorte Press, 2004

Reading Level: . . . . Grades 6–8
Genre: . . . . Realistic fiction
Themes: . . . . Survival, refugees, war and destruction

Plot Summary

When civil war comes to the village where Tiger and her foreign-aid worker parents are staying, they must flee on foot to cross the border and return to their home country. The journey is told from the perspective of the young child who has never known another home and is both intrigued and concerned about the trip they are about to undertake. As Guide loads his loyal donkey with the basic supplies and belongings for the several days' walk, Tiger finds a fish barely floating in the remains of a very muddy pond, washed out from the river with the monsoon rains. The fish is rescued, and all agree that it can join the trip, kept alive in a securely closed pot of water, wrapped in Tiger's backpack. The trip is arduous, difficult, perilous, and frightening as the four travelers are refused entry at the normal border checkpoint and must change their route, walking over difficult terrain that is both desert dry and mountainous and treading through a muddy deep river. Through it all, Tiger describes each obstacle they must overcome and endure to reach safety. They encounter unfriendly and murderous soldiers, teeter close to the edge of a cliff as the path narrows greatly, and run out of food and water. The donkey's amazing animal instinct on which Guide relies for their direction and its sure footing over treacherous ground, together with the metaphorical aspect of the fish's survival as Tiger falls and the water supply spills and is consumed, demonstrate faith and perseverance in this survival story against incredible odds. The exhausting escape dramatically concludes with parents and child, barely able to continue the last stretch of their twelve-hour hike down the mountain, finally reaching the other side of the border.

Main Characterization

Tiger's innocence and trust are continually challenged and altered as she worries over conversations she overhears between her father and Guide while their journey increases in danger. Yet when she is separated from her parents and left to save herself from the three violent soldiers, she is smart enough to control her fear and hide from them. She gains fortitude from both the encouragement she receives from the adults but also the responsibility she feels to keep her fish alive at all costs. The incredible scene of using her mouth as a last effort to keep the fish wet parallels the travelers' formidable struggle to walk the final twelve hours without food, water, or rest.

Themes

The devastation and destruction that result during and after war are portrayed in this survival story uniquely told from a child's perspective.

Books with Similar Issues or Themes

Whelan, Gloria. *Goodbye, Vietnam*. New York: Random House, 1992.

Thirteen-year-old Mai relates her family's escape through the swamps of the Mekong Delta and aboard one of the numerous overcrowded fishing boats at the height of the Vietnam War.

Holm, Anne. *I Am David*. New York: Harcourt Children's Books, 2004.

David escapes on foot from his twelve-year-long life in an Eastern European prison camp, traveling through a world he does not understand, hoping to cross the border to Denmark.

Mead, Alice. *Adem's Cross*. New York: Bantam Doubleday Books, 1996.

This survival story tells of a fourteen-year-old boy living in Serbian-controlled Kosovo who escapes across the mountains after his family is brutally singled out and persecuted.

Mikaelsen, Ben. *Tree Girl*. New York: HarperCollins, 2004.

Witnessing a massacre from the safety of the tree she loves to climb, Guatemalan Gabriela spends months alone, avoiding more violence from the soldiers who killed her family and eventually seeking refuge across the border in Mexico where her sister Alicia lives.

Discussion Questions

For *Fish*

1. Where do you think this story might take place?

2. What does Tiger's description of their journey on foot help you understand about the situation?

3. What dangers do the characters encounter, and how were they able to overcome each one?

4. What does the fish represent in the story?

5. How does the fish's appearance change and symbolically reflect the travelers' situation?

6. Why is the fish's survival important for all the characters, including Guide?

7. How does the release of the fish in a river parallel the escape of Tiger and her family?

8. What does this story tell you about humanity and the will to survive?

9. What feelings did you have while reading this story?

Flipped

By Wendelin Van Draanen

New York: Alfred A. Knopf, 2001

Reading Level: . . . . Grades 6–8

Genre: . . . . Realistic fiction

Themes: . . . . Coming of age, self-reflection, ethical behavior, respect for handicapped

Awards: . . . . School Library Journal Best Books

Plot Summary

Bryce Loski and Juli Baker have been neighbors and classmates since the second grade. They tell of their turbulent relationship over the years in alternating voices and with individual perspectives on how circumstances and situations have dramatically changed their feelings and attitude toward one another by the eighth grade. Bryce has always had a problem coping with Juli's in-your-face, pushy, confident. and imposing personality. He has spent days avoiding her, ignoring her, trying to get her to disappear from his life. On the other hand, Juli has had a crush on Bryce and his beautiful blue eyes from the day he moved in across the street when they were just seven years old. As the school years progress, Bryce watches Juli from a distance somewhat intrigued, but never quite understanding her motives and reasons for doing things. When Juli takes to climbing an old, very large sycamore tree near the school bus stop each morning, Bryce thinks she is behaving like a maniac monkey. But Juli's view of the world from her high perch makes her feel wonderfully alive, watching the beauty of nature and the colors of the sunsets. When the owner of the land where the tree stands hires a company to cut it down for a new house, Juli takes a bold stand and refuses to climb down, causing quite a commotion and rewarding her with a picture on the front page of the local paper. Her brave attempt at saving the tree, although unsuccessful, impresses Bryce's grandfather, who sees a girl, much like his late wife, with spunk and an admirable character. Juli has been raised in a home that believes in hard work and taking care of family. Her retarded adult uncle is the responsibility of her father and somewhat of a financial drain on the family. But love and support are foremost in her parent's values. Bryce, on the other hand, comes from a family that has done well financially. His father has a low tolerance for those less fortunate and a poor understanding of the mentally disabled. When Bryce's father learns of Juli's family circumstances and openly refers to the Bakers as "trash," his rude, discriminatory remarks upset and embarrass the entire family, especially Bryce. His grandfather is able to shed light on certain values and ethics for Bryce, and the two bond to develop a better understanding of their neighbors. In the meantime, Juli sees a different side of the Loski family and, hurt and angry, refuses to continue pursuing a friendship with Bryce. It takes a family dinner invitation and a whole lot of humbleness on Bryce's part to mend a relationship through apologetic words and a very special gift of a new sycamore tree. Not surprisingly, Bryce literally flips his attitude and develops a new affection for Juli, seeing the warm and insightful girl, described several months before by his grandfather.

Main Characterization

Bryce Loski is the average boy who only wants to appear normal to his male buddies and works hard to stay within the limits of peer acceptance. He is more disturbed by Juli's liveliness and for several years cannot see beneath the outwardly weird behavior she displays. It requires his grandfather's experience and wisdom to teach Bryce that Juli's inner beauty is her strength of character and happy, self-sufficient attitude.

Julianna Baker lives in her own world of values and ideals gleaned from her family's subtle approach to life. Her goal is always to strive to be and do the best she can.

Mr. Loski and his intolerance is an unfortunate example of how incorrect assumptions can be made leading to disrespect and even prejudicial attitudes. His closed-minded behavior leads him to label people, as he does with Juli's uncle and brothers, disrespectfully referring to them as "retard" and "drug pushers," respectively.

Chet Duncan, Bryce's grandfather, serves as a positive male role model in a divided household. His ethics and loneliness combine to pave the way for Juli and Bryce to gain a better understanding of each other.

Themes

Juli and Bryce mature and take a new look at each other's values and thinking as they come of age. The events in their year before high school, including the sycamore tree incident, the egg fiasco, and the final fundraising campaign, all serve to help the characters reflect on the ideals with which they have been raised. Ethical behavior and respect for the less fortunate or handicapped are also shown.

Books with Similar Issues or Themes

Hyppolite, Joanne. *Seth and Samona*. Illustrated by Colin Bootman. New York: Delacorte Press, 1995.
> Seth, a quiet Haitian American boy, and Samona, a wild and free-spirited girl in the fifth grade, build an unlikely friendship despite their very different families.

Holt, Kimberley Willis. *When Zachary Beaver Came to Town*. New York: Henry Holt, 1999.
> Thirteen-year-old Toby Wilson works through his own coming-of-age issues during the summer when a traveling side show stops in his town and he meets Zachary Beaver, "the world's fattest boy."

Nelson, Theresa. *Ruby Electric: A Novel*. New York: Atheneum, 2003.
> Ruby, a smart and well-behaved girl, must contend with two boys at school, Big Skinny and Mouse, who help her to uncover her true feelings about her father's disappearance through a series of misunderstood yet well-meaning endeavors.

Paterson, Katherine. *Bridge to Terabithia*. New York: Crowell, 1977.
> A country boy and a city girl become close friends through their imaginative play.

Author-Related Sources

Interview with Wendelin Van Draanen: http://www.writerswrite.com/journal/dec01/vandraanen.htm (accessed 2 March 2005).

"Wendelin Van Draanen." In vol. 122 of *Something about the Author*. Farmington Hills, MI: Gale Group, 2001, 213–7.

Discussion Questions

For *Flipped*

1. What kind of girl is Julianna Baker?

2. What kind of boy is Bryce Loski?

3. Why is it difficult for them to become friends?

4. What does the sycamore tree represent to Juli?

5. What does Bryce learn from his grandfather about making choices and doing the right thing?

6. Why is it important for Juli to clean up her yard? How does this have a positive impact on the Loski household?

7. What does Juli realize after her visit with her father at her uncle's group home?

8. What difficulties does the Loski family have despite the fact that they seem to have a good middle-class lifestyle?

9. What does Bryce learn about himself and his family by observing Juli and her way of life?

10. What is the significance of the title *Flipped*? What does it mean, beyond the idea that Bryce has fallen in love with Juli?

Gideon's People

By Carolyn Meyer

New York: Harcourt, Brace, 1996

Reading Level: . . . . Grades 4–6
Genre: . . . . Historical fiction
Themes: . . . . Friendship, religious convictions, cultural differences
Awards: . . . . YALSA Best Books for Young Adults

Plot Summary

Two boys from very religiously different families are brought together through an accident. Twelve-year-old Isaac Litvak is hurt when the horse, pulling the wagon his peddler father uses to sell his wares, is spooked by a thunderstorm on the property of Gideon's Amish family farm in early-twentieth-century Lancaster, Pennsylvania. Isaac is taken in by Gideon's family and nursed back to health over a two-week period, while his father must return to their Orthodox Jewish home and care for Mameh and the new baby. The two lifestyles, paradoxically very different and similar in terms of religious conviction, are reflected in Isaac's experience with his host family. Sixteen-year-old Gideon is considered to be *dopplig* ("dreamy") by his stern father, with whom he has a difficult, if not volatile, relationship. Gideon is very interested in the world outside their Amish community; he has refused thus far to commit to his religion by the traditional baptism which would then require him to follow all the rules in their rigid and restrictive *Ordnung* and is planning to leave the community for another, more liberal one where his uncle lives. Thrust into a very different life from his Jewish world, Isaac must remember to keep to his religious rules, particularly those pertaining to eating kosher food. Both families represent strong religious values with similar convictions, and the boys are able to make comparisons and distinctions as they observe each other over the two-week period. Gideon's personal need to lead a more openly acceptable life without being chastised for his unorthodox ways brings him both confusion and anger as he decides his only choice is to leave, no matter how much he will miss his mother and little sister Annie. Isaac feels increasingly uncomfortable in the Amish surroundings despite the caring and loving attention he has received as he struggles to understand the corporal punishment to which Gideon is subjected by his father for his alternative way of thinking. The experience brings to both boys emotional growth and a mutual respect for the divergent ways of each other's families.

Main Characterization

Isaac is a twelve-year-old Jewish boy eager to begin to learn his father's trade and excited to be allowed on this first peddler's trip. When placed in the care of an Amish family, he is hesitant and nervous, never having been separated from his family before and never having spent the Sabbath without them. He clearly remembers his place in the world and the culture and traditions he must keep; he does his best to explain what he is allowed to eat as he compares religious rules with the Amish family. He is also disturbed by the harsh and different ways of showing love and respect from which Gideon is running away.

Gideon is an angry sixteen-year-old, looking to find a way to stay Amish but live a less restrictive life in a more modern world. He is curious about the outside world and is interested to learn about "worldly ways." He resents his father's blind acceptance of their lifestyle and his unreasonable expectations.

Annie, Gideon's little sister, acts as a liaison between the Orthodox Jewish and the Amish lifestyles. She is able to equate and compare the religious rules and helps her family understand Isaac's needs. Like her brother, Annie would like to explore a less rigid and more modern way of life and helps to keep Gideon's secret safe despite her fears for losing him.

Themes

Cultural differences depicted through each family's religious convictions is the main theme in this story of two boys who develop a cautious and respectful friendship. Friendship and respect are also displayed in the way each father welcomes and takes care of a boy from outside his community. Not only is Isaac looked after on the Amish farm, but Gideon is also brought to Isaac's home for a traditional Jewish Sabbath meal.

Books with Similar Issues or Themes

Carmi, Daniella. *Samir and Yonatan*. Translated from the Hebrew by Yael Lotan. New York: Scholastic/Arthur A. Levine Books, 2000.

> Two boys, one Jewish and the other Palestinian, meet in a hospital in Israel and become friends despite their different cultures and prejudicial views.

Books about the Amish and Jewish Cultures

Israel, Fred L. *The Amish*. New York: Chelsea House, 1996.

An overview of the Amish culture and way of life.

Brown, Tricia. *L'Chaim: The Story of a Russian Émigré Boy*. New York: Henry Holt, 1994.

A look into the Orthodox Jewish world of a young boy.

Author-Related Sources

Berger, Laura Standley, ed. *Twentieth-Century Young Adult Writers*. Detroit, MI: St. James Press, 1994, 453–5.

"Carolyn Meyer." In vol. 142 of *Something about the Author*. Farmington Hills, MI: Gale Group, 2002, 99–120.

Hipple, Ted, ed. *Writers for Young Adults*. New York: Charles S. Scribner's Sons, 2000, 175–84.

Discussion Questions

For *Gideon's People*

1. Isaac and Gideon live in different communities and follow different religions but still have many things in common. What do you think are their similarities?

2. How does Gideon feel about continuing his life in the Amish tradition?

3. What concerns does Gideon have about completely leaving the Amish world?

4. How does Isaac feel about living with Gideon's family for two weeks?

5. What does the custom of "shunning" accomplish when a member of the Amish community doesn't obey the rules?

6. What do both boys gain from living with each other for the two-week period?

7. What does Isaac's father mean when he says, "Remember who you are" before leaving Isaac in the care of Gideon's family?

8. Why does the peddler Jakob help Gideon despite it conflicting with his religious observance on the Sabbath? What does this mean to Gideon and to Isaac?

9. Sometimes real-life situations bring a need for compromise. How do Gideon, Isaac, Jakob, and Annie all compromise to live their lives within their religion while achieving certain goals?

The Giver

By Lois Lowry

Boston: Houghton Mifflin, 1993

Reading Level: . . . . Grades 6–8
Genre: . . . . Science fiction
Themes: . . . . Diversity, controlled society, free choice, utopia
Awards: . . . . Newbery Medal

Plot Summary

Jonas lives in a unique community, run by the elders, with rules and controls devised to maintain a normal, safe, peaceful life. The elders of this community believe sameness and the lack of free choice guarantee an error-free world, removing the difficulty and pain of living. All of life's ugliness—poverty, inequality, war, rebellion—is eliminated through a system that does not allow free thinking. Even death is considered and referred to as a form of "release." The inhabitants of this community all live their very controlled life happily, unaware of the reality of a world with choices, both good and bad. Families are created according to a strict plan. Children are schooled and then assigned a lifelong career at the age of twelve, chosen by the elders at an annual ceremony. Twelve-year-old Jonas is excited and apprehensive about his upcoming assignment and is quite confused, even embarrassed, when at the time, he is passed over by the Chief Elder. But Jonas is special and possesses a talent that makes him a strong candidate for the most important position, "the receiver of memories." The current Receiver is very old and must train a new person, someone who has the ability to see beyond, as Jonas can. Jonas then becomes "the Receiver" and begins his long training with "the Giver" to learn and experience all of the memories of a past life. He begins to see and feel emotions he has never truly had through the realistic visions the giver passes on to him. Jonas is exposed to both the wonders of life—natural beauty, love, laughter, and enjoyment through a colorful and spiritual awareness—and to the harsh brutalities of war, disease, famine, death. and destruction. These painful episodes and the clarity of what his community has done to its inhabitants disturb Jonas, causing strong conflict within him and resulting in the most difficult choice of his life. Jonas must decide whether he can continue as the Receiver and live a life of loneliness, filled with both wonderful and unbearable knowledge or leave the community for "elsewhere."

Main Characterization

Jonas believes in everything he has learned from his parents, teachers, and the community but is also a curious and bright boy who tends to question even before he is given the ability to do so by the Giver. It is this ability to question and evaluate that ultimately forces him to make the decision to leave.

The Giver represents the knowledge of all past life, both good and evil. Although his obedience has allowed him to maintain his position for so many years, he accepts the honor, yet refuses to use his power of so much knowledge to change things. Only when confronted by the death of his own daughter is the Giver able to allow Jonas the opportunity to leave for the good of the community.

Themes

Sameness versus diversity in a controlled society is the premise in this story. The elders of this society have a parental attitude, eliminating free choice and error to maintain peace and tranquility and a form of utopia.

Books with Similar Issues or Themes

Cormier, Robert. *Fade*. New York: Delacorte Press, 1988.
Thirteen-year-old Paul Moreaux inherits the power to become invisible and struggles with the possibilities. Is it a curse or a gift?

Farmer, Nancy. *The Ear, the Eye, and the Arm*. New York: Orchard Books, 1994.
In the future, technologically controlled society of Zimbabwe, year 2194, three children leave to discover both wonders and horrors of other societies as they are pursued by mutant detectives.

Haddix, Margaret Peterson. *Among the Hidden*. New York: Simon & Schuster, 1998.
Luke, a "shadow child" in a society that permits only two children per family, is the third and must hide his identity. When he meets ten other "thirds," they join forces to challenge their totalitarian society.

Lowry, Lois. Sequels to *The Giver: Gathering Blue* (2000) and *Messenger* (2004).

Author-Related Sources

Berger, Laura Standley, ed. *Twentieth-Century Young Adult Writers*. Detroit, MI: St. James Press, 1994, 408–10.

Daniel, Susanna. *Lois Lowry*. New York: Rosen Central, 2003.

Hipple, Ted, ed. In vol. 2 of *Writers for Young Adults*. New York: Charles S. Scribner's Sons, 1997, 269–70.

"Lois Lowry." In vol. 72 of *Children's Literature Review*. Farmington Hills, MI: Gale Group, 2002, 196 206.

"Lois Lowry." In vol. 111 of *Something about the Author*. Farmington Hills, MI: Gale Group, 2000, 121–8.

"Lois Lowry Autobiography." In vol. 127 of *Something about the Author*. Farmington Hills, MI: Gale Group, 2002, 134–50.

Lois Lowry's Web site: http://www.loislowry.com/ (accessed 27 February 2005).

Lowry, Lois. *Looking Back: A Book of Memories*. Boston: Houghton Mifflin, 1998.

Marcus, Leonard S., ed. *Author Talk: Conversations with Judy Blume et al.* New York: Simon & Schuster, 2000, 58–63.

Markham, Lois. *Lois Lowry*. Santa Barbara, CA: Learning Works, 1995.

Discussion Questions

For *The Giver*

1. How does this community differ from one in our world? What makes it better or worse?

2. What is the difference between having power and having honor?

3. Why does the Giver think the role of the Receiver is one of great honor without power?

4. What power do the elders possess? Does it benefit the community residents?

5. Why do the elders prevent the residents from making their own choices?

6. What keeps the residents so happy in a community without color, pain, or a past? How are the emotions they experience different from what Jonas feels as the Receiver?

7. What does Jonas realize after he has received a year's worth of training and memories? How does his training affect his relationship with his parents?

8. Why is leaving the community important for Jonas? What other choices could he have made?

9. Why is the Giver able to keep his role for so many years, yet Jonas is unable to continue after only one year? What is the most important thing the Giver passes on to Jonas?

10. What do you think happened to Jonas and Gabriel at the end?

11. Why do we need to have our memories, good and bad, to live a complete life?

12. Is it wrong for a society to be controlled by a small group of "elders"? How does free choice empower a society to be productive and hopeful despite the possibility of making poor choices?

13. Do you think a Utopian society can be truly free?

The Gold Cadillac

By Mildred Taylor, Illustrated by Michael Hays

New York: Dial Books for Young Readers, 1987

Reading Level: . . . . Grades 3–4

Genre: . . . . Historical fiction

Themes: . . . . Prejudice, racial bias, race relations, materialism

Plot Summary

The American dream for 'lois and Wilma's daddy is to own a beautiful new Cadillac, which he buys against their mother's better judgment. On the day he brings the shiny new car home, this African American family is awed and proud of their father's achievement, but when Daddy insists on driving the car down to visit relatives in Mississippi, the pleasurable experience and satisfaction of success is marred by the prejudice and persecution of the segregated South of the 1950s. As the family crosses over the Mississippi border, they are stopped by a white police officer who accuses Daddy of stealing the car. Falsely arrested and taken to the police station, the family waits in the car for three hours until the charges are dropped after ownership of the car is proven. Shaken by the experience, the family leaves the car close by with other relatives and continues the trip in a less showy Chevy. Following the trip home, Daddy sells the Cadillac, to the protests of his family, settling for the transportation of a less expensive car and the less obvious sign of success.

Main Characterization

Daddy works hard, is proud of his achievement, and feels he has a right to display his honest efforts by purchasing a Cadillac. But when his family is placed in danger because of this materialistic expression of success, he alters his thinking.

'lois relates the family's experience through her proud, young, and innocent voice. Both she and her father learn a difficult lesson about intolerance and humility.

Themes

Prejudice, racial bias, and race relations all come through in this story of a family's success kept in check by the intolerance of others.

Books with Similar Issues or Themes

Clements, Andrew. *The Jacket*. New York: Simon & Schuster, 2002.
> Wrongly accusing an African American boy for stealing his brother's jacket, Phil learns a hard lesson about ingrained prejudice.

Vander Zee, Ruth. *Mississippi Morning*. Illustrated by Floyd Cooper. Grand Rapids, MI: Eerdmans Books for Young Readers, 2004.
> The shock of Klan violence in Depression-era Mississippi is difficult for James William to accept when he realizes his father is a member and partially responsible for the cruelty and possible murders of many in the local black community.

Woodson, Jacqueline. *The Other Side*. Illustrated by Earl B. Lewis. New York: Putnam's, 2001.
Two girls, one white, one black, become friends over their property-dividing fence under the watchful and suspicious eyes of their parents.

Author-Related Sources

Berger, Laura Standley, ed. *Twentieth-Century Young Adult Writers*. Detroit, MI: St. James Press, 1994, 635–6.

Hipple, Ted, ed. In vol. 3 of *Writers for Young Adults*. New York: Charles S. Scribner's Sons, 1997, 273–82.

"Mildred Taylor." In vol. 135 of *Something about the Author*. Farmington Hills, MI: Gale Group, 2003, 205–10.

"Mildred Taylor." In vol. 90 of *Children's Literature Review*. Farmington Hills, MI: Gale Group, 2004, 119–49.

Murray, Barbara. *Black Authors and Illustrators of Books for Children and Young Adults,* 3rd edition. New York: Garland, 1999, 375.

Silvey, Anita, ed. *Children's Books and Their Creators*. Boston: Houghton Mifflin, 1995, 638–9.

Discussion Questions

For *The Gold Cadillac*

1. What does owning a Cadillac represent to the father in this story?

2. Why is it important for Daddy to drive the car to Mississippi? Why does he later change his mind?

3. Why do the uncles try to warn Daddy about driving the car south? What did they mean by using the word "lynch"?

4. Why does Daddy decide to sell the car after returning from the trip? Do you think he should have?

5. Why is having material possessions not always a sign of success?

6. What civil rights were denied to Daddy when the police stopped him?

7. What does this story help you understand about African American history, prejudice, and persecution in our country?

8. What is the meaning of this story for you?

Granny Torrelli Makes Soup

By Sharon Creech

New York: Joanna Cotler Books/HarperCollins, 2003

Reading Level: . . . . Grades 3–5
Genre: . . . . Realistic fiction
Themes: . . . . Self-reflection, friendship, visual disabilities
Awards: . . . . ALA Notable Children's Book

Plot Summary

The ups and downs of special friendship are told through the conversations between Rosie and her grandmother during visits filled with soup and pasta making. Together they discuss joy, sadness, jealousy, and love balanced by the wise words of Granny Torrelli's reminiscence of a childhood friend in Italy. Rosie's best friend in the world is her neighbor Bailey, a boy she has known since birth who is as close to her as a brother. Bailey's visual impairment does not interfere with their caring and endearing relationship until it is time for school. Accustomed to doing everything together, Rosie must adjust to attending a different school. But their playtime together and her visits with Granny Torrelli never change. As the children grow, Rosie is curious about how Bailey reads in Braille and, wanting to please him and hoping to surprise him, she struggles to learn Braille only to face his rebuke and anger. Rosie is upset and confides in her granny, who commiserates and helps her to understand Bailey's reasons with a story about her childhood friend, Pardo. Similarly, when a new girl, Janine, moves in on the block, Rosie is disturbed and even jealous of the interest she develops in Bailey until Granny Torrelli recounts another episode that includes Pardo and a new girl, Violetta. Granny Torrelli's paralleled and insightful stories help to straighten things out between Rosie and Bailey, two friends with an unbreakable bond.

Main Characterization

Rosie, a spunky, sensitive, and caring girl, is comfortable and confident with her two important confidantes, Bailey and Granny.

Bailey has learned to be independent and is proud of his ability to read and work despite his disability.

Granny Torrelli is wise and loving, using her recipes for soup and pasta to mend broken hearts and soothe misunderstandings.

Themes

Both Rosie and Bailey become better acquainted with themselves and with each other's feelings as they work through recent misconceptions, benefiting from Granny's experience and perspective.

Books with Similar Issues or Themes

Cameron, Ann. *Gloria's Way*. Illustrated by Lis Toft. New York: Garrar, Straus & Giroux, 2000.
In six vignettes, Gloria shares her adventures with friends Julian, Huey, and Latisha and solves her own frustrations and problems with the wise help of the adults who surround her.

Horvath, Polly. *The Trolls*. New York: Farrar, Straus & Giroux, 1999.
When their parents take a trip to Paris, ten-year-old Melissa, eight-year-old Amanda, and six-year-old Frank enjoy time with their babysitter, Aunt Sally, who tells wonderfully fantastic and true stories of their family history.

Hurwitz, Johanna. *Oh No, Noah*. Illustrated by Mike Reed. New York: SeaStar Books, 2002.
Klutzy Noah, new to the neighborhood, makes friends with Mo, the nosy girl next door, but still feels he must do something special to impress everyone in her group.

Author-Related Sources

Hipple, Ted, ed. *Writers for Young Adults*. New York: Charles S. Scribner's Sons, 2000, 29–36.

Interview with Sharon Creech: http://www.bookwire.com/bookwire/MeettheAuthor/Interview_Sharon_Creech.htm (30 May 2004).

"Sharon Creech." In vol. 89 of *Children's Literature Review*. Farmington Hills, MI: Gale Group, 2003, 22–52.

"Sharon Creech." In vol. 139 of *Something about the Author*. Farmington Hills, MI: Gale Group, 2002, 67–73.

Sharon Creech's Web site: http://www.sharoncreech.com/novels/01.asp (accessed 30 May 2004).

Silvey, Anita, ed. *Essential Guide o Children's Books and Their Creators*. Boston: Houghton Mifflin, 2002, 109–10.

Discussion Questions

For *Granny Torrelli Makes Soup*

1. Why does Bailey become angry with Rosie for learning to read Braille?

2. How does Rosie feel about Bailey? Why does she want to learn to read Braille?

3. How do Granny Torrelli's stories help Rosie understand her friendship with Bailey?

4. What does Rosie learn about feelings and anger from Granny Torrelli?

5. Why is Rosie and Bailey's friendship so special?

6. What does Rosie find out about herself through Granny Torrelli's stories about Pardo?

7. How does Rosie's friendship help Bailey to function despite his blindness?

8. Why is it important to have a pasta party at the end of the book?

Habibi

By Naomi Shihab Nye

New York: Simon & Schuster, 1997

Reading Level: . . . . Grades 6–8
Genre: . . . . Realistic fiction
Themes: . . . . Palestinian/Israeli conflict, cultural differences
Awards: . . . . ALA Notable Children's Book, YALSA Best Books for Young Adults

Plot Summary

The comfortable, middle-class life that fourteen-year-old Liyana and her younger brother Rafik enjoy in St. Louis, Missouri, is about to change in ways they cannot envision when their father, Doctor Abboud, announces his decision to move his family to his native Palestine and live in Jerusalem. Doctor Abboud, called Poppy by his children, came to America twenty years before with the intention of attending medical school but stayed after marrying and starting a family. Wanting to offer his children and American wife the knowledge and experience of their mixed heritage from within his home country, they arrive in Israel with feelings of curiosity and apprehension. Greeted by their grandmother, Sitti, and the entire extended Abboud family, Liyana and Rafik are introduced to some of the old Arabic customs of their ancestors and must adjust their liberal American upbringing to the more restrictive aspects of the culture. Liyana is not permitted to wear shorts or have a casual relationship with boys. Their father joyously wants to show them the wonders of the country—the food, the customs—as the children make a reluctant effort to follow along and please him. In fact, by the twenty-ninth day, Liyana recounts how her life has changed by listing the things she has accomplished. Her new friends at her Armenian school treat her nicely, she can write the proper heading on all her school papers, she has learned to read and write the Arabic alphabet, she knows exactly where to go during the daily hour and a half lunch period, and she is able to give tourists in the street directions. Rafik seems to have assimilated more easily, but Liyana is lonely and misses her American teen life and friends. On her daily lunch break, she has taken to wandering around the school neighborhood and enters a ceramics shop that sells beautiful pottery and meets Omer. Mistaking him for Omar, another Arab boy, they begin a conversation in English, and Liyana boldly accepts an invitation to meet him on Saturday afternoon in the old city. As it turns out, Omer is a Jewish boy, a bit older, and unconcerned about their different cultures. Liyana is intrigued by this boy, who talks of peace, harmony, and acceptance. Omer wishes to meet her grandmother and after much discussion and persuasion with her father, the whole family takes Omer outside Jerusalem to visit Sitti and the relatives. Most of them welcome Omer, but there is tension, particularly with an uncle who sees Omer as simply another Jew who will join the occupying government and Israeli army. The unfortunate reality of hatred and discrimination becomes frighteningly evident and personal to the Abboud children when their father becomes embroiled in an army raid at a Palestinian refugee camp near their home following a suicide bombing and is then arrested. Clearing his involvement and name takes several hours, but the family remains determined to live peacefully as Liyana, her parents and brother, Omer, and Sitti share a meal days later.

Main Characterization

As a girl, Liyana must contend with the restrictive constraints that an Arabic society imposes on females. Not only must she alter her way of dress to one of unadorned modesty, she must also try to comply with new expectations her father has developed concerning appropriate and conservative behavior. The cultural differences are something of an awakening for her, especially when she is introduced to the more modern lifestyle of western Jerusalem, the Jewish part of the city. Paradoxically, her brother Rafik has an easier time adjusting because, as a male, he is afforded a different status in society. He is not expected to change his behavior or style of dress and finds school "a piece of cake."

Omer is a secular Jewish boy who believes in judging people individually and genuinely wants to develop a relationship not only with Liyana, but with her family as well. He believes the history between Arabs and Jews is a difficult and cruel one but that peace is still possible.

Themes

Doctor Abboud has good intentions to introduce a wonderful culture to his family, but the Palestinian-Israeli conflict is always in the forefront as the Abboud family must deal with a suicide bombing. Their American identity becomes secondary to their Arabic one as they face the realities of war and a nation in self-defense. Liyana's adjustment to her new home and country bring out the cultural differences of her two countries and their people.

Books with Similar Issues or Themes

Banks, Lynne Reid. *Broken Bridge*. New York: Morrow Junior Books, 1995.
> After witnessing the murder of her visiting cousin Glen by the hand of a Palestinian terrorist, Israeli Nili chooses to conceal the identity of the killer as payment for sparing her life.

Clinton, Cathryn. *A Stone in My Hand*. Cambridge, MA: Candlewick Press, 2002.
> When her father is killed on a public bus attacked by a terrorist's bomb in Israel, Malaak, a Palestinian girl living in Gaza, withdraws into a silent world. But she must soon come back to reality to try and reach her militant brother, who has become involved with a group of radicals.

Levine, Anna. *Running on Eggs*. Chicago: Front Street/Cricket Books, 1999.
> Two girls living in Israel, one a Jewish girl on a Kibbutz, the other a Palestinian girl in a nearby village, meet on an Arab-Israeli track team and develop a friendship despite the disapproval of their families.

Miklowitz, Gloria D. *The Enemy Has a Face*. Grand Rapids, MI: Eerdmans Books for Young Readers, 2003.
> Newly arrived in Los Angeles, Israeli Netta Hoffman is befriended by a Palestinian boy in her middle school and must confront her fears that terrorists are not responsible for her brother's mysterious disappearance.

Author-Related Sources

Holtze, Sally Holmes, ed. *Seventh Book of Junior Authors and Illustrators*. New York: H. W. Wilson, 1996, 240–1.

"Naomi Shihab Nye." In vol. 59 of *Children's Literature Review*. Farmington Hills, MI: Gale Group, 2000, 43–59.

"Naomi Shihab Nye." In vol. 147 of *Something about the Author*. Farmington Hills, MI: Gale Group, 2004, 169–77.

Naomi Shihab Nye, interview with Bill Moyers, October 11, 2002: http://www.pbs.org/now/transcript/transcript_nye.html (accessed 3 March 2005).

Discussion Questions

For *Habibi*

1. How does Liyana's life change after moving to Jerusalem?

2. What is most difficult for Liyana during her first year in Jerusalem?

3. Why is Liyana's brother able to adjust to their new life more easily than she can?

4. What is Poppy trying to accomplish by bringing his family to Jerusalem? How do some of the cultural differences make it difficult for them?

5. Liyana's mother compares the people living in Israel and Palestine with a family that is always fighting. What do you think she is trying to say?

6. Why is Omer interested in visiting Liyana's family? What does he believe?

7. How does Omer feel about living in Jerusalem? What does he mean when he tells Liyana, "a place is inside you—like a part of your body"?

8. How does Liyana's extended family feel about Omer and why?

9. Why do Liyana and Omer feel their friendship is important and must continue despite their different backgrounds?

10. What does the luncheon with Liyana, her parents, Omer, and Sitti represent at the end of the book?

Hachiko Waits

By Leslea Newman, Illustrated by Machiyo Kodaira

New York: Henry Holt, 2004

Reading Level: . . . . Grades 3–5
Genre: . . . . Historical fiction, cultural fiction
Themes: . . . . Devotion, loyalty, hope, friendship

Plot Summary

Professor Ueno lives a peacefully quiet, routine, orderly life in 1924 Japan. He acquires his eighth puppy and names him Hachi, the word for "eight" in Japanese. Hachi is an Akita, a Japanese dog breed known for its intelligence, good behavior, and loyalty to their masters. Each workday, Hachi accompanies the professor to the station, watches him board the commuter train, and then dutifully returns home to await his return. At three o'clock, Hachi instinctively knows to return to the station to wait and greet his master, as the professor descends from his train. Hachi is treated well by Professor Ueno, rewarded for his good, loyal behavior with kind words and gestures of praise. The professor and Hachi meet a young boy, Yasuo, and his mother in the train station and after becoming acquainted, they see each other most days on their way to work and school. One afternoon, Hachi comes to the station to wait on the platform as usual, and when the train arrives, the professor does not descend from the train. As each train arrives, Hachi waits patiently for a master who will never return; Professor Ueno has suffered a heart attack at work and died. Yasuo notices the dog alone, and when he learns of the professor's unfortunate fate, he tries to adopt the dog, but Hachi is unhappy and runs away. Each day, Hachi returns to the station a few minutes before 3 P.M. to wait for his master in vain. Over the course of ten years, he is fed and cared for by the train station supervisor and the daily commuters. The dog comes to represent a symbol of dedication and loyalty to the people of Japan. Articles in newspapers talk about his continual devotion, and he is given the honored name of Hachiko. Upon the dog's death, a statue is created for the train platform commemorating the dog's life and love for his master. A novelization based on a true story.

Main Characterization

Hachi is a devoted, loyal pet who behaves in the only way he knows: to obey his master exclusively. His animal persona instills a sense of sympathy, caring, and respect for a dog so persistent in his daily habitual expectation.

Yasuo is a gentle, caring, boy who displays a sense of responsibility and concern for his new charge and is unwilling to give up even when the dog refuses to live in his home.

Themes

Hachiko's persistent daily routine of waiting for a master who will never return symbolizes devotion and loyalty. Beyond his behavior, the themes are demonstrated in the willingness of Yasuo and the people surrounding the dog to continue to take care of him. In addition, hope and friendship are exhibited as well, as Hachiko never loses hope that his master and friend will return.

Books with Similar Issues or Themes

Burnford, Sheila. *The Incredible Journey*. Boston: Little, Brown, 1961.
> Three house pets, a Siamese cat, a Labrador retriever, and a bull terrier, follow their instinct and travel 250 miles west to rejoin their loving family, surviving weather, wild animals, and starvation through the Canadian wilderness.

Cleary, Beverly. *Henry and Ribsy*. New York: Morrow Junior Books, 1954.
> From the classic author, a story of a boy, his dog, and how they try to stay out of trouble on a fishing trip.

Gardiner, John Reynolds. *Stone Fox*. New York: Crowell, 1980.
> Willy trains daily for the National Dogsled Race with his devoted dog Searchlight, hoping to use the prize money to help pay the back taxes and save his grandfather's farm.

Kjelgaard, Jim. *Big Red*. New York: Holiday House, 1945.
> This is the story of the love and devotion between Danny and his dog, Red.

Rawls, Wilson. *Where the Red Fern Grows*. New York: Bantam Books, 1961.
> Classic story of Billy Colman and his two coonhound pups, Old Dan and Little Ann.

Author-Related Sources

"Leslea Newman." In vol. 134 of *Something about the Author*. Farmington Hills, MI: Gale Group, 2003, 124–7.

Leslea Newman's Web site: http://www.lesleanewman.com (accessed 3 December 2004).

Discussion Questions

For *Hachiko Waits*

1. How remarkable is it that Hachi instinctively knew when to come back each day to the station? What does this true story tell us about our pets?

2. Why does Hachi continue to come back, day after day, for so many years without seeing his master?

3. Why are the regular train commuters willing to help take care of Hachi even though he is now a stray dog?

4. What impression does Hachiko make on Yasuo's life?

5. Can this story be considered one specific to Japanese culture, or could it have taken place anywhere else in the world?

6. Why does Hachiko become a symbol for the Japanese people?

7. Why is it important to live with a certain amount of hope in your life?

The Hundred Dresses

By Eleanor Estes, Illustrated by Louis Slobodkin

New York: Harcourt Brace Jovanovich, 1974

Reading Level: . . . . Grades 3–4
Genre: . . . . Realistic fiction
Themes: . . . . Poverty, teasing, cultural differences
Awards: . . . . Newbery Honor

Plot Summary

Polish immigrant child Wanda Petronski feels out of place in her school, not just because of her different cultural background, but also because of her poor economic status. Wearing the same clean, faded blue dress that never hangs right, Wanda would like to fit in and have friends. One day when a crowd of girls gathers around Cecile to admire her new dress, Wanda is enveloped in the circle and impulsively tells Peggy that she, too, has a hundred dresses all lined up in her closet. The incredulous and cynical Peggy begins to taunt and tease, shouting out Wanda's unbelievable statement to the rest of the children. From that day on, Peggy and Maddie question Wanda on her "collection of dresses," always receiving the same answers. Wanda says that her dresses are lined up in the closet, they are of many different colors and materials, for different occasions, but that she cannot wear them to school. Thinking Wanda is a liar, the children are all surprised to discover that her collection is indeed real in the form of a variety of beautiful drawings and designs—one hundred to be precise. Wanda's talent earns her the prize in the school's annual drawing and color contest. But Wanda has moved away with her family to a more diverse neighborhood. Maddie has always felt uncomfortable about Peggy's gibes and is upset that Wanda's move means they won't have the chance to apologize. Instead the two write a letter, hoping Wanda will accept; in return, they receive a reply with drawings of two girls who have a strong likeness to them, both wearing beautiful dresses.

Main Characterization

Wanda's role in this story is the focus of the conflict. She is a quiet, sad, motherless girl, always on the outside, with dreams of acceptance and success.

Maddie, the narrator, is a girl who unconsciously knows her participation in taunting Wanda is wrong. She feels guilt and remorse yet cannot stand up to Peggy for fear of losing her acceptance and friendship. Wearing hand-me-downs, she is closer to Wanda's economic situation and can appreciate the family's struggle to afford new clothes.

Peggy, with her advantage of popularity, leads the group in mild although hurtful mockery of Wanda's original claim. She never quite feels the pain and sadness that Maddie experiences in losing what could have been a good friend.

Themes

Poverty and cultural differences foster a situation that involves the cruelty of teasing at the expense of someone less fortunate.

Books with Similar Issues or Themes

Cohen, Barbara. *Molly's Pilgrim*. Illustrated by Michael J. Deraney. New York: Lothrop, Lee & Shepard, 1983.
    Russian immigrant Molly brings in a homemade pilgrim to class that is different from the traditional American Thanksgiving figure and is embarrassed by her classmates' reaction.

Kline, Suzy. *Song Lee in Room 2B*. Illustrated by Frank Remkiewicz. New York: Viking, 1993.
    Korean-born, sweet-tempered Song Lee finds a way to be accepted by her classmates despite her shyness.

Marsden, Carolyn. *The Gold-Threaded Dress*. Cambridge, MA: Candlewick Press, 2002.
    Trying to fit in with her new classmates, Oy, a girl from Thailand, brings in a much-valued traditional silk dress that becomes the subject of misunderstood behavior when the special garment is unfortunately ripped.

Author-Related Sources

Berger, Laura Standley, ed. *Twentieth-Century Children's Writers*. Detroit, MI: St. James Press, 1995, 324–5.

"Eleanor Estes." In vol. 70 of *Children's Literature Review*. Farmington Hills, MI: Gale Group, 2001, 26–57.

"Eleanor Estes." In vol. 91 of *Something about the Author*. Farmington Hills, MI: Gale Research, 1997, 65–9.

Hopkins, Lee Bennett, ed. *More Books by More People*. New York: Citation Press, 1974, 147–52.

Silvey, Anita, ed. *Children's Books and Their Creators*. Boston: Houghton Mifflin, 1995, 226–7.

Discussion Questions

For *The Hundred Dresses*

1.   What emotions do Wanda, Peggy, and Maddie express?

2.   Why does Wanda want Peggy to know about her hundred dresses?

3.   Why doesn't anyone believe Wanda's statement about the hundred dresses?

4.   Why is Maddie able to understand Wanda better than Peggy can?

5.   What does Maddie realize about Peggy's teasing? Why couldn't she do anything to stop it?

6.   What do the hundred dresses represent to each of the girls—Peggy, Maddie, and Wanda?

7.   What do the girls learn from Wanda's drawings?

8.   In the end, what does Wanda have that both Peggy and Maddie never would?

9.   Why is Maddie so sad right to the end of the book?

10.   What does this story mean to you?

Journey to Jo'burg: A South African Story

By Beverley Naidoo, Illustrated by Eric Velasquez

New York: J. B. Lippincott, 1985

Reading Level: . . . . Grades 4–6
Genre: . . . . Historical fiction
Themes: . . . . Apartheid, race relations

Plot Summary

The apartheid environment of South Africa has separated thirteen-year-old Naledi, her brother Tiro, and little sister Dineo from their widowed mother, who must work as a maid for a white family in the city of Johannesburg, three hundred kilometers from their village. Dineo has taken seriously ill and might die if she is not taken for medical treatment soon. But Nono, their granny, has no money to take her to the doctor or to the hospital in the next village. Desperately afraid that Dineo will succumb to the fever, Naledi makes a bold decision to walk with Tiro to Johannesburg to find their mother and bring her back. The walking trip is much further than Naledi had realized, but fortunately they are offered a ride with a kind truck driver who brings them to the center of the city, where they must then take a bus to reach their destination. Naledi's sheltered life in her village has not prepared her for the reality of apartheid, and she is immediately reprimanded when she tries to board a bus for whites only. Rescued again, this time by a kind maid, Grace, who works on the same street as their mother, they learn to board the "blacks only" bus and are able to reach their mother in time. Mother must leave work to the annoyance of her employer, travel back with the children to the village, and take Dineo to the hospital. Throughout, Naledi and Tiro are introduced to the numerous hardships blacks have suffered under apartheid rule. Naledi's brave decision has saved her sister's life, but the family is now even more financially behind with mother's loss of workdays combined with all of the doctor bills. Nevertheless, Naledi has gained new insight into the plight of her people and is inspired to dream about a different future for herself, maybe even with a better education.

Main Characterization

Naledi is a serious girl, determined to do the right thing, who assumes responsibility for the well-being of her little sister. Her innocence regarding the political situation in her country is jarred and challenged as she witnesses the segregation and listens to Grace's explanations about the protests and rallies. But Naledi is also awakened to a new sense of hope and determination that things can change with the support and strength of many who are willing to question and take risks.

Themes

Apartheid and race relations are clearly portrayed through a girl's encounter with the realities of a segregated lifestyle.

Books with Similar Issues or Themes

Gordon, Sheila. *The Middle of Somewhere: A Story of South Africa*. New York: Orchard Books, 1990.
>   In South Africa during the apartheid period, Rebecca and her family are forced out of their home and village to make room for a new expensive white suburb.

Maartens, Maretha. *Paper Bird: A Novel of South Africa*. New York: Clarion Books, 1991.
>   A young black boy leaves his village every day despite the dangers of traveling in white South Africa to sell newspapers as a means of support for his family.

Silver, Norman. *An Eye for Color*. New York: Dutton Children's Books, 1991.
>   Twelve stories of a Jewish boy as he grows up in Capetown, South Africa, revealing the increasing awareness of the cruelty and disparity of apartheid.

Somewhere Tenderness Survives: Stories of Southern Africa. Selected by Hazel Rochman. New York: Harper & Row, 1988.
>   Ten stories and autobiographical accounts by both black and white authors describing life in South Africa's apartheid government.

Author-Related Sources

Berger, Laura Standley, ed. *Twentieth-Century Young Adult Writers*. Detroit, MI: St. James Press, 1994, 479–80.

"Beverley Naidoo." In vol. 29 of *Children's Literature Review*. Farmington Hills, MI: Gale Research, 1993, 160–7.

"Beverley Naidoo." In vol. 135 of *Something about the Author*. Farmington Hills, MI: Gale Group, 2003, 155–9.

Beverley Naidoo's Web site: http://www.beverleynaidoo.com/index2.html (accessed 27 February 2005).

Holtze, Sally Holmes, ed. *Seventh Book of Junior Authors and Illustrators*. New York: H. W. Wilson, 1996, 234–5.

Discussion Questions

For *Journey to Jo'burg: A South African Story*

1. What does Naledi learn about her country and her people on the trip?

2. How is education different for black children in the small villages of South Africa compared with whites who live in the cities?

3. What gives Naledi the encouragement to dream about a better life with a better education at the end of the story?

4. How does the trip to Johannesburg change Naledi?

5. How does the concept of apartheid compare with America's history of slavery?

6. What does freedom mean to a girl like Naledi?

Lizzie Bright and the Buckminster Boy

By Gary D. Schmidt

New York: Clarion Books, 2004

Reading Level: . . . . Grades 6–8

Genre: . . . . Historical fiction

Themes: . . . . Race relations, prejudice, coming of age

Awards: . . . . Newbery Honor, Printz Honor

Plot Summary

Turner Buckminster, son of the newly hired preacher in the seaside town of Phippsburg, Maine, has difficulty adjusting to his new home. Everything seems different from his hometown of Boston. Daunted by the wicked pitching of the boys he has met, Turner cannot play his usual game of baseball and is too scared to follow them, diving from atop a high granite edge. To make matters worse, his father expects him to dress and behave properly as the son of a preacher should, setting a good example for this 1911 coastal community. But Turner is unable, through one mishap after another, to comply and quickly learns to keep to himself as much as possible, avoiding the cruel torments and beatings of some of the town boys along with the chastising from some of the town elders. Assigned by his father to spend time with the aged Mrs. Cobb, reading to her and playing the organ as she awaits her impending death, Turner enters an unexpected friendship, his first in his new town. As the summer days grow longer and hotter, Turner spends time near the shore and meets Lizzie Bright Griffin, a down-to-earth, feisty girl who lives on the Malaga Island off the Maine coastline with her grandfather and other descendants of former slaves. The two develop a bond, each giving the other a view of life through their mutual experiences. Lizzie begins to join Turner at Mrs. Cobb's to listen to his organ playing as Turner visits Lizzie at her grandfather's, appreciating the simplicity of their livelihood through fishing, crabbing, and faith. As their relationship grows and becomes apparent to the senior members of the town council, racial prejudice fueled by a greed to turn the coastal town into a tourist resort sets off an underhanded campaign, led by the thieving, villainous Mr. Stonecrop, to remove forcefully Lizzie and the rest of the inhabitants of the island. Mrs. Cobb dies and bequeaths her home to Turner, who in turn wants to give it to Lizzie. As the pressure mounts on Turner, his father, seeing the injustice, chooses to uphold his son's decision rather than support his employers, the town deacons. The bigotry and hate climax in an unfortunate fatal conclusion with the death of both the Reverend Buckminster and Lizzie and the burning of the shanties on Malaga Island. Turner and his mother move into the Cobb house while the rest of the town attempts to recover from the ramifications of the horrific event.

Main Characterization

Turner Buckminster's status as preacher's son and newcomer, immediately places him in a vulnerable position. His city upbringing has left him unprepared for the small coastal lifestyle of Phippsburg. He feels trapped and isolated living within a rigidly conservative community and prefers solitude along the beach. Lizzie's friendship becomes a way for him to validate his own way of thinking and to learn to appreciate the beauty of his new environment.

Lizzie Bright Griffin is used to taking care of herself and her own. She is astute, bold, and brave, with genuine goodness. She is accepting of the racial prejudice surrounding her as she tells Turner that she will never be allowed to live in Mrs. Cobb's house. Despite that, she enjoys the freedom she has, moving between the mainland and the island, and although her death is not explained, it may be assumed that the forced confinement of the asylum might have contributed to the abrupt end to her life.

Reverend Buckminster at first is accepting of the town elders' views and expectations but becomes increasingly supportive of a combined religious and secular outlook on life as he observes and then becomes fatally involved in his son's struggle with the racism of the town majority.

Mrs. Cobb's loneliness has been relieved by the unexpected relationship she quietly develops with Turner and Lizzie. She is a surprising ally in Turner's struggle.

Willis Hurd, at first one of Turner's tormentors, becomes a secret ally after his grandmother is forcibly removed from her home for the profit of the deacons and is then drawn to respect the Buckminsters' ethical behavior when his family loses all their money and Turner's mother offers them shelter.

Themes

Race relations and prejudice combine with coming-of-age issues in this story based on a true incident in Maine history. Turner comes away from the tragedy with a deeper sense of justice and responsibility.

Books with Similar Issues or Themes

Cooney, Caroline. *Burning Up*. New York: Delacorte Press, 1999.

> Fifteen-year-old Macy and new friend Austin uncover the dark secret behind the 1959 burning of a barn, which was once the home of the only black high school teacher in the town of Shell Beach.

Hesse, Karen. *Witness*. New York: Scholastic, 2001.

> Through the poetic voices of several characters, the story of how the arrival of the Ku Klux Klan to this 1924 Vermont town changed the lives of one black girl, Leanora Sutter, and one Jewish girl, Esther Hirsch.

Staples, Suzanne Fisher. *Dangerous Skies*. New York: Farrar, Straus & Giroux, 1996.

> Like brother and sister since the age of twelve, Buck Smith, son of a white farm owner, and Tunes Smith, the motherless child of a black family that has served the Smiths for generations, are torn apart as the murder of a farm-labor manager is blamed on Tunes in a racially divided town.

Author-Related Sources

"Gary D. Schmidt." In vol. 135 of *Something about the Author*. Farmington Hills, MI: Gale Group, 2003, 186–9.

Discussion Questions

For *Lizzie Bright and the Buckminster Boy*

1. What brings Lizzie and Turner together, and why do they become good friends?

2. Why does Mrs. Cobb leave her house to Turner?

3. What is special about the relationship between Turner, Mrs. Cobb, and Lizzie?

4. What do you think Mrs. Cobb thinks about what the town leaders are trying to do on Malaga Island?

5. Why does Willis Hurd secretly become Turner's ally?

6. Why do you think Lizzie dies so quickly after arriving at the Pownal Home for the Feeble-Minded?

7. What do Turner's parents learn to appreciate from their son's behavior?

8. What does Turner realize about his father's view of the world around him despite his religious beliefs?

9. What do the whales represent to Turner? How does his experience with them help him cope with the deaths of Lizzie and his father?

10. Turner goes out to the whales again and thinks these words: "there is nothing in the world more beautiful and more wonderful in all its evolved forms than two souls who look at each other straight on." What has he come to understand about the look in his father's eyes?

11. How do the tragic events in this story change some of the residents of Phippsburg?

Much Ado about Aldo

By Johanna Hurwitz, Illustrated by John Wallner

New York: Morrow Junior Books, 1978

Reading Level: . . . . Grades 3–4
Genre: . . . . Realistic fiction
Themes: . . . . Vegetarianism, animal rights

Plot Summary

Aldo is a very interested third-grade student. He enjoys just about every subject his creative teacher, Mrs. Dowling, introduces and is particularly excited about the new class terrarium housing several crickets. Aldo especially likes the science of animal study, maintains his household responsibility for the care of the family's two cats, Peabody and Poughkeepsie, and might even become a veterinarian one day. In the days following the introduction of the crickets to the two terrariums, the class spends time observing their behavior, assigning names to the insects, and maintaining their man-made environment. Then Mrs. Dowling incorporates a new component to the class project, chameleons, which by natural instinct eat crickets. Unlike the rest of the class, Aldo is quite disturbed by this development and is immediately uncomfortable when a discussion of the food chain led by his teacher makes him realize his own participation every time he eats meat. So Aldo embarks on a new mission to eat only vegetarian meals and somehow save the crickets from their natural demise. Sneaking into his empty classroom during lunch to rescue the crickets only produces a serious infraction with his teacher and the principal. Aldo's heartfelt plea and explanation are rewarded with a compromise. Having accomplished the food chain lesson, Mrs. Dowling will raffle off the chameleons as pets to Aldo's classmates and free the crickets in the park.

Main Characterization

Aldo is an animal lover, unaware of nature's food chain and determined to make his own choices about what he eats. He is also quite bold, taking steps to right what he perceives is a cruel way to treat the creatures involved in the class experiment. Although not quite an activist, he speaks his mind and is able to state his thoughts effectively.

Themes

Basic themes of animal rights and vegetarianism are introduced in this classroom scenario.

Books with Similar Issues or Themes

Capeci, Anne. *Food Chain Frenzy*. Illustrated by John Speirs. New York: Scholastic, 2003.
 A "Magic School Bus chapter book in which Miss Frizzle's class learns much about ecosystems and eating habits.

Korman, Gordon. *The Chicken Doesn't Skate.* New York: Scholastic, 1996.
> When Milo's science project demonstrating the food chain involves a chicken named Henrietta, the other students adopt her as a hockey mascot and pet.

Rockwell, Thomas. *How to Eat Fried Worms.* Illustrated by Emily McCully. New York: Franklin Watts, 1973.
> A group of boys carries out an experiment to prove that worms are edible.

Author-Related Sources

Berger, Laura Standley, ed. *Twentieth-Century Children's Writers.* Detroit, MI: St. James Press, 1995, 481–3.

Holtze, Sally Holmes, ed. *Sixth Book of Junior Authors and Illustrators.* New York: H. W. Wilson, 1989, 145–6.

"Johanna Hurwitz." In vol. 113 of *Something about the Author.* Farmington Hills, MI: Gale Group, 2000, 84–9.

Marcus, Leonard S., ed. *Author Talk: Conversations with Judy Blume et al.* New York: Simon & Schuster, 2000, 42–8.

Silvey, Anita, ed. *Children's Books and Their Creators.* Boston: Houghton Mifflin, 1995, 335–6.

Discussion Questions

For *Much Ado about Aldo*

1. What disturbs Aldo about the science lesson that Mrs. Dowling is teaching?

2. Why do the crickets and chameleons become more than just science specimens to Aldo?

3. What does the principal mean when he tells Aldo that hunting for food is different from hunting to kill?

4. When it comes to the natural order of the food chain, why do humans and animals participate differently?

5. What do you think would happen if we didn't allow the food chain to progress naturally?

Olive's Ocean

By Kevin Henkes

New York: Greenwillow/HarperCollins, 2003

Reading Level: . . . . Grades 5–7
Genre: . . . . Realistic fiction
Themes: . . . . Coming of age, self-reflection, death

Plot Summary

An unexpected connection to the accidental and tragic death of a classmate becomes a turning point in twelve-year-old Martha's life. It is the end of the summer and vacation time. Martha's Wisconsin family is ready to leave for their usual retreat by the ocean at their grandmother's New England home. Just before they leave, the doorbell rings, and Martha greets Mrs. Barstow, Olive's mother, a lonely and isolated girl from her class who was recently killed on her bicycle in an automobile accident. Mrs. Barstow hands Martha a page from Olive's journal, stating three desires. The first, is to be a writer; the second, to see the ocean; and the third and most important, to get to know Martha better because "she is the nicest person in my whole entire class." The gesture and gift of the diary page is both haunting and mystifying to Martha, who begins to think about Olive in a new way. Later, at Godbee's house, Martha's special relationship with her grandmother unfolds as they take turns each day of the vacation week revealing something new and personal about each other. Martha reveals her wish to be a writer, but keeps Olive and the diary page a secret from everyone, including Godbee. There is another family living next door to Godbee with boys who have become friends of Martha's brother, Vince, over the last few summers. This year, the oldest, fourteen-year-old Jimmy, is involved in a new project, making a film with his own video camera. Martha and Vince spend time with the Manning boys. Martha notices Jimmy and believes he has an interest in her when he extends an invitation to view the portion of the video he has completed and then maneuvers her into a first kiss. Unaware that he is taping his version of "love" and that the kiss is also part of a bet he made with his brothers, Martha is quite embarrassed and hurt when she realizes Jimmy's real motive. Through her thoughts and turmoil, Martha cannot be consoled even by her grandmother's unassuming and lovingly patient support. Martha remembers the diary portion where Olive states her love of the ocean and in an inspiring moment, collects some seawater in a jar to present to Olive's mom on their return. The kiss and her hateful feelings toward Jimmy's betrayal are somewhat tempered with her anticipation of returning with a gift for Olive's mother. As the vacation week comes to an end, however, Tate, Jimmy's younger and more sensitive brother, manages to take the tape away and in a noble gesture gives it to Martha. Arriving at the Barstow home only to learn that she has moved away, Martha uses the seawater to paint Olive's name symbolically on the doorstep and says goodbye to a friend she never knew she had as she watches the water writing evaporate in the heat.

Main Characterization

Martha's typical middle school life is jarred as she is involved in the emotional release and response of Olive's mother. The words in the simple journal entry indicate the common threads in the two girls' lives that would never be tied together. Like Martha, Olive wished to be a writer, loved the ocean, and wanted to know and understand this distant girl. The naïve and trusting Martha is sub-

293

jected to a cruel and hurtful prank that challenges her sensitivity yet forces her to face a reality of the meaning of true friendship.

Godbee's wise, old, calm way of communicating with Martha helps her regain a new confidence in her aspirations for the future.

Themes

Coming of age and understanding one's thoughts and feelings through self-reflection are portrayed through the everyday moments and episodes of this girl's summer vacation. Death as an unfortunate reality of life is also portrayed through both Olive's accident and Godbee's elderly philosophical view.

Books with Similar Issues or Themes

Frank, E. R. *Friction: A Novel*. New York: Atheneum Books for Young Readers, 2003.
Unfounded rumors about a favorite teacher's sexual advances forces twelve-year-old Alex to consider the realities of truth and falsehoods.

Juby, Susan. *Alice, I Think*. New York: HarperTempest, 2003.
A home-schooled girl enters a public high school and must adjust to society as a result of participating within a learning and social community.

Langston, Laura. *A Taste of Perfection*. Toronto: Stoddard Kids, 2002.
Twelve-year-old Erin Morris spends the summer at her grandmother's farm where she learns about the breeding and training of dogs and discovers her own fortitude when her show dog Blue suffers an accident.

Mitchel, Mariane. *Finding Zola*. Honesdale, PA: Boyds Mills Press, 2003.
Thirteen-year-old Crystal copes with the death of her father in a car accident and her own parapalegic status as she helps to pack and close her recently deceased grandmother's home.

Author-Related Sources

Holtze, Sally Holmes, ed. *Sixth Book of Junior Authors and Illustrators*. New York: H. W. Wilson, 1989, 123–4.

"Kevin Henkes." In vol. 23 of *Children's Literature Review*. Farmington Hills, MI: Gale Group, 1991, 124–31.

"Kevin Henkes." In vol. 108 of *Something about the Author*. Farmington Hills, MI: Gale Group, 2000, 105–10.

Kevin Henkes's Web site: < http://www.kevinhenkes.com/ > (18 August 2004).

Silvey, Anita, ed. *Children's Books and Their Creators*. Boston: Houghton Mifflin, 1995, 303–4.

Discussion Questions

For *Olive's Ocean*

1. What kind of person do you think Olive was?

2. How does Martha's life change after Mrs. Barstow gives her the page from Olive's journal?

3. Why do you think Martha never tells anyone about the journal entry?

4. What do you think about the way Jimmy makes his films?

5. Who are Martha's real friends that summer and why?

6. What does Martha learn about herself by talking with Godbee?

7. What does the author mean when he writes after Martha's near drowning, "The world can change in a minute, and at the same time remain unchanged"? What changed for Martha at that point? What remained the same?

8. What did the seawater mean to Martha, and why was it important not to keep it when she could not give it to Mrs. Barstow?

9. How does Olive's awful death affect Martha's life positively?

10. How did this story make you feel after you finished reading it? Why?

The Prince of the Pond

By Donna Jo Napoli, Illustrated by Judith Byron Schachner

New York: Dutton Children's Books, 1992

Reading Level: . . . . Grades 3–5
Genre: . . . . Fantasy
Themes: . . . . Family relationships, responsibility, loyalty

Plot Summary

In this fractured fairytale, we meet the Frog Prince, newly transformed and very confused about his amphibious change by the old wicked Hag. Discovered and described by a female frog, he is unable to talk properly with his long frog tongue and calls himself "the fawg pin." To his new friend, Pin is a peculiar frog who behaves oddly and is clumsy at hopping and simply getting around. Curious and somewhat intrigued by this large, green, familiar creature, the female frog helps him to become accustomed to his body, eventually teaching him about the ways and differences of the animals of the pond and encouraging him to mate. All seems alien to Pin, who still has the mind and emotions of a human being. With hesitation and trepidation, Pin begins to adjust, using his unusually large size and bold behavior to challenge and outsmart enemies such as other predators and the old hag. He eventually mates with his female partner whom he calls Jade and creates a family, teaching Jade in turn about the responsibilities of parenthood and the emotional bonds developed by loving and caring for a family. When the hag threatens the family and kidnaps Jimmy, Pin's favorite son, the entire frog family works together to free him, but as Jimmy finds himself near a real princess and is picked up and caressed, Pin hurls himself up at the princess, knocking Jimmy down and receives the inevitable kiss, thus breaking the spell of the old hag and allowing him to return to his human, although naked self. He leaves his frog family to rejoin his human life while retaining a certain fondness for his amphibious offspring and wife.

Main Characterization

The Fawg Pin is human in his way of thinking despite his amphibious form and thus displays a variety of human emotions including courage, fortitude, dedication, love, devotion, unhappiness, and some pretty clever thinking that overshadows the rest of the pond life.

Jade behaves with a certain curiosity, intrigue, and awe, allowing her male counterpart to take charge even though her frog judgment is against it.

Themes

Disguised as an animal story, this creative version, written from the point of view of a typical frog, cleverly introduces family responsibility, human relationships, and loyalty for one's group.

Books with Similar Issues or Themes

Napoli, Donna Jo. *Jimmy the Pickpocket of the Palace.* Illustrated by Judith Byron Schachner. New York: Dutton Children's Books, 1995.
    In this sequel, Jimmy, Pin and Jade's frog son, enters the palace and is transformed into a human boy.

Scieszka, Jon. *The Frog Prince, Continued.* Illustrated by Steve Johnson. New York: Viking, 1991.
    Another fractured picture-book style version in which the frog prince prefers his amphibian life and changes back to live with his frog princess.

Traditional versions:

Ormerod, Jan. *The Frog Prince.* New York: Lothrop, Lee & Shepard, 1990.

Tarcov, Edith. *The Frog Prince.* Illustrated by James Marshall. New York: Four Winds Press, 1974.

Author-Related Sources

"Author Donna Jo Napoli" [Web site]: http://www.donnajonapoli.com/ (accessed 30 May 2004).

"Donna Jo Napoli." In vol. 51 of *Children's Literature Review.* Farmington Hills, MI: Gale Group, 1999, 152–68.

"Donna Jo Napoli." In vol. 137 of *Something about the Author.* Farmington Hills, MI: Gale Group, 2003, 154–60.

Hipple, Ted, ed., *Writers for Young Adults.* New York: Scribner's, 2000, 217–26.

Silvey, Anita, ed. *Essential Guide to Children's Books and Their Creators.* Boston: Houghton Mifflin, 2002, 320.

Discussion Questions

For *The Prince of the Pond*

1. How does Pin live his life as a frog?

2. What do Jade and Pin teach each other?

3. Jade talks about the "true happiness of a frog." Why do you think the author indicates that frogs are always happy?

4. If Pin is family-conscious and responsible, why does he "jump" at the chance to be kissed by the princess, ending the spell?

5. Why can't Pin ever adjust to frog life?

6. How does the author use the traditional fairytale to tell her own story?

7. How does the author use certain situations to make the story seem humorously plausible, even though it is a fairytale?

8. Why is this story considered a fractured fairytale?

Sarah, Plain and Tall

By Patricia Maclachlan

New York: Harper & Row, 1985

Reading Level: . . . . Grades 3–4
Genre: . . . . Historical fiction
Themes: . . . . Family, trust, bonding, emotions
Awards: . . . . Newbery Medal

Plot Summary

On their prairie farm, Anna continually answers her younger brother Caleb's questions about the mother he never knew; both children miss her in their own ways. When their father, Jacob, writes for a mail-order bride from the East, the children begin to anticipate a new life with a new mother who calls herself, Sarah, plain and tall. Sarah comes for a month's trial visit in the summer, bringing her cat Seal, and samples of shells and rocks as reminders of the beautiful sea she left behind in Maine. Throughout the visit, the children and Papa explore the differences and similarities of eastern and frontier life. Longing to make Sarah feel welcomed and happy so she will want to stay, the children cautiously look for clues in her questions and statements about living with them. Anxiety and concern escalate as Sarah expresses her homesickness, missing the ocean and family, finally convincing Caleb and Anna of her desire to begin a new life with them and their father.

Main Characterization

Anna, older sister to Caleb, treats him with a motherly affection. Her patience and calmness balance the younger boy's eager peskiness. Both siblings share a desire for a mother's love, guidance, and warmth, hoping that Papa's mail-order bride will be the stepmother of their dreams. Anna narrates their family story with heartfelt emotion as she describes the actions and reactions of her brother, Papa, Sarah, and herself.

Sarah is a practical woman, ready to make a change in her life. She brings all of the qualities of a perfect mother to the household, including her New England sensibility, courage, and tenderness.

Themes

Family love, bonding, and trust are all intertwined themes expressed through a variety of emotions displayed in the actions and words of the characters.

Books with Similar Issues or Themes

Dalgliesh, Alice. *The Courage of Sarah Noble*. Illustrated by Leonard Weisgard. New York: Scribner, 1954.

> The classic story of a young girl who sets out to build a home in the Connecticut wilderness after her mother's death.

Erdich, Louise. *The Range Eternal*. Illustrated by Steve Johnson and Lou Fancher. New York: Hyperion Books for Children, 2002.

> A woman recalls the blue enamel stove of her childhood home in the mountains of North Dakota and its representation of family and love.

Maclachlan, Patricia. Sequels to *Sarah, Plain and Tall*: *Skylark* (1994), *Caleb's Story* (2001), *More Perfect than the Moon* (2004)

Turner, Ann Warren. *Dakota Dugout*. Illustrated by Ronald Himler. New York: Macmillan, 1985.

> A description of prairie life on the Dakota frontier.

Turner, Ann Warren. *Grass Songs*. Illustrated by Barry Moser. San Diego, CA: Harcourt Brace Jovanovich, 1993.

> Seventeen poems describe the lives of women who chose the unsettled west in nineteenth-century America.

Author-Related Sources

Berger, Laura Standley, ed. *Twentieth-Century Children's Writers*. Detroit, MI: St. James Press, 1995, 617–18.

Holtze, Sally Holmes, ed. *Sixth Book of Junior Authors and Illustrators*. New York: H. W. Wilson, 1989, 183–4.

"Patricia MacLachlan." In vol. 14 of *Children's Literature Review*. Farmington Hills, MI: Gale Research, 1988, 177–86.

"Patricia MacLachlan." In vol. 107 of *Something about the Author*. Farmington Hills, MI: Gale Group, 1999, 128–32.

Patricia MacLachlan's official Web site: http://www.harperchildrens.com/authorintro/index.asp?authorid=12425 (accessed 14 February 2005).

Silvey, Anita, ed. *Children's Books and Their Creators*. Boston: Houghton Mifflin, 1995, 427–9.

Discussion Questions

For *Sarah, Plain and Tall*

1. How do Anna and Caleb feel about Sarah coming to visit?

2. Why is Caleb so worried about Sarah's visit?

3. How does Sarah feel about her visit?

4. What clues does Sarah give about wanting to stay with Jacob and his children?

5. How does Maggie, Sarah's new friend, help her understand her sadness?

6. What does Maggie mean when she tells Sarah, "There are always things to miss … no matter where you are"?

7. Why is it important for Sarah to learn how to ride a horse and drive a wagon?

8. Why does Sarah bring back colored pencils?

9. How did reading this story make you feel?

Seedfolks

By Paul Fleischman, Illustrated by Judy Pedersen

New York: HarperCollins, 1997

Reading Level: . . . . Grades 6–8

Genre: . . . . Realistic fiction

Themes: . . . . Poverty, hope, community, friendship, self-fulfillment, multicultural relationships, diversity

Awards: . . . . School Library Journal Best Books

Plot Summary

In this small, episodic book, readers meet thirteen people of different cultural backgrounds and ages, all living separate lives in a rundown and poor neighborhood. Each voice tells of how a community garden brought them out to share their hopes, aspirations, and cautious friendships, inspiring feelings of reward and self-fulfillment.

Main Characterization

Kim is a nine-year-old Vietnamese girl who chooses to honor the dead father she never knew by planting some bean seeds in the vacant lot. Understanding that her father was a farmer, Kim creates her small bean garden as a way to connect and remember the man who died before she could get to know him. Her actions first seem strange to the others living and passing by, but soon her persistence serves as inspiration for twelve other people who have their own unique reasons and interests in planting and gardening.

Voices of the other gardeners include Ana, an elderly white woman; Wendell, another white resident in the building; Gonzalo, a Guatemalan boy; Leona, an African American woman; Sam, a retired Jewish man; Virgil, a Haitain boy; Sae Young, a Korean woman; Curtis, a black man trying to woo an old girlfriend; Nora, a British nurse for Mr. Myles, who has had a stroke; Maricela, a pregnant Mexican teenager; and Florence, a descendent of the first black family in the county.

Themes

Poverty, community, diversity, and friendship are intertwined in this novella of personal voices. Hope and fulfillment are subthemes as the last voice of Florence wonders, at the end of the long winter, if the digging will begin anew. As the gardeners connect in some way each day, friendships and multicultural relationships develop that might otherwise never have blossomed.

Books with Similar Issues or Themes

Bulla, Clyde. *The Chalk Box Kid*. New York: Random House, 1987.
> In his new urban neighborhood, Gregory creates a garden on a wall with his chalk paintings as a substitute for the real thing.

Bunting, Eve. *Smoky Night*. Illustrated by David Diaz. San Diego, CA: Harcourt, 1994.
A group of multicultural residents develops a new understanding of each other during the Los Angeles riots.

Di Salvo-Ryan, Dyanne. *City Green*. New York: Morrow Junior Books, 1994.
A version for younger readers of how a little girl transforms a neighborhood by starting a community garden.

Thesman, Jean. *Nothing Grows Here*. New York: HarperCollins, 1994.
Moving to a neglected apartment building from her suburban house following her father's death, twelve-year-old Maryanne develops new friendships with a new garden.

Author-Related Sources

Berger, Laura Standley, ed. *Twentieth-Century Children's Writers*. Detroit, MI: St. James Press, 1995, 214–16.

Hipple, Ted, ed. *Writers for Young Adults*. New York: Charles S. Scribner's Sons, 2000, 47–58.

"Paul Fleischman." In vol. 66 of *Children's Literature Review*. Farmington Hills, MI: Gale Group, 2001, 44-76.

"Paul Fleischman." In vol. 110 of *Something about the Author*. Farmington Hills, MI: Gale Group, 2000, 89–93.

Paul Fleischman's official Web site: http://www.paulfleischman.net/ (accessed 10 January 2005).

Discussion Questions

For *Seedfolks*

1. What was the community like before Kim began the garden?

2. What does the garden mean for each of the gardeners? Why did each one decide to plant a section?

3. How does the language of the garden help the people communicate with one another, even when some don't speak the same language?

4. What do the different people learn about each other through the garden?

5. How does the garden change the residents of the community?

6. How does the garden represent the diversity of the community?

7. Who is your favorite voice in the community? Why?

8. What is the most important result of the Gibb Street garden?

Stone Fox

By John Reynolds Gardiner, Illustrated by Marcia Sewall

New York: Crowell, 1980

Reading Level: . . . . Grades 3–4
Genre: . . . . Realistic fiction
Themes: . . . . Death, family responsibility, dedication, fairness

Plot Summary

Ten-year-old Little Willy lives with his grandfather on a potato farm in Wyoming. Grandfather has taken to his bed for the last three weeks, unable to move or speak. Doc Smith says Grandfather is not sick but has given up hope of paying the tax collector and saving his farm. Willy works hard, harvesting the potatoes with the help of his dog, Searchlight, pulling the plow. He tries to earn what he can but knows he will never be able to raise the $500 in back taxes. His only chance is winning the $500 prize at the National Dogsled Race with his fast and loyal dog. But Willy has stiff competition from Stone Fox, a large, resentful Indian man with a team of beautiful Samoyeds who has never lost a race. Willy and Searchlight practice the ten-mile run for the next couple of weeks, never losing hope or confidence. On the day of the race, most of the townsfolk are out cheering and supporting Willy and Searchlight, who does his very best to run the fastest and the strongest. Then, just one hundred yards from the finish line, the extreme effort causes Searchlight's heart to burst, leaving him dead on the route. Stone Fox, just feet behind, stops the race and creates a new finish line right at the fallen dog's place, thus allowing Willy to win the prize money and pay the tax collector for his grandfather.

Main Characterization

Little Willy is stubborn and strong-minded, persistent in his goal to keep the farm going and win the money for the tax bill. His youthful idealism does not allow him to give up as his grandfather has but brings hope and pride to the man who finally leaves his bed to stand by the window to watch for Willy as the racers pass by.

Searchlight's dedication and devotion is evident in his determination to help Willy plow the potato field and run his best, last race.

Stone Fox appears to be a formidable opponent and harsh individual who ultimately behaves with fairness and compassion for his youthful fellow competitor.

Themes

Willy faces the reality of death with his grandfather's depression and his dog's participation in the race. Unwilling to compromise, Willy is dedicated to his surrogate parent and takes on family responsibility to save his grandfather and farm.

Stone Fox's display of fairness following the death of Searchlight counters Willy's ultimate sacrifice, the loss of his beloved dog.

Books with Similar Issues or Themes

Blake, Robert J. *Ariak: A Tale from the Iditarod*. New York: Philomel Books, 1997.
Ten-year-old lead dog, Ariak, defies all odds to win her last race.

O'Dell, Scott. *Black Star, Bright Dawn*. New York: Ballantine, 1988.
An Eskimo girl takes her deceased brother's place in the Iditarod in Alaska and depends on her team of dogs to survive the brutal conditions and the race.

Van Steenwyk, Elisabeth. *Three Dog Winter*. New York: Doubleday, 1999.
A boy adjusts to his father's death and mother's remarriage with the determination to be a champion dog-sled racer.

Author-Related Sources

Holtze, Sally Holmes, ed. *Sixth Book of Junior Authors and Illustrators*. New York: H. W. Wilson, 1989, 91–2.

"John Reynolds Gardiner." In vol. 64 of *Something about the Author*. Farmington Hills, MI: Gale Research, 1991, 64.

Silvey, Anita, ed. *Children's Books and Their Creators*. Boston: Houghton Mifflin, 1995, 264.

Discussion Questions

For *Stone Fox*

1. Why is Grandfather sick even though Doc Smith could not find anything physically wrong with him?

2. Why does Willy refuse to give up the farm and allow Mrs. Peacock to take care of Grandfather?

3. Why is it important for Willy to keep his college money?

4. Why does Willy feel he had to use his college money to enter the race?

5. Why does Stone Fox change the finish line and allow Willy and Searchlight to be the winners?

6. How does Willy feel after the race is over? What regrets might he have?

7. What does Willy win and lose in the race? Is it worth the sacrifice?

8. What do you think happened after the race ended?

9. Who is the hero in this story?

Toliver's Secret

By Esther Wood Brady, Illustrated by Richard Cuffari

New York: Crown, 1976

Reading Level: . . . . Grades 3–5
Genre: . . . . Historical fiction
Themes: . . . . Adventure, courage, loyalty

Plot Summary

Everything about Ellen Toliver makes her unlikely to be a spy. A ten-year-old girl with little experience outside her home, she has never traveled alone. But when her grandfather hurts his ankle and cannot fulfill a mission to help pass an important message to General George Washington, unlikely or not, Ellen is given the task. Her mother has hidden a secret message inside a snuffbox and baked it within a loaf of bread. Ellen dresses as a boy, cuts her hair, and sets out on the planned route her grandfather has given her to board one of the fishing boats at Front Street and cross over to Elizabeth-town, where she is to bring the bread to its first courier, Mr. Shannon, owner of the Jolly Fox Tavern. Setting out with grandfather's assurances that her trip will be easy and uneventful, everything that could possibly go wrong does. Ellen misses all the boats and is practically abducted by a group of Redcoats, taken aboard one of their ships and released in Perth Amboy. She is chased and teased by older boys who grab the bread and toss it back and forth. Losing her way, she must walk the thirteen miles to Elizabeth-town, is given a ride on a horse, and nearly has her precious cargo eaten by a large pig. Struggling to keep calm, to push forward, and to keep her promise to her grandfather, Ellen finally arrives at the tavern late but nevertheless with the bread and snuff box intact. With her mission done, she returns the next day under the care of Mrs. Shannon and is invigorated with a new urge to help in the cause of the Revolutionary War.

Main Characterization

Ellen Toliver's love and devotion to her grandfather help her overcome her fear to take on a mission that becomes more perilous with each step. She is sometimes foolishly impulsive and yet bold enough to take the risks necessary to keep her secret and deliver the message as planned.

Themes

Courage and loyalty work together in this adventurous glimpse of Revolutionary War life.

Books with Similar Issues or Themes

Collier, James Lincoln. *War Comes to Willy Freeman*. New York: Delacorte Press, 1983.
    After the Redcoats kill her father and take her mother, Willy, a free black girl, disguises herself as a boy and goes to New York City to search for her mother.

Griffin, Judith Berry. *Phoebe the Spy*. New York: Scholastic, 1989.
    Disguised as General George Washington's housekeeper, Phoebe will double as a spy to find out information concerning death threats on the general's life.

O'Dell, Scott. *Sarah Bishop*. Boston: Houghton Mifflin, 1980.
    When her father and brother support opposite sides in the Revolutionary War and are both killed, Sarah flees to the wilderness.

Woodruff, Elvira. *George Washington's Socks*. New York: Scholastic, 1991.
    At a camp outing, two children are transported back in time to the scene at Valley Forge during the famous Revolutionary War battle.

Author-Related Sources

"Esther Wood Brady." In vol. 31 of *Something about the Author*. Detroit, MI: Gale Research, 1983, 35.

Discussion Questions

For *Toliver's Secret*

1. How does Ellen feel at first about helping her grandfather?

2. Why is the mission her grandfather gave her important for Ellen to accept, despite her feelings of fear and reluctance?

3. How does Ellen overcome her timidity and fear?

4. What does the British Redcoat Mr. Higgins give Ellen in addition to a "fat silver coin"?

5. What does Ellen learn about herself as she makes her way?

6. How does the trip change Ellen's way of thinking and behaving?

Tuck Everlasting

By Natalie Babbitt

New York: Farrar, Straus & Giroux, 1975

Reading Level: . . . . Grades 4–6
Genre: . . . . Fantasy
Themes: . . . . Eternal life, death

Plot Summary

Ten-year-old Winnie Foster lives a sheltered, boring life with her parents and grandmother in a little house at the edge of a forest in a place called Treegap. Forbidden to leave her enclosed yard, Winnie dreams about venturing out to do something important, to make a difference in the world. Standing by her fence thinking her thoughts, she is unaware that her life is about to change in an unforgettable way. A peculiarly inquisitive stranger dressed in a yellow suit approaches her and asks about others who might live in the area. As her grandmother approaches, eager to dismiss the stranger, an enchanting music is heard distantly from within the forest. The music, unbeknownst to the Fosters, comes from a music box that belongs to the Tuck family, who lives deep within the forest.

The Tucks are unique. They have eternal life as a result of accidentally drinking from a magical spring close to Winnie's home more than a hundred years earlier. The next day, Winnie challenges herself to venture out beyond her yard and comes to a large tree next to a spring. There she encounters Jesse Tuck, the seventeen-year-old younger son of Mae Tuck, who is really 104 years old but has remained a youth since drinking from the spring. Winnie is intrigued by the boy, but when her thirst moves her to drink from the spring, Jesse stops her just as his mother, Mae Tuck, and his older brother, Miles, arrive with their horse to meet him. Mae, thinking that their secret of eternal life has been exposed, panics and kidnaps the little girl and brings her back to the Tuck cabin twenty miles within the forest.

The Tucks are good people and have decided that common knowledge of the spring's magic would be a terrible thing to allow. They explain their story to Winnie, who at first is unbelieving, and then they promise to return her home if she keeps their secret. At the same time Jesse has given Winnie a proposal to think about. He asks her if she will drink the water when she turns seventeen so they can have eternal life together. Winnie is both confused and uncomfortable. The Tucks seem kind and caring, but their story is very strange. At the same time, Winnie's kidnapping is witnessed by the man in the yellow suit who has also overheard the story and is now satisfied that he has found what he was searching for. In a greedy gesture, the man in the yellow suit makes a deal with Winnie's father to buy the property just outside their home with the tree and spring, in exchange for the information on Winnie's whereabouts and kidnappers.

As the constable and the man approach the Tuck home, Mae again panics, realizing that the man's greedy and vicious plan to sell the water will have a terribly immoral result. She shoots and kills the man with the yellow suit and is arrested. Knowing her trial will surely end at the gallows, and that death is not possible for Mae, the Tucks and Winnie devise an escape plan for her to preserve the secret of their eternal life. In an epilogue, the Tucks return after a generation to a much-changed Treegap, to find that Winnie chose to live a normal life and died at the age of seventy-eight, rejecting Jesse's idea to drink the water and gain eternal life.

311

Main Characterization

Winnie Foster is an innocent, sheltered young ten year old, who learns to distinguish quickly between evil and good. She develops a fondness, even a love, for the Tuck family, during her two-day stay and understands the important role she must play in maintaining their secret.

The Tuck Family, although folksy, ignorant, and even a bit simpleminded, are wise in the sense of what the knowledge of their secret might unleash if given to an evil and possibly less prudent person.

Themes

The joy and trepidation of living an eternal life are explored in this fantasy.

Books with Similar Issues or Themes

Dickinson, Peter. *Eva*. New York: Delacorte Press, 1989.
> Following a terrible car crash, fourteen-year-old Eva wakes up to find her brain has been recovered from her smashed broken body and placed within the head of a chimpanzee by her scientist father, who wishes to keep her soul and spirit alive.

Haddix, Margaret Peterson. *Turn About*. New York: Simon & Schuster, 2000.
> A scientific experiment gives the elderly Melly and Anny Beth an injection to reverse their aging, and as they grow progressively younger, they must find a way to avoid death and reverse the process once more so that their life will continue.

Lasky, Kathryn. *Star Split*. New York: Hyperion Books for Children, 1999.
> In the year 3028, gene research has eliminated terminal diseases, and cloning has provided the ability for a brain to live indefinitely. When Darci discovers she is a clone, she wonders whether her existence can continue without a soul.

L'Engle, Madeleine. *A Wrinkle in Time*. New York: Farrar, Straus & Giroux, 1962.
> Meg, her brother Charles, and their friend Calvin embark on a space travel odyssey to find their scientist father who has disappeared while working on a tesseract project.

Author-Related Sources

Berger, Laura Standley, ed. *Twentieth-Century Children's Writers*. Detroit, MI: St. James Press, 1995, 49–50.

Hopkins, Lee Bennett, ed. *More Books by More People*. New York: Citation Press, 1974, 24–9.

"Natalie Babbitt." In vol. 53 of *Children's Literature Review*. Farmington Hills, MI: Gale Group, 1999, 20–39.

"Natalie Babbitt." In vol. 106 of *Something about the Author*. Farmington Hills, MI: Gale Group, 1999, 24–8.

Silvey, Anita, ed. *Children's Books and Their Creators*. Boston: Houghton Mifflin, 1995, 42–4.

Discussion Questions

For *Tuck Everlasting*

1. How do Winnie and each of the Tucks feel about eternal life?

2. Why does Winnie choose to give the frog in the yard eternal life?

3. What important thing does Winnie do in her life that might have made a difference in the world?

4. Why does Winnie break the law and help Mae escape? How do you feel about her breaking the law?

5. Why do you think Winnie chose to live a normal life span rather than drink the water and live with Jesse eternally?

6. What do you think might have happened if Jesse and Winnie had lived together eternally?

7. Why is it important to keep the secret?

8. What do you think might have happened if the man in the yellow suit had succeeded in selling the water to people who "deserved it" for a high price?

9. What does Tuck mean by "the wheel of life" and that we "can't have living without dying"?

The View from Saturday

By E. L. Konigsburg

New York: Atheneum Books for Young Readers, 1996

Reading Level: . . . . Grades 4–6

Genre: . . . . Realistic fiction

Themes: . . . . Friendship, self-reflection

Awards: . . . . Newbery Medal, ALA Notable Children's Book, School Library Journal Best Books

Plot Summary

Four sixth graders and one teacher are brought together through serendipity and circumstance for a triumphant Academic Bowl victory. When Noah Gershom spends time with his grandparents in southern Florida while his parents take a cruise, he participates in the wedding of one of their neighbors, Izzy Diamondstein, as the best man, substituting for Mr. Diamondstein's son, Allen, who breaks his ankle in a mishap just before the big day. Allen Diamondstein is newly divorced and the father of Nadia. Izzy is about to marry Margaret Draper, grandmother of Ethan Potter.

Noah, Nadia, and Ethan all live in Epiphany, New York, go to the same school, and have been assigned to the same homeroom with Mrs. Olinski. The class has a new student and resident to the town, Julian Singh, whose father, a cruise ship chef, has just purchased the old Sillington farmhouse and plans to renovate it and open a bed and breakfast inn. As Julian boards the bus on the first day of school, his East Indian appearance, British-style school clothing, and accent alert the other students and encourage some mockery. Julian takes a seat next to Ethan and much to the latter boy's reluctance, the two develop an initial relationship.

As the year progresses, Julian initiates an invitation to Noah, Nadia, and Ethan for a Saturday afternoon tea party and a bonding and special friendship develop. Observing from her teacher's position, Mrs. Olinski, coach for the sixth-grade Academic Bowl team, notices the unique chemistry between the four students and selects Noah, Ethan, Nadia, and Julian for the team. Mrs. Olinski, victim of a car accident and confined to a wheelchair, teaches and coaches this team with a resolve and conviction that they will be the first sixth-grade team to not only win at their school level, but triumph at the state tournament as well.

Main Characterization

Mrs. Eva Marie Olinski has had a difficult and unfortunate event in her life, losing her husband and her mobility in a car accident, but she continues to teach and guide her students with a positive and determined attitude.

Noah Gershom is resentful of losing out on his chance to take a cruise vacation with his parents, but he enjoys his stay with his grandparents and comes away with both the experience of being a best man and the new art of calligraphy, learned from his grandmother in charge of wedding invitations.

Nadia Diamondstein is adjusting to her newly divorced parents, a move to her mother's hometown, Epiphany, and to new friendships.

Ethan Potter, long-time resident of Epiphany, has been drawn to Noah and Nadia through his grandmother Margaret's wedding to Nadia's grandfather, Izzy. Ethan, usually a loner, prefers to live his life quietly but is pulled into a combined relationship with Julian's efforts of initial politeness and kindness. Ethan, against his better judgment, cannot stand by and watch the continual mockery of the new boy Julian and takes certain steps to shield his new acquaintance.

Julian Singh, raised in a different environment of British boarding schools, behaves appropriately and is able to bring an influence of justice and kindness to the other characters.

Themes

Friendship and self-reflection are both present in this novel of four short-story scenarios featuring characters with complicated personalities and their own perceptions on life. The stories are part of a larger plot sequence that involves winning an academic contest and the importance of friends, neighbors, and family.

Books with Similar Issues or Themes

Grunwell, Jeanne Marie. *Mind Games*. Boston: Houghton Mifflin, 2003.
> Six members of a science club investigate extrasensory perception and win the Maryland science fair.

Klise, Kate. *Regarding the Fountain: A Tale in Letters, of Liars, and Leaks*. Illustrated by Sarah M. Klise. New York: Avon Books, 1998.
> Students at the Dry Creek Middle School uncover a mystery behind the leaky fountain through clues given by newspaper articles, letters, invoices, and other numerous items in a paper trail.

Howe, James. *The Misfits*. New York: Atheneum, 2001.
> Four kids who are teased and called names for a variety of reasons join to form "the gang of five" and create a third party of candidates for the school elections.

O'Connor, Barbara. *Beethoven in Paradise*. New York: Farrar, Straus & Giroux, 1997.
> With the help of best friend Wylene, new friend Sybil, and grandmother Hazeline, Martin manages to pursue his love of music in spite of his father's mean-spirited attitude.

Slepian, Jan. *The Alfred Summer*. New York: Macmillan, 1980.
> Four middle school kids, two with disabilities, come together to help build a boat and discover the meaning of heroism, freedom, and courage.

Author-Related Sources

Ambroook, Renée. *E. L. Konigsburg*. New York: Rosen, 2005

Berger, Laura Standley, ed. *Twentieth-Century Children's Writers,* 4th ed. Detroit, MI: St. James Press, 1995, 533–4.

"E. L. Konigsburg." In vol. 81 of *Children's Literature Review*. Farmington Hills, MI: Gale Group, 2002, 122–79.

"E. L. Konigsburg." In vol. 126 of *Something about the Author*. Farmington Hills, MI: Gale Group, 2002, 127–33.

Hanks, Dorrel Thomas. *E. L. Konigsburg*. New York: Twayne, 1992.

Hopkins, Lee Bennett. *More Books by More People: Interviews with Sixty-Five Authors of Books for Children*. New York: Citation Press, 1974, 234–8.

Marcus, Leonard S., ed. *Author Talk: Conversations with Judy Blume et al.* New York: Simon & Schuster, 2000, 49–57.

Scholastic Authors: E. L. Konigsburg: http://www2.scholastic.com/teachers/authorsandbooks/ authorstudies/authorhome.jhtml?authorID=644&collateralID=5205&displayName= Biography (accessed 30 May 2004).

Silvey, Anita, ed. *Children's Books and Their Creators*. Boston: Houghton Mifflin, 1995, 377–8.

Discussion Questions

For *The View from Saturday*

1. Why does Julian choose to invite Noah, Nadia, and Ethan to tea and not other members of the class?

2. Noah, Nadia, Ethan, and Julian are all different, yet they are able to become good friends. Why do you think this is so?

3. What does friendship mean to each character, including Mrs. Olinski?

4. What statement does this novel make about friendships and how they are formed?

5. Why do the four kids choose the name "The Souls" for their tea-time group?

6. How does the name "The Souls" reflect the group's purpose and time together?

7. What reasons do you think Mrs. Olinski might have had to select the members of the team?

8. What do Noah, Nadia, Ethan, and Julian all have that makes their team work well to win?

9. The author, E. L. Konigsburg, chose to name the town Epiphany. What symbolic reference do you think she had in mind in making this choice?

10. What do the characters gain in the end, besides their triumphant win in the state Academic Bowl tournament?

Voices in the Park

By Anthony Browne

New York: DK, 1998

Reading Level: . . . . Grades 3–4
Genre: . . . . Contemporary fiction/picture book
Themes: . . . . Personal perspective from different voices
Awards: . . . . School Library Journal Best Books, ALA Notable
Children's Book

Plot Summary

Four individuals—two parents and two children—take a walk in the park and view their outing from four perspectives. The first voice is that of a mother, walking with her dog and son. Upon arriving at the park, she instructs her son, Charles, to sit with her on a bench and becomes annoyed with a "scruffy mongrel" to which her pristine canine Victoria is attracted. Charles, on the other hand, appears to be talking with a "rough-looking child." Mother, son, and dog leave the park. The second voice is of an unemployed dad who arrives at the park with his daughter, Smudge, and their dog, a rambunctious, fun-loving mutt named Albert. The third voice belongs to Charles, bored being home without friends and eager to connect with a friendly, playful girl he meets named Smudge. Finally, the fourth voice is that of Smudge, who encourages Charles, much to his mother's objections, to let loose a little. She is observant of the other three and enjoys herself, laughing at her dog, Albert, as he takes a swim in the park fountain.

Main Characterization

Voice 1, Mother, is snobbish, standoffish, and unwilling to allow her child to play or make friends with others who do not seem of her social status.

Voice 2, Father, is concerned about his unemployment but hopeful and willing to keep trying as he proceeds to read the want ads.

Voice 3, Charles, is a lonely child, bored and interested in exploring new things and new relationships.

Voice 4, Smudge, is a chatty, happy child willing to take risks and enjoy life as it comes.

Themes

Individual views on life and the different perspectives that both adults and children may have are clearly portrayed in this unique picture book through both words and art.

Books with Similar Issues or Themes

Beattie, Ann. *Spectacles.* Illustrated by Winslow Pels. New York: Workman Publishing, 1985.
Wearing the glasses belonging to her great-grandmother, who is sick in bed, Alison is able to view a younger life and proposal of marriage from the old woman's perspective.

Myers, Christopher. *Wings*. New York: Scholastic Press, 2000.

 Ikarus Jackson has wings that make him different, yet special and beautiful in this story celebrating individuality.

Van Allsburg, Chris. *The Sweetest Fig*. Boston: Houghton Mifflin, 1993.

 Bibot, a cold-hearted, presumptuous dentist, gets his comeuppance when he and his suffering dog reverse roles through some magical intervention.

Author-Related Sources

"Anthony Browne." In vol. 19 of *Children's Literature Review*. Farmington Hills, MI: Gale Group, 1990, 59–70.

Berger, Laura Standley, ed. *Twentieth-Century Children's Writers*. Detroit, MI: St. James Press, 1995, 159–61.

Holtze, Sally Holmes, ed. *Sixth Book of Junior Authors and Illustrators*. New York: H. W. Wilson, 1989, 44–5.

Silvey, Anita, ed. *Children's Books and Their Creators*. Boston: Houghton Mifflin, 1995, 98–9.

Discussion Questions

For Voices in the Park

1. How do the four voices differ from each other?

2. What concerns do each of the four voices express?

3. How do you think each character lives his or her life?

4. Which character do you like best?

5. How does the author-artist use his paintings to reflect the mood and personality of each voice?

6. How do the illustrations change and alter for each character's voice?

7. How are the words and printing used to tell each character's view?

8. Why do you think the children and dogs have names, but the adults do not?

9. What is author Anthony Browne trying to say in this book?

The Whipping Boy

By Sid Fleischman, Illustrated by Peter Sis

New York: Greenwillow Books, 1986

Reading Level: . . . . Grades 3–4
Genre: . . . . Humorous fiction/adventure
Themes: . . . . Behavior, maliciousness, friendship
Awards: . . . . Newbery Medal

Plot Summary

Prince Horace is known and thought of as a brat, always in trouble or causing trouble but never suffering the punishment because he has the benefit of a whipping boy, Jemmy, to endure corporal punishments. Prince Brat is equally difficult with his tutor, never learning his lessons, unable to read, write, or do sums. Paradoxically, Jemmy, the son of a rat catcher, clever and resourceful, has learned right along with the frustrated tutor and has had quite enough of the prince's spoiled attitude, bad behavior, and whippings, hoping to be dismissed from his post as whipping boy. But Prince Brat has other plans and engineers an escape from the castle at night, forcing Jemmy to go with him where they are promptly kidnapped by the notorious highwaymen, Hold-Your-Nose Billy and Cutwater. Things go from bad to worse for the prince as his kidnappers mistakenly think Jemmy is the real prince because Prince Brat cannot read or write. An adventurous caper ensues as Jemmy continually tries to outmaneuver both the bumbling kidnappers and the unfortunately inexperienced and naively spoiled prince in several foiled escape plans, eventually ending back at the castle with a much changed prince and possible friend.

Main Characterization

Prince Brat (Horace) is on the outside a caricature of a spoiled, mischievous fellow maliciously misbehaving for the fun of watching the beatings of his poor whipping boy. On the inside, however, he is a lonely, sad individual, afraid to express his true feelings until he is thrust into a completely uncontrolled environment. Forced to follow Jemmy, the streetwise rat catcher's son, he learns to respect and understand the concept of friendship and camaraderie.

Jemmy, wise, clever, and resourceful takes care of himself pretty well but is also responsibly protective of the prince, unable to leave him stranded, despite the several chances he is given.

Themes

Behavior, maliciousness, and friendship are woven together in this adventure of two seemingly different boys who find out they can live together with certain harmony and respect for each other.

Books with Similar Issues or Themes

King-Smith, Dick. *The Toby Man*. Illustrated by Lynette Hemmant. New York: Crown, 1991.
Tod Golightly teams up with four animal friends to form a robber band, holding up travelers on the "toby," or road, in eighteenth-century England.

Scieszka, Jon. *Knights of the Kitchen Table*. Illustrated by Lane Smith. New York: Viking Penguin, 1991.
The first in the Time Warp Trio series, offering a humorous and perilous adventure in King Arthur's Court.

Van Draanen, Wendelin. *Shredderman Secret Identity*. Illustrated by Brian Biggs. New York: Alfred A. Knopf, 2004.
Nolan Byrd puts his nerd reputation aside and emerges with his secret superhero persona to confront the class bully, Alvin Bixby, known as Bubba.

Author-Related Sources

Berger, Laura Standley, ed. *Twentieth-Century Children's Writers*. Detroit, MI: St. James Press, 1995, 357–8.

"Sid Fleischman." In vol. 15 of *Children's Literature Review*. Detroit, MI: Gale Research, 1988, 101–13.

"Sid Fleischman." In vol. 148 of *Something about the Author*. Farmington Hills, MI: Gale Group, 2004, 71–9.

Sid Fleischman's Web site: http://www.sidfleischman.com/ (accessed 3 January 2005).

Silvey, Anita, ed. *Children's Books and Their Creators*. Boston: Houghton Mifflin, 1995, 245–7.

Discussion Questions

For *The Whipping Boy*

1. How are the prince and Jemmy different from each other?

2. What do the prince and Jemmy have in common?

3. Why does Prince Brat want to run away from the castle?

4. What is Prince Brat really hoping to find away from the castle?

5. What does Prince Brat learn from his time away from the castle?

6. Why does Jemmy change his feelings toward Prince Brat?

7. What do Jemmy and the prince realize about both their lives after they return to the castle?

8. How does the adventure change the boys' relationship?

The Witch of Blackbird Pond

By Elizabeth George Speare

Boston: Houghton Mifflin, 1958

Reading Level: . . . . Grades 6–8
Genre: . . . . Historical fiction
Themes: . . . . Persecution, religious freedom, prejudice
Awards: . . . . Newbery Medal

Plot Summary

Raised by her grandfather until his death in the more liberal environment of the island of Barbados, Kit Tyler travels alone to the shores of Wethersfield, Connecticut, to live with her aunt's family in their 1687 Puritan household. Scandalously out of place with her wildly colorful gowns, ability to read and write, and outspoken way of thinking, Kit is immediately sanctioned by the other women of the town and viewed suspiciously. Resolved to make the best of her situation and not to cause problems for her Aunt Rachel, Kit learns the ways of the family and tries to alter her behavior modeled after her cousins, Judith and Mercy. But her loneliness and homesickness for the green and turquoise colors of the island lead her one afternoon to a meadow near Blackbird Pond, where she finds a bit of sanctuary amid its natural beauty. Kit also encounters the old widow name Hannah, a Quaker, regarded with much hate and suspected of performing witchcraft by the ignorant and uneducated Puritan members of the town. Kit's secret visits with Hannah help her relax and feel comfortable. There Kit becomes reacquainted with Nathaniel Eaton, the son of the captain of the ship she sailed to Connecticut, and Prudence, a little girl who is not permitted to attend school by her fearfully restrictive mother.

Kit continually places herself in trouble with the townsfolk who always misunderstand her approach. Teaching school with Mercy, she must curtail her storytelling and refrain from straying from the teachings of the Bible. When the town suffers a serious epidemic and several people and children die of a fever, both Kit and Hannah are blamed for their witchcraft. Hannah escapes onboard Nat's ship as her house along the pond is burned. But Kit must endure the indignity of a witch trial, where her abilities as a good teacher come through and prove that Prudence is able to learn and read as well as anyone else. The story ends with the romantic weddings of both Judith and Mercy along with a promise of betrothal for Kit and Nat, who have found in each other a similar outlook on life in a town filled with ignorance, fear, and hysteria.

Main Characterization

Kit (Katherine) Tyler is an independent thinker and forthright person forced to temper her unconventional ways to gain acceptance from both her family and new neighbors. Her wider view of the world based on the upbringing and teachings of her grandfather allows her to see things with a clear, unprejudiced eye.

Hannah is old, wise, and misunderstood in a world that cannot and will not tolerate difference. Her sound advice serves as a way for Kit to balance her own liberal ideology with the strict, rigid Puritan lifestyle.

Nat Eaton is the young, adventurous captain's son, a logical romantic interest for Kit, who appreciates his open-mindedness and forward way of thinking. He eventually becomes a strong ally, helping to rescue Hannah and remove Kit from her Puritan uncle's household.

Themes

Kit's altered and unconventional upbringing place her squarely in a position of suspicion and danger as her free thinking is abhorred equally with the religious beliefs of non-Puritans, such as Quakers. Hannah's and Kit's situations and their friendship display themes of persecution, religious freedom, intolerance, and prejudice.

Books with Similar Issues or Themes

Hurst, Carol Otis and Rebecca Otis. *A Killing in Plymouth Colony*. Boston: Houghton Mifflin, 2003.
> A fictional mystery of the first murder and trial in the Plymouth Colony during the year 1630.

Rees, Celia. *Witch Child*. Cambridge, MA: Candlewick Press, 2000.
> After her grandmother is condemned and hung for witchcraft in England in the year 1659, Mary Newbury is offered passage to America and records her experiences in the colonial community as she struggles to uphold her disguise as a true Puritan girl.

Author-Related Sources

Berger, Laura Standley, ed. *Twentieth-Century Young Adult Writers*. Detroit, MI: St. James Press, 1994, 606–8.

"Elisabeth George Speare." In vol. 8 of *Children's Literature Review*. Detroit, MI: Gale Research, 1985, 204–11.

"Elisabeth George Speare." In vol. 62 of *Something about the Author*. Farmington Hills, MI: Gale Research, 1990, 163–8.

Hopkins, Lee Bennett. *More Books by More People: Interviews with Sixty-Five Authors of Books for Children*. New York: Citation Press, 1974, 330–5.

Silvey, Anita, ed. *Children's Books and Their Creators*. Boston: Houghton Mifflin, 1995, 615–7.

Discussion Questions

For *The Witch of Blackbird Pond*

1. How does Kit's life change when she moves to her Aunt Rachel's house?

2. Why is it difficult for both Kit to adjust to her new surroundings and for the townsfolk to accept her?

3. What does the meadow represent to Kit?

4. Why is Kit's relationship with Hannah so important to both of them?

5. How does Hannah's advice help Kit sort out her feelings?

6. How does Kit help Prudence understand Hannah when Kit tells her, "people are afraid of things they don't understand"?

7. Why do the townsfolk believe that Hannah is a witch?

8. What positive influence does Kit have over some of the people in the town?

9. How do fear and ignorance fuel hatred and religious intolerance in this town?

10. Even though witch trials are a thing of the past, how can the message of this story be applied in our world today?

Suggested Readings

Bauermeister, Erica, and Holly Smith. *Let's Hear It for the Girls: 375 Great Books for Readers*. New York: Penguin Books, 1997.

Brooks, Bruce." "Will Boys Be Boys?" *VOYA* (June 2000): 88–92.

Cooper-Mullin, Alison. *Once upon a Heroine: 450 Books for Girls to Love*. Chicago: Contemporary Books, 1998.

Dodson, Shireen, and Teresa Baker. *The Mother-Daughter Book Club*. New York: HarperCollins, 1997.

Dodson, Shireen. *100 Books for Girls to Grow On*. New York: HarperCollins, 1998.

Fineman, Maria. *Talking about Books: A Step-by-Step Guide for Participating in Book Discussion Groups*. Rockville, MD: Talking About Books, 1997.

Gambrell, Linda B., and Janice F. Almasi, eds. *Lively Discussions! Fostering Engaged Reading*. Newark: International Reading Association, 1996.

Gurian, Michael. *The Wonder of Boys*. New York: Putnam, 1996.

Gurian, Michael, and Terry Trueman. *What Stories Does My Son Need?* New York: Penguin Putnam, 2000.

Jacobsohn, Rachel W. *The Reading Group Handbook: Everything You Need to Know, From Choosing Members to Leading Discussions*. New York: Hyperion, 1998.

Maughan, Shannon." "You Go, Guys." *Publisher's Weekly* (May 7, 2001): 41.

Moore, Ellen, and Kira Stevens. *Good Books Lately: The One-Stop Resource for Book Groups and Other Greedy Readers*. New York: St. Martin's Press, 2004.

O'Dean, Kathleen. *Great Books for Boys*. New York: Ballantine Books, 1998.

O'Dean, Kathleen. *Great Books for Girls*. New York: Ballantine Books, 2002.

Slezak, Ellen, ed. *The Book Group Book*, 3rd edition. Chicago: Chicago Review Press, 2000.

Smith, Michael W., and Jeffrey D. Wilhelm. *Reading Don't Fix No Chevys: Literacy in the Lives of Young Men*. Portsmouth, NH: Heinemann, 2002.

Sullivan, Michael." "Why Johnny Won't Read." *School Library Journal* (August 1, 2004): 36–9.

Wilhelm, Jeff. " "Getting Boys to Read, It's the Context!" *Instructor* (October 2002): 16–19.

Author Index

Genre Index

Adventure

Cultural Fiction

Fable

Fairy Tale

Fantasy

Historical Fiction

Humorous Fiction

Mystery

Picture Book

Poetic Format

Realistic Fiction

Science Fiction

Short Stories

Grade Level Index

Note: Both reading and discussion level are considered

Grade 7

Grade 8

Theme and Subject Index

Honor

Kite Rider, 206
The Master Puppeteer, 209

Honesty

Gooney Bird Greene, 112
The Hundred Dresses, 281
Jim Ugly, 203
The Million Dollar Shot, 212
The Real Thief, 55
Ronia, the Robber's Daughter, 58
A Single Shard, 70

Hope

Bud, Not Buddy, 173
Baseball in April and other Stories, 9
Hachiko Waits, 278
Maniac Magee, 42
Seedfolks, 302

Idealism

Maniac Magee, 42

Identity

Jip, His Story, 35
Lydia, Queen of Palestine, 127

Imagination

James and the Giant Peach, 200
Ruby Electric, 145
Sector 7, 67

Immigration

In the Year of the Boar and Jackie Robinson, 121
Lydia, Queen of Palestine, 127
Yang the Youngest and His Terrible Ear, 86

Independence

Catherine, Called Birdy, 95
The Chocolate War, 179
Ella Enchanted, 102
Lydia, Queen of Palestine, 127

Individuality

Gooney Bird Greene, 112

Ida B … and Her Plans to Maximize Fun, Avoid Disaster, and (Possibly) Save the World, 118
Yang the Youngest and His Terrible Ear, 86
Yolonda's Genius, 163
Wringer, 242

Ingenuity

Frindle, 185
James and the Giant Peach, 200
Rumpelstiltskin's Daughter, 148
Shadow Spinner, 154

Interpersonal Relationships

Lizzie Bright and the Buckminster Boy, 287
Seedfolks, 302
Smoky Night, 74

Interracial Friendship

Dave at Night, 182
Grape Thief, 188
Lizzie Bright and the Buckminster Boy, 287
Maniac Magee, 42
The Other Side, 49
Pink and Say, 52
Seedfolks, 302
Smoky Night, 74
Taking Sides, 233
Yolonda's Genius, 163
Yang the Youngest and His Terrible Ear, 86

Intimidation

The Chocolate War, 179
Wringer, 242

Inventiveness

Frindle, 185

Jealousy

Feathers and Fools, 25
Jacob Have I Loved, 124

Loneliness

Because of Winn-Dixie, 15
A Girl Named Disaster, 105
Ida B … and Her Plans to Maximize Fun, Avoid Disaster, and (Possibly) Save the World, 118

Prejudice

An Island Far from Home, 197
Feathers and Fools, 25
The Gold Cadillac, 269
Journey to Jo'burg, 284
Lizzie Bright and the Buckminster Boy, 287
Maniac Magee, 42
Ronia, the Robber's Daughter, 58
Taking Sides, 233
Weasel, 236
The Witch of Blackbird Pond, 323

Problem Solving

Chasing Vermeer, 19

Race Relations

Dave At Night, 182
The Gold Cadillac, 269
Journey to Jo'burg, 284
Lizzie Bright and the Buckminster Boy, 287
Maniac Magee, 42
The Other Side, 49
Pink and Say, 52
Grape Thief, 188
Seedfolks, 305
Smoky Night, 74
Taking Sides, 233
Weasel, 236
Yolonda's Genius, 163

Racism

Bud, Not Buddy, 173
The Gold Cadillac, 269
Journey to Jo'burg, 284
Lizzie Bright and the Buckminster Boy, 287
Maniac Magee, 46
Taking Sides, 233
Weasel, 236

Refugees

Fish, 257
Lydia, Queen of Palestine, 127
Run, Boy, Run, 215

Religious Faith

Gideon's People, 263
Grape Thief, 188
The Witch of Blackbird Pond, 323

Resistance

The Cats in Krasinski Square, 251

Respect for Others

Flipped, 260
Henry Hikes to Fitchburg, 32
Olive's Ocean, 293
Samir and Yonatan, 64
A Single Shard, 70
Smoky Night, 74

Responsibility

The Enormous Egg, 22
Ereth's Birthday, 254
Grape Thief, 188
Kite Rider, 206
The Master Puppeteer, 209
Prince of the Pond, 296
The Real Thief, 55
Stone Fox, 305
Wringer, 242
The Young Man and the Sea, 245

Revenge

The Clock, 98
Matilda, 130
Weasel, 236

Risks

Harris and Me, 191
Singularity, 218
Soup, 221
The Watertower, 77
The Young Man and the Sea, 245

Rivalry

Ronia, the Robber's Daughter, 58
Singularity, 218

Rural Life

Harris and Me, 191
Soup, 221
Squashed, 157

Sadness

Because of Winn-Dixie, 15
Love That Dog, 39

Title Index

About the Author

RITA SOLTAN, an independent Library Youth Services Consultant, is a former children's librarian of New York and Michigan, where she also supervised youth services departments for 15 years. An active member of ALA/ALSC, Soltan currently chairs the Education Committee of this group. She is Past Chair of the Children's Services Division of the Michigan Library Association; and she has written for the *MLA Forum*, the electronic journal for the Michigan Library Association. Soltan also reviews children's books for *Kirkus Review* and *School Library Journal*.